Marriage at Midlife

Counseling Strategies and Analytical Tools

Doug Kelley, PhD, is associate professor of communication studies at Arizona State University's West campus. Professor Kelley studies communication in personal relationships, with a specific emphasis on marital interaction. His recent work has appeared in such outlets as the *Journal of Social and Personal Relationships*, the *Journal of Applied Gerontology*, and *Communication Quarterly*. He is co-author, with Vince Waldron, of *Communicating Forgiveness*. In addition, Professor Kelley finds particular enjoyment in teaching and mentoring college students and conducting community workshops on various aspects of healthy relationships. Doug lives near the mountains in central Phoenix and spends most of his leisure time hiking, swimming, and kayaking with his wife, Ann, his two boys, Daniel and Jonathan, and his two dogs, Allen and Billy.

Vince Waldron, PhD, is professor and director of graduate studies for the Communication Studies program at Arizona State University where he also is affiliated with the program in Aging and Lifespan Development. He researches the communication processes that promote longevity, satisfaction, and justice in personal and work relationships. Dr. Waldron's recent research publications include the book *Communicating Forgiveness* (with Douglas Kelley) and articles in such outlets as the *Journal of Social and Personal Relationships*, the *Journal of Applied Gerontology*, and *Communication Quarterly*. Professor Waldron founded the Osher Lifelong Learning Institute at Arizona State University and continues to serve as its research director. A dedicated teacher, Dr. Waldron is the recipient of a *Professor of the Year* award from the Carnegie Foundation for the Advancement of Teaching. Vince lives in Glendale, Arizona, with his wife Kathleen and his daughters Emily and Laura.

Marriage at Midlife

Counseling Strategies and Analytical Tools

VINCENT R. WALDRON, PhD
DOUGLAS L. KELLEY, PhD

SPRINGER PUBLISHING COMPANY
New York

Springer Publishing Company, LLC
11 West 42nd Street
New York, NY 10036
www.springerpub.com

Acquisitions Editor: Sheri W. Sussman
Production Editor: Wendy Druck
Cover Design: Mimi Flow
Composition: Aptara Inc.

09 10 11 / 5 4 3 2 1
Ebook ISBN: 978-0-8261-2563-7

Library of Congress Cataloging-in-Publication Data

Waldron, Vincent R.
    Marriage at midlife : counseling strategies and analytical tools / Vincent
R. Waldron, Douglas L. Kelley.
        p. cm.
    Includes bibliographical references and index.
    ISBN 978-0-8261-2562-0
    1. Marriage—United States. 2. Married people—United
States—Psychology. 3. Middle-aged persons—United States—Psychology.
4. Marriage counseling—United States. I. Kelley, Douglas L. II. Title.
    HQ1059.5.U5W247 2009
    306.810973—dc22
                                                        2009001391

Printed in the United States of America by Hamilton Printing Company.

Contents

PART II: RETOOLING: ADAPTING TO MIDLIFE EVENTS   111

5   New Career Directions: Coping With Job Loss and Returning to School   113

7 Relocation at Midlife: Marking a New Era 179
Dayna Kloeber and Vincent R. Waldron

Contributors

Dayna Kloeber is a graduate student in the Communication Studies program at Arizona State University. Her research addresses conditional forgiveness in romantic and intergenerational family relationships with an emphasis on the dynamics of power and relational morality. Communication in families with children who face health and disability challenges is another research interest. Through her teaching, mentoring, and community outreach activity, Dayna provides practical support to practitioners and families. Dayna lives in Peoria, Arizona, with her husband, two sons, and daughter.

Kathleen Waldron is director of the School of Aging and Lifespan Development at Arizona State University, where she also teaches courses on such topics as caregiving, family relationships, sexuality and aging, and gerontological research methods. Ms. Waldron organizes community education seminars on aging issues and facilitates a support group for family members caring for older parents. Kathleen lives in Glendale, Arizona, with her husband Vince and their two daughters.

Preface

This book is intended as a professional resource for those who provide counsel to married clients experiencing the challenges and opportunities of middle age, which is the period of life we have labeled "centerstage." These professionals encounter middle-aged clients in a multitude of settings such as private counseling practices, community service agencies, faith communities, university student services offices, hospitals and healthcare agencies, and job retraining centers.

The centerstage of marriage begins when a couple realizes that their children will soon be leaving home. Its ending point is less certain, but for many couples, the decision to retire signals the end of this marital era and the beginning of another. This middle period of married life is marked by startling opportunities for growth and renewed intimacy. But for many veteran couples, it also brings daunting challenges, including illness, job loss, problematic relationships with adult offspring, and caregiving burdens. This is particularly true at the present moment in American history when traditional visions of midlife stability no longer apply. To note just a few American trends, middle-aged workers are losing their jobs and long-term couples are joining the ranks of the divorced at higher rates than in the past. One result: More couples and individual partners are seeking professional assistance. Distressed middle-aged clients are showing up with increased frequency at the offices of counselors, therapists, religious advisors, and other helping professionals. For many, this is the "make or break" point in a lifelong relationship.

Despite these trends, few existing books are designed to help professionals understand the dynamics of the centerstage marriage. Even fewer provide practical, research-based suggestions for practitioners.

WHY THIS BOOK NOW?

As we researched the communication practices of veteran couples over the last few decades, the need for this book became obvious. A massive generation of married Americans, the baby boomers, is solidly middle aged, with its leading edge now approaching retirement age. The generation immediately after is on its cusp, contemplating a midlife landscape in rapid transformation. Indeed, as they have with so many of our social institutions, baby boomers are changing the definition of what it means to be middle aged, married, with adult kids. Many rejected the traditional childraising practices of their parents. But now, they struggle with the inevitable questions that follow the launching of children, an event that is particularly troubling for a generation defined by hyper-self awareness and high-intensity parenting. How do I find meaning in life now that I am no longer at the center of my kids' universe? Changing social trends raise disconcerting questions that rarely bothered their parents. Questions like: What do I do now that I have lost my job at the age of 51? What do we do about adult children who continue to live at home? Should we try to recapture the intimacy we lost years ago, or simply "hang it up" after 2 decades of marriage?

Unfortunately, the existing literature is largely unhelpful to the professionals who hear these kinds of questions in their practices. Marriage researchers have been somewhat preoccupied by the conflicts experienced early in marriage or the challenges faced by elderly partners. Although important studies of middle-aged couples have been conducted, most are too dated to be of use with the current generation. Popular books tend to oversimplify the centerstage of marriage. The overused metaphor of the empty nest is an inadequate characterization of this rich period of married life. Midlife clients, those roughly 40 to 65 years old, often have more on their minds than the fact that their children no longer live at home. Of course, many welcome the launching of children into adulthood, and some find that the "nest" is frequently reoccupied by boomerang children.

WHAT TOPICS ARE COVERED?

Chapter 1 introduces the analytical tools we use when interpreting the experiences reported by centerstage couples. We bring a life span perspective to our work, focusing on the communication practices that help couples mange relational tensions, negotiate changing roles, resolve lingering disputes, renew intimacy, and adapt to changing circumstances. We also take a resilience-based approach, focusing less on limitations and more on the strengths and resources that help couples preserve long and satisfying relationships.

Subsequent chapters are divided into two sections. The first section provides research-based insights and practical resources for helping clients with the process of *recoupling*—the conscious effort to reinvent and deepen the marriage through improved communication (chapter 2), forgiving past transgressions (chapter 3), and the development of new and meaningful shared activities (chapter 4). The chapters in the second section address *retooling*—the adaptations couples make when faced with challenging midlife circumstances, such as job loss and returning to school (chapter 5); redefined relationships with "boomerang kids," adult children, and grandchildren (chapter 6); midlife relocation (chapter 7); and the stresses of illness and caregiving (chapter 8).

A brief final chapter emphasizes the importance of relational metaphors in helping clients reimagine their marriage. We address the implication for counseling practice of the recoupling, retooling, and centerstage metaphors. We end the book by revisiting the best practices of resilient centerstage couples.

HOW TO USE THIS BOOK

The book is organized to help you quickly find and apply the information you need in your counseling work. It is grounded in research, but we intentionally avoided long lists of research citations. Key concepts are often summarized in tables and textboxes, labeled with headings like, "*How do I use it?*" and "*What you might hear from clients.*" We ground our work in the experiences of real couples, so you will see plenty of illuminating examples and quotations from the couples we have interviewed over the past decade.

With the exception of the introductory and concluding chapters, each chapter conforms to a standardized structure. The common organizational scheme helps readers quickly locate the issues that concern them and their clients. For example, those interested in fostering resiliency in clients will always find a resiliency heading in the *Applying the Analytical Frameworks* section of each chapter. Specific suggestions for practice are labeled *Working With Clients*. Each chapter includes the following sections:

Opening Narrative

We begin with an opening narrative, which grounds the chapter in the lived experiences of clients. These brief stories are from couples who participated in our studies or class assignments. Some are based on couples we know personally. All stories have been altered to disguise identities. The opening narratives, along with other brief stories, are used to illustrate key concepts from the text.

Chapter Introduction

The first section of each chapter introduces the topic, grounds it in a social and family context, explains its importance to clients and counselors, and briefly discusses relevant research findings.

Sources of Distress

Here, we address the reasons why clients seek counseling and therapy. We consider the relational and individual challenges typically reported to us by couples in our studies and some of the likely causes of their distress.

Analytical Tools

Our approach to understanding centerstage couples is guided by three analytical frameworks: relational dialectics theory, resilience theory, and role theory. Each framework provides counselors and clients with a unique language for interpreting the experience of midlife marriage. We apply at least two of the analytical frameworks in each chapter.

Working With Clients

In this section, the reader finds a streamlined set of suggestions and "tasks" to incorporate in counseling sessions or workshops. We provide many practical suggestions throughout each chapter, but the primary purpose of the *Working With Clients* section is to make these easily accessible for the professional reader.

Questions for Clients

We provide a list of questions for your clients to consider. Linked to key themes raised in the chapter, these questions are designed to prompt reflection and productive discussion during counseling sessions.

Exercises

This section provides activities to incorporate in your counseling sessions or workshops. These have been formatted to be easily copied for client use.

References

This book is based on our own research and that of other scholars, but for the purposes of readability, we limit the number of research citations. The reference list includes key research sources for the interested reader.

Resources

For every chapter we have included resources (in Appendix A at the back of the book) for you and your clients. In some cases, you can refer your clients directly to these sources as a supplement to counseling. We include links to useful internet sites, assessments and inventories, popular and professional books, inspirational stories, organizations, government programs, and myriad other sources of assistance.

We are university researchers and teachers who study how romantic relationships change and persist over the life span. Our research focuses mainly on the communication practices of resilient couples—those who manage to sustain, and even optimize, their partnerships as they progress together through the life course with its many transitions and obstacles. You can learn more about our perspective in chapter 1, but it is important to know that our own research informs the book. For nearly 20 years, we have published studies based on interview and survey data collected from hundreds of couples, many of them marriage veterans of 3 or more decades, and some married as many as 80 years (e.g., Kelley & Waldron, 2005; Waldron & Kelley, 2005,). Our recent book, *Communicating Forgiveness*, presents our work on the role of forgiveness in preserving long marriages (Waldron & Kelley, 2008).

In recent years, we have turned our attention to the dynamics of marriage at midlife. We adopted the term "centerstage" because the metaphor works at several levels of meaning. The first is temporal. Many of the couples we report on in this book are middle aged—at the "temporal center" of what they hope will be a long life of 8 or 9 decades. At a second level of meaning, the metaphor says something about the center of attention. With their active parenting years behind them, these couples have the time and opportunity to reassess the opportunities and challenges of marriage. Concerns about the quality of the relationship, which may have been relegated to a peripheral position in a busy child-filled life, now move up the priority list. In the language of the theater, marriage moves from the wings to center stage.

We are joined in this effort by Kathleen Waldron, a life span scholar and highly successful teacher at Arizona State University's School of Aging and Lifespan Development. Kathleen took primary responsibility for chapter 6, which addresses relationships with boomerang children and adult offspring, as well as the special relational challenges that sometimes accompany grandparenting.

We have engaged many of our students in our efforts to more fully understand the experiences of centerstage couples. We have learned enormously from the personal stories of our middle-aged students, and from the hundreds of relational narratives our students have collected from "centerstage" friends, parents, and relatives. Dayna Kloeber, one of the most dedicated and insightful graduate students, has been instrumental in the development of this book. She is the primary author of chapter 7, which focuses on relocation at midlife.

Marriage at Midlife is our effort to translate years of research into a resource that is accessible, useful, and grounded in the experiences of real couples. We hope you find it helpful in your efforts to guide clients through the sometimes turbulent transitions that characterize the centerstage of married life.

Acknowledgments

The authors thank graduate student, Dayna Kloeber, the lead author of chapter 7 and the primary architect of the Appendix, who contributed in myriad ways to the creation of the book. We are thankful for Dayna's creativity, enthusiasm, and amazing work ethic. In addition, thanks to Colleen McQuade for her diligence in locating internet and print resources, running down research references, and responding cheerfully to innumerable requests for assistance.

The original proposal for this book was refined through conversations with colleagues in the Communication Studies department at Arizona State University. We are grateful to work in such a supportive and collegial environment. In addition, a number of professional counselors gave feedback and encouragement as we refined the book proposal during the early stages. These include Marian Hopkins-Busby, Anne Conser, and Natalie Keller.

Much of what we have learned about midlife marriage comes from the many veteran couples who agreed to share their experiences in interviews and surveys. We cannot thank them enough for their generosity. The authors also acknowledge the students who worked with us over the years on this and other marriage projects. Their efforts to interview, record, and analyze the experiences of veteran couples yielded rich insights, for them and for us.

Finally, at Springer Publishing Company, Senior Editor Sheri W. Sussman was encouraging, responsive, and insightful from the moment we shared our ideas for this book. Sheri challenged us to write a research-based book that would be truly useful to counselors. With her considerable assistance, we were able to do just that.

Vince Waldron offers special thanks to his spouse Kathleen, whose unyielding support and sense of adventure make her the perfect companion for a ride on the roller coaster that is midlife marriage.

Doug Kelley is especially grateful to Ann, his wife of 27 years, for being an exciting and challenging partner as they have worked to keep their marriage centerstage.

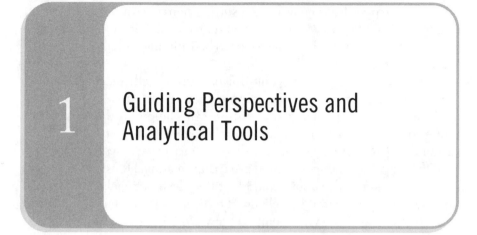

1 Guiding Perspectives and Analytical Tools

We always got along pretty well, despite a few rough spots. Anna was very involved with the kids, even though she always had a part-time job. I helped out too, with coaching and boy scouts, that kind of stuff. But my job was 24/7, especially during the early years. We had fun on vacations and had dinner together most nights of the week. I thought Anna and I made a pretty good team. The kids are out of the house now, and I thought it would be fun. But, Anna went back to school, and she wants to be a nurse. She is gone a lot, and we don't really have much time for the fun things I thought we would be doing. Anna kind of has another life she is building up, with new friends at school. After all these years, my job is boring me. It pays the bills, but it's gotten routine. In some ways, we have more to talk about—its not just the kids, so that is good. But we are arguing a lot. To be honest, things are confused right now. It's not what we expected.

Joe and Anna, who have been married for 26 years, are among the millions of couples discovering that the "middle years" of marriage can be both perplexing and challenging. Inspired by the stable relationships their parents enjoyed, Joe and Anna launched their marriage with a lifetime commitment firmly in mind. However, the societal forces that supported their parents' long marriages are largely obsolete. The stigma of divorce is a thing of the past. Fewer couples are staying married simply to avoid the disapproval of religious leaders. Expectations are higher. Veteran spouses like Joe and Anna want their marriages to be fulfilling and happy, not just stable and long.

Faced with this changing cultural backdrop, with marriage bonds fraying and the "empty nest" years now upon them, Anna and Joe recognized the need for change and enlisted the help of a therapist. The therapist helped this baby-boomer couple realize that the practices that sustained their marriage during those hectic early years were no longer working. Together they confronted recurring relational tensions, renegotiated unrealistic expectations, and identified dysfunctional communication patterns. "Our world had changed radically," Joe confided, "and we needed to change if we were going to grow old together." Their counseling continues, and Anna and Joe are growing more hopeful about what the future holds for them.

DEFINING THE "CENTERSTAGE" MARRIAGE

In recent decades, the once stalwart ideal of lifelong marriage has been battered by changing cultural tides. Even experienced couples are sometimes knocked off course as they navigate tricky and sometimes treacherous trends: Boomerang children. Job insecurity. Friends divorcing. Change in gender roles. Care for long-lived parents. But compared to their younger and older counterparts, middle-aged couples are expected to negotiate these challenges with surprisingly little assistance from family, church, or other sources. Moreover, research on the marriages of middle-aged people is relatively thin and increasingly out of date. As a counseling professional, you likely recognize the need for a deeper and different understanding of what we call "centerstage" marriages.

As researchers who study the communication patterns of experienced partners, we collect "relational narratives" from couples like Joe and Anna. Different in important ways from those describing younger and older relationships, these stories reveal the unique stresses and opportunities that arise during the middle years of long marriages. Our research confirms what one of our marriage counselor friends has observed in her practice—that this is a "make or break" period for many of her married clients.

BOX 1.1 THE EMPTY NEST—AN EMPTY METAPHOR?

We use the term *empty nest* sparingly in this book, preferring the term *centerstage marriage*. Although widespread, the empty nest metaphor distorts important aspects of a complex and lengthy phase of married life. We object to the implication that a marriage is emptied of meaning because children no longer live in the home. The empty nest label ignores the ongoing and sometimes difficult relationships parents have with adult children, some of whom actually return to the "nest." Empty nest language focuses attention on loss rather than opportunity. Some couples do grieve the passing of their active parenting years, but many others find this stage of married life to be freeing and even exhilarating. The period of married life that starts as the children begin to leave and ends with the onset of older age, the centerstage, can be a time of challenge, growth, and renewed intimacy, not emptiness.

So what do we mean by *centerstage* marriage? First, the term *centerstage* emphasizes a period of time, the middle period of a lengthy relationship. Second, centerstage is a metaphor. By using it, we emphasize that midlife is a time when couples reexamine their marriage, as if it were under a spotlight. With parenting responsibilities receding, relationship concerns move from the periphery to the center of attention, from backstage to centerstage. The lengthy centerstage of a marriage begins as parents first confront a new reality: Their children will soon be (relatively) independent adults. Its onset is signaled by bittersweet emotions: The heady anticipation of new freedoms mixed with a palpable grief over the loss of the joint mission of parenting. But what has popularly been known as the empty nest syndrome (see Box 1.1) is just one in a cascade of changing conditions that couples negotiate at midlife. The first of these concerns is relational identity. What kind of a marriage will we have now that our identity as "coparents" is fading? In the wake of this identity question comes a series of others. What kinds of activities will bring us fulfillment in this next stage of our lives? Should we move to a new home or stay where we are? How will we respond when our adult children need help? What adjustments will we make in response to job loss, a partner's return to college, or the needs of elderly relatives? How will we cope when one of us becomes seriously ill?

Our research examines how successful couples answer these questions and many others. Most of the couples we study are marriage veterans. Having reached the centerstage of marriage, they have been together between 20 and 40 years. These are, in most cases, *first* marriages with partners ranging in age from the mid-40s to the mid-60s. Couples who have chosen not to be parents deserve more attention from researchers and clinicians. Nevertheless, in the interests of clarity and brevity, this book focuses on the unique experiences of those who are parents.

OUR RESEARCH: HOW DID WE LEARN ABOUT CENTERSTAGE MARRIAGES?

This book is based on our research with veteran married couples. Through interviews, anonymous surveys, and even personal observations, we have studied their communication practices for nearly 2 decades. Much of this research focuses on times of trouble in resilient marriages. How do marriages survive, even thrive, in the face of serious challenges? Our results are reported in traditional journal articles and also in books, such as *Communicating Forgiveness* (Waldron & Kelley, 2007), a volume written for researchers and students.

As we recorded the stories of veteran couples, we often heard about the adjustments they were required to make during the newlywed years. Older age certainly brought its own trials and tribulations, but we were surprised by the large number of couples who reported significant relational changes, and sometimes serious difficulties, *at midlife*. Of course, we expected to hear about adjustment to the empty nest, and we did. But many of the challenges were encountered well after the kids left home. Some described trying times of tumult, despair, and stress; others experienced profoundly positive turning points in once satisfying marriages that had simply gone stale. Intrigued, we delved back into the interview data. We also invited our college students to join us in the quest by interviewing their parents and friends; the ensuing audiotaped interviews and written accounts were rich sources of insight. The data convinced us that the challenges and relational accomplishments of centerstage couples were frequent, varied, and underappreciated. Adapting to the "empty nest" was only the beginning of a long period of adjustment.

FIVE COUPLES: FIVE DIFFERENT CHALLENGES

Consider Rafer and Vielka. Two of their three sons have left for college and the youngest, Noah, is leaving soon. Devoted parents, this couple's conversation has been mostly devoted to the kids for better than 2 decades. The house is already strangely quiet. Vielka wonders what she and Rafer will talk about after Noah leaves. Will they find a new "project" to share? Will they drift apart?

Regina and Dallas face a different challenge. Their kids left too—but now one is back. Their daughter Riki graduated from college and quickly found a new job. But the economy turned for the worse, and Riki was laid off. Unable to pay the rent, she asked to move back home until she could get back on her feet. Her parents were certainly willing to help out in the short term. However, it has been 9 months since Riki settled back into her old room and tensions are mounting. Dallas wants to be firm in setting a move-out date, but Regina disagrees. She argues that "patience will pay off." Regina feels certain that as the economy improves, Riki will find a job and their relationship with her will be better for having been supportive during her time of crisis.

Raul and Teresa are in their mid-50s. Both are working hard, trying to build up the retirement fund that was neglected during the child raising years. Recently, Raul's mother Maria fell and broke her hip. The couple invited Maria into their home where they could help her recover. Using limited vacation time, one of them leaves work whenever Maria must be driven to one of her many medical appointments. Now, having filed for divorce, their oldest daughter is moving home too, with her three children.

Judy has been married for 30 years to her husband Sean who is faithful, stable, and supportive. After raising two kids and working for nearly a decade as a clerk at the local courthouse, Judy admits to being bored with life. At her recent high school reunion, she became reacquainted with Scott, a high school flame, who left their small town to attend college on the East Coast. The pair talked deep into the night, laughing about old times and lamenting missed opportunities. The conversation continued by e-mail. Divorced and single, Scott asked Judy to visit him some weekend. She is mulling the offer and its implications for her marriage.

After years of hard work, Dean and Sally are about 10 years from retirement. Dean dreams of a move south—anywhere the weather is warm and the golf courses are open all year. Sally wants to live close to their current home in the suburbs of a midwestern city. She enjoys the company of her daughters and grandchildren and has been offered a part-time position by the large bank that employs her. "Easing into" retirement suits Sally.

Veteran couples commonly benefit from a store of relational goodwill and a history of mutual problem-solving. Nevertheless, these five couples, and your own midlife clients, are facing unfamiliar challenges. They often need the assistance of counselors and other professionals as familiar strategies fail and stresses start to mount. In this book, we provide the information you need to help them.

THIS BOOK'S ORGANIZATION

This book can be read as a whole, but we anticipate that many readers will select chapters to read based on their professional needs at a given moment in time. For that reason, chapters 2 through 8 are designed to stand alone as useful resources for your professional practice. Chapter 1 provides you with the analytical tools that we use to interpret the experiences reported by centerstage couples. It also shares some of the "best practices" of resilient couples. The bulk of the book is organized in two parts: Recoupling and Retooling. The first examines fundamental processes that help couples reassess, and sometimes redesign, a midlife marriage. This recoupling period often requires partners to improve communication (chapter 2), forgive past transgressions (chapter 3), and locate new and meaningful activities to share (chapter 4).

The second part examines the adjustments couples must make as they encounter difficult life events. This retooling occurs when partners experience job loss or return to school (chapter 5). Changing family obligations also challenge midlife couples. Chapter 6 addresses "boomerang children," difficult relationships with adult offspring, and stressful grandparenting. Relocation can be a source of marital stress at midlife. Chapter 7 addresses the challenges and opportunities of midlife moving. Finally, illness and care giving burdens can profoundly change a marriage, as we discuss in chapter 8.

The brief closing chapter challenges couples and counselors to think more creatively about the opportunities offered by midlife marriage. We offer several provocative metaphors and leave the reader with an enriched understanding of the best practices of centerstage couples.

Each chapter is designed around a common structure so you can easily find the information you need. After an introductory section, you will find sections labeled *Sources of Distress*, *Analytical Tools*, and *Working With Clients*. Prior to an intentionally brief set of research *References*, you will find sections entitled *Questions for Clients* and *Exercises*. These are designed to help you apply the chapter concepts in your counseling sessions or workshops. Finally, we provide a detailed Appendix A, with links to books, organizations, and Web sites that should prove useful to your clients.

The chapters are research-based but intentionally light on research jargon and technical references. The references we do include are chosen for their relevance and applicability. To increase interest and utility, each chapter features a special section labeled *"How do I use it?"* and *"What you might hear from clients."* The conceptual material in each chapter is "fleshed out" by stories and examples from the midlife couples we have observed (names and identifying details are altered).

A GUIDING PERSPECTIVE: COMMUNICATING ACROSS THE LIFE COURSE

Our understanding of couples, like the five mentioned previously, is grounded in our work as communication researchers and teachers. We believe that careful observation of communication patterns reveals a lot about the dynamics of a marriage. Underlying emotions and attitudes can often be detected in marital discourse—the patterns of talk that define a marriage. Relational messages about trust, power, respect, and intimacy are often communicated nonverbally, sometimes without awareness. Indeed, habitual patterns of everyday communication sustain both functional and dysfunctional marriages. In our view, counselors and therapists play the crucial role of helping partners identify dysfunctional patterns while increasing the capacity to engage certain kinds of constructive communication such as expressing emotion, negotiating conflict, or forgiving transgressions.

The development of improved communication practices helps a marriage adapt to changing conditions, including those encountered at midlife. Of course, a couple's satisfaction at midlife is only partly determined by current events and interactions. It is also a product of roles that the partners have embraced or rejected, adaptation to changing social norms, career trajectories, and the many other forces that build as the decades pass. With other researchers who find relevance in this larger historical picture, we operate from what is frequently called a *life course perspective*. Four life course principles emerge from the stories told to us by midlife couples.

Partners Develop and Change

Change is (ironically enough) a constant in human relationships. Although acknowledging that personality, cohort characteristics, and social structure remain relatively stable, life span researchers assume that people and their social arrangements are constantly developing. Change in intimate relationships is driven by the development of individual partners as they mature, adapt to changes, and pursue new goals. One implication is that spouses need to adjust the expectations they have for themselves, their partners, and the marriage.

Time Matters

Time is an important consideration as we try to understand the current status of a relationship. We consider the past. In relational narratives, couples often recount "critical incidents" and "turning points." They reveal how currently dysfunctional practices might have been useful in the past. But we also consider the future. The content of current interactions may reveal fear, uncertainty, or excitement about what lies ahead. Veteran couples often benefit from long experience, and they can see some relational phases unfold over long periods of time. In our research on long-term marriages (over 40 years in duration), we noted that even happy older couples describe surprisingly long periods of dissatisfaction. One implication is that patience sometimes pays off in the long run.

However, we also noticed that fall-out from serious transgressions often lasted years, even decades. Angela's story illustrates how the passing of time changes perspective.

When my husband first confessed to having an affair, the emotions were so raw I wasn't sure how I would survive, much less how our marriage would. Even now, I can recall the pain. It was the kind that takes your breath away, makes your knees buckle, takes years to digest. But now, some 15 years later, I see that time has allowed a great deal of healing and in a weird way, that incident made us appreciate each other more because we realized how much we wanted a future for ourselves and our family. It made us stop to work on it. Our life together isn't perfect, but that almost makes it better. We have two amazing children who have not only brought enormous joy to our lives but also provided the initial incentive to work toward forgiveness. I'm so glad we took the time.

Marriages Have "Turning Points"

Life span perspectives acknowledge that critical events punctuate relational development. Parenthood, childrearing, death of a parent, leaving or entering the workforce, children leaving the home—all of these bring stress as well as opportunities for relational growth. We often think of relationship development as a gradual and steady process. But when couples tell their stories, they sometimes describe these events as important turning points when relationship quality rapidly improved or declined. A key lesson is that surviving these turning points requires adaptability and the willingness to retool the marriage.

External Circumstances Will Change

A new marriage is inevitably influenced by prevailing cultural values. Once adopted, these persist over time, determining the practices that seem normal for a given cohort of married people. Even the most traditional of marriages can be stressed by a failure to adapt to changes in the larger culture. Relaxed gender roles, economic upheaval, adjustments in parenting expectations, new definitions of old age, expanded communication technologies, and other macroforces can alter the expectations of one or more partners. They also influence the couple's relations with others, including extended family. The importance of adaptation to changing circumstances became obvious as we studied nearly 500 older couples who had decided to relocate late in life (see Box 1.2). Those who were willing to use communication technologies maintained their social support networks, despite a radical change in living arrangements. Those who did not were more likely to report social isolation.

How does a life span approach change things? For researchers, it means looking beyond simple survey assessments—snapshots of the current state of the relationship. Instead, we collect richer data about the relationship's past and its developmental trajectory, often by collecting extended relationship narratives. Life span researchers also separate cohort effects from the simple effects of age. A group of married people in their 50s may share similar beliefs about marriage, not because they are the same age, but because they were all married during a particular cultural period. Their collective approach to marriage was shaped by common role models, mass media depictions, and family norms. However, the next generation of 50-year-olds may hold quite different views.

BOX 1.2 RESEARCH EXEMPLAR: GENDER ROLES AND ADJUSTMENT TO RELOCATION

In a longitudinal study of more than 500 husbands and wives (aged 50 and older), we examined how long-distance relocation affected a couple's social ties with family and friends (Waldron, Gitelson, & Kelley, 2005). The study demonstrated the importance of gender roles in a couple's adjustments to major life changes. It appeared that wives were more profoundly affected by the disruption of existing family and friend relationships. They reported reductions in supportive social ties after relocation, while men reported little or no reduction. In fact, males appeared to increase social connectedness after moving to the new community, probably because they started the study with few close relationships. Perhaps more important, persons of either sex who used electronic communication to stay in touch with distant family and friends reported higher levels of social support. This study of "later midlife" couples illustrates the importance of being able to maintain supportive relationships. These results not only illustrate how gender norms influence responses to a major life event, but they also provide insight about how environmental factors, such as communication technology, can impact relational health.

An understanding of these generational differences is critical during counseling. Couples married in the late 1960s and early 1970s may express different attitudes about money and sex, than those married earlier and later. Table 1.1 presents several American generations, their average age at marriage, and historical/cultural factors that influence attitudes about marriage. Interestingly, although there are many differences between the generations, we were surprised in our interviews by number of couples, across generations, who had sought counseling during the middle stage of their marriage.

ACCOUNTING FOR DIFFERENCES AMONG CLIENTS: CULTURE, GENDER, AND RELIGION

Thus far, we have made the marital dyad our primary focus and assumed that despite their differences midlife couples grapple with similar developmental events, such as the cessation of active parenting or the need to care for aging parents. However, as any experienced counselor will attest,

Table 1.1

GENERATIONAL DIFFERENCES AND MARRIAGE		
World War II	Born 1910–1920s	Age at marriage: 18–20 years, rigid gender roles; valued formality and authoritarian parenting style
Window ("Silent")	1930s–1945	Age at marriage: 20 years; valued conformity; valued extended family ties
Baby Boomers	1946–1964	Age at marriage: 22 years; raised in suburban families; value androgyny and individuality
Generation X	1965–1970s	Age at marriage: 26 years; children of divorce; leery of romantic commitments; value informality
Generation Y	1980s	Age at marriage: 26 years; highly individualistic; value technology

no two marriages are the same. The inevitable variation is explained in part by the unique blend of personalities that defines a marriage and by the patterns of interaction that sustain it. But another important consideration is the larger cultural context in which a marriage is embedded. Similar to many other authors (see, e.g., the recent volume edited by Szinovacz & Davey, 2007), we encourage counselors to consider a midlife client's cultural background, gender, and religious orientation. It is certainly true that that the middle years bring changes and challenges to nearly every life, but it is obvious from our research that some spouses are impacted more, or differently, than others.

The effects of culture and gender in relationships are examined within three research traditions (for an accessible review, see Wilmot & Hocker, 2007). The *behavior differences* approach looks for unique patterns of relational behavior displayed by men and women, either religious or nonreligious, or those of different cultural backgrounds. Certainly, counselors should expect such variation, as the research suggests, example, that women sometimes prefer indirect approaches to conflict, whereas men prefer more competitive communication styles. However, considerable research supports another perspective, the *behavioral similarities* approach. Proponents argue that research results showing differences tend to be of modest statistical strength and that similarities often outweigh differences. For example, although some faiths encourage the value of forgiveness, it appears that religious people are only modestly more forgiving of an unfaithful spouse than their nonreligious counterparts. Behavioral similarities theorists argue further that variations *within* a cultural group may outweigh any differences *between* groups. For example, Hispanic and Asian clients may experience different types and levels of intergenerational conflict due to cultural differences in familial values. But a more important factor might be the degree of acculturation *within* a given Hispanic or Asian family. In this way, Hispanic clients who are less identified with their culture of origin will report different experiences, compared to Hispanic clients who remain heavily identified. These differences may be indicated by factors such as their choice of language or participation in cultural rituals.

A third approach, the *perceptual filters* approach assumes that the effects of culture are not so noticeable in patterns of behavior but in the ways that behavior is interpreted and evaluated. From this approach, clients of different genders or cultures might report similar patterns with different social consequences. For example, due to prevailing gender norms, the caregiving behavior offered by a female client may simply be "expected" by her extended family, whereas similar behavior by her husband may be regarded as heroic or unselfish. The perceptual filters approach may be particularly useful in counseling, as spouses often are aware of differences in their behavioral responses to midlife challenges but sometimes need assistance in understanding that the very same behaviors may be evaluated differently due to the cultural, gender, and religious filters used by the couple, their friends, and family members.

For this volume, we have chosen not to include a separate chapter on client differences. Instead, we address gender and culture differences in places where they seemed to matter most in our observations of midlife couples. For example, an extended discussion appears in chapter 8, which addresses the role of cultural differences in caregiving obligations and responses to illness. The interested reader will find many other examples. With regard to gender, we explore how women are more likely than men to assume the responsibilities of custodial grandparenting (chapter 6) and, as suggested earlier, women are more likely to experience social isolation due to long-distance relocation (chapter 7). Mothers and fathers may react differently to the loss of a job or a return to school (chapter 5). We encourage counselors to also take religious orientation into account. Some clients will be motivated by religious principles to forgive past transgressions (chapter 3). Others will find that the religious practices that served them well during the parenting years are less meaningful in later life (chapter 4).

In short, every midlife transition is likely to be influenced, in some way, by the cultural values of the individual partners, the couple, and the larger social networks to which they belong.

UNDERSTANDING CENTERSTAGE COUPLES: THREE FRAMEWORKS

Centerstage marriages are sometimes distressed by threats to familiar patterns of living and relating. Buffeted by changes in the external environment, married clients may report feelings of confusion, frustration, or powerlessness. We have found three analytical frameworks to be particularly helpful in understanding centerstage couples. Readers may find one or more of these useful in their own professional work. The *why* of relational distress, the underlying causes and explanations, often become clearer as a framework is applied. The three frameworks presented here differ, but each focuses attention on certain variables while pushing others into the background.

The Relational Dialectics Framework

An interesting and useful way to think about the dynamics of centerstage marriage emerges from the *dialectical tradition*, rooted in the work of philosopher Mikhail Bakhtin (1981). Dialectical theory encourages us to question the assumption that relationships "progress through" stages. Instead, marriage is in a state of continuous flux and negotiation. Leslie Baxter (2003), a prominent relationship researcher, emphasizes the central themes of contradiction and dialogue. *Contradiction* involves the co-occurrence of relational qualities and traits that are opposites, such as openness versus closedness, vulnerability versus protection, interdependence versus autonomy, or novelty versus predictability. Table 1.2 introduces some of the commonly observed relational dialectics. Tensions emerge inevitably because these opposing qualities are both desirable and incompatible. Successful partners find ways to manage or integrate them into the marriage. During a period of relational distance, for example, they might disclose previously unexpressed emotions, a move which reduces psychological distance and increases vulnerability. Subsequently, they might choose to edit or "tone down" negative feelings until things have "cooled off" a bit. This behavior temporarily moves the relationship to a more closed and protective stance.

Table 1.2

SOME COMMONLY OBSERVED RELATIONAL DIALECTICS

DIALECTIC	DESCRIPTION
Openness vs. closedness	Ambivalence about revealing information or keeping it private
Vulnerability vs. protectedness	Competing needs to reveal the self and shield the self from hurt
Interdependence vs. autonomy	Wanting to collaborate and wanting to act with freedom from constraint
Novelty vs. predictability	Wanting predictability and comfort as well as uncertainty and new experiences
Real vs. ideal	Pragmatic relational concerns are considered against romanticized views

Applying the Dialectical Framework

For theorists like Baxter, relational contradictions are *dialogic*. In other words, they are *not* located in the psychological perceptions of individual partners; rather, they emerge in the patterns of discourse that express and manage contradictory relational states. Counselors better understand the dynamics of a middle-stage marriage by listening for dialectics embedded in *language* used by clients. For example, the interdependence versus autonomy dialectic often appears when couples discuss the empty nest. As a collective activity, childrearing requires considerable interdependence and joint action. Having largely completed the childrearing task, a mother may desire new levels of autonomy. However, these efforts to gain freedom of action may trigger anxiety in a mate who prefers close consultation.

It is essential to recognize four approaches that couples use to deal with dialectical tensions (Baxter & Montgomery, 1996). The *sequence or separate strategy* allows contradictory impulses to be expressed in the marriage, but they are enacted at different points in time or in different contexts. By sharing some decision-making responsibilities (e.g., childcare, family budgeting) and entrusting others to individual members (e.g., home maintenance decisions, managing in-law relationships), partners experience both autonomy and interdependence.

A second approach is to *embrace* one relational quality while actively suppressing its opposite. Partners who insist on "total honesty" are choosing vulnerability over protectedness. *"What they don't know can't hurt them*," is a relational maxim that expresses the opposite position. A third approach is the *integration* of the opposites. Some communication practices allow simultaneous expression of contradictory relational needs. Couples may find predictability in certain "ritualistic" practices, such as taking the dog for a walk every evening, but they may also find novelty by changing the topics they discuss along the way. Finally, contradictions are sometimes *reframed* in marital discourse. For example, a young adult may approach parents for a loan when purchasing a first home but may chafe at the conditions offered "as part of the deal." Should the parents seek influence in this purchasing process or should they take a hands-off approach? As an alternative to viewing this situation as a struggle between autonomy and interdependence, the parties might label it as a "period of growth" in the family. This kind of reframing makes issues of control less salient even as it creates opportunities for family members to express maturity, mutual learning, and openness to change.

A Resilience Framework

Grounded in the growing "positive psychology" movement (see, e.g., Park, Peterson, & Seligman, 2004), resilience is the idea that people possess a great capacity to withstand life challenges. Rather than focus on losses and deficits, resilience perspectives focus on the relational resources and communication tools that help couples bounce back from challenges and thrive in the face of change. Resilience is also fostered by certain kinds of community resources. Specifically, counselors and other professionals can help clients discover and exploit sources of resilience.

What are the components of resilience? In answering that question, we are guided by the research of the nationally known *Resilience Solutions Group* (2008), located at Arizona State University. Researchers find that resilience includes these seven components:

1 *Optimism:* Resilient people focus on positive results. When faced with a crisis, they are hopeful rather than despairing. They imagine positive rather than negative outcomes.
2 *Flexibility:* Adaptation to changing circumstances is essential. Even as they embrace lessons of the past, resilient people make adjustments in light of new requirements and conditions.
3 *Determination:* A strong commitment to future success is another characteristic, which is accompanied by perseverance, patience, effort, and resolve.

4 *Sustainability:* Good stewardship of one's personal and relational resources is another feature of resilience. This involves a long-term commitment to healthy behavior and the cultivation of a broad-based sense of well-being.

5 *Diversity:* Resilience is fostered when people perceive a range of alternatives and options. Resilient people draw on a variety of skills and past experiences. They imagine a variety of potential outcomes to problematic situations.

6 *Balance:* Stability, centeredness, and harmony contribute to a sense of composure in resilient people. Living a balanced life leads to psychological and physical balance.

Applying the Resilience Framework

The components of resilience provide concrete ways to help couples thrive despite the challenges of centerstage marriage. For example, some couples have adapted their communication patterns to sustain their marriage after the children leave home. Our data frequently reveal couples who "flexed" when a spouse unexpectedly became ill. The healthy partner accepted new caretaking tasks and the ill partner adjusted to unfamiliar feelings of dependency. A couple that loves dancing may find new pleasure in watching old movies together. The resilience framework is an inventive and optimistic one. In using it, counselors help clients inventory their own strengths, imagine more hopeful futures, and connect to helpful resources.

BOX 1.3 HOW DO I USE IT? APPLYING RESILIENCY CONCEPTS

■ Focus on client resources, strengths, opportunities, and hopeful outcomes, not just their losses and limitations.
■ Prompt reflection on unnecessarily limiting or pessimistic assumptions.
■ Encourage clients to identify positive role models in their relationship network.
■ Help clients locate past experiences that could prove helpful now.
■ Connect clients with information and resources in the community.
■ Encourage clients to practice new behaviors that promote flexibility, sustainability, and balance in their relationships.

The Roles Framework

The notion of the social role is one of the most familiar explanations for human behavior (see Blumer, 1969). We use it throughout this book because role changes experienced by one or both partners often appear as significant events in the relational narratives of veteran couples. As we use the term, a *role* is simply a set of regularly expected behaviors. Learned through exposure to family, cultural, and religious norms, a role provides structure and predictability in social relations. Much of human behavior is role guided, including behavior exhibited by married partners.

BOX 1.4 HOW DO ROLES CAUSE DISTRESS?

Role conflict:	Incompatibility of multiple roles such as parent or student
Role Loss:	Valued roles are given up or taken away, as with job loss
Role Ambivalence:	Uncertainty about the desirability of a role, such as grandparent
Role Resistance:	Unwillingness to adopt a new role, such as patient or caregiver
Role Rigidity:	Inflexible role performance, as when a spouse refuses to share responsibility for financial decision making.
Role Ambiguity:	Uncertainty of role requirements, such as that experienced by a middle-aged spouse returning to college.

Applying the Roles Framework

Distress at midlife often involves role stress. When couples share narratives about midlife challenges, role dynamics are often implicated. Relinquishing parenting duties, loss of a job, career changes, a spouse returning to school, caretaking for parents, relocation to a new community, health challenges—these events all imply role change. Roles influence marriages in a variety of ways. Partners who are unable or unwilling to meet changing role expectations may experience anxiety, guilt, or

rejection. Role rigidity makes a person impervious to changes in partner needs. Some roles are incompatible, as couples sometimes discover
when they try to balance work and caretaking obligations. Professionals
can assist centerstage couples in diagnosing role-related stressors and
help them renegotiate roles.

BEST PRACTICES OF CENTERSTAGE COUPLES

Having studied many successful couples, we approached this book with
the spirit of hope, for it is certainly the case that many of your clients will
overcome the challenges we describe in the following chapters. The centerstage of marriage is often a time of positive transition and relational
growth. We wrote this book, in part, because we wanted to share the
experiences of the resilient couples we have encountered in our various
research projects. Each chapter integrates some of that accumulated wisdom with our own analysis. But before proceeding, we offer this summary
of seven best practices of successful midlife couples. Derived from our
own research and that of other researchers (Mackey & O'Brien, 1996),
these practices are applicable to each of the transitions and life events
described in this book. Of course, there exists no one magical communication formula. Centerstage couples will need your assistance in adapting
these ideas to their own circumstances as they explore new terrain *beyond
the empty nest*.

1. Renew Relationship Commitment

Many couples told us "recommitment stories," tales of trying times or
wavering allegiances, followed by pledges of renewed commitment to
the marriage. Having entered a new stage of life, spouses may need to
"rechoose" their partnership. One couple implemented this process by
drawing a line on a piece of paper, and placing an X toward the middle.
In the space before the X, they wrote descriptions of the "old couple"
and their child-raising years; the space after the X described possibilities
for their future. They committed to seek that future together. As they
would say, new commitments breed hope. Hope creates the possibility
of change. Recommitment is an important theme in chapter 3, which
examines the process of forgiveness.

2. Prioritize the Relationship

Faced with new opportunities and changing obligations, some midlife couples can find their relationship slipping down the list of priorities. Careers often peak at this time of life. A return to school or a new career can be exhilarating, but also time-consuming. Family obligations, such as caring for elderly parents, can be emotionally exhausting. Nevertheless, we find that successful couples continue to make their marriage the highest priority, even in the midst of such challenges as job loss and a return to school (chapter 5). They look for the warning signs of neglect and talk about them. Relationship time is built in to their schedules, the health of their relationship is a major consideration when making important decisions, and regular communication is used to navigate these dynamics.

3. Negotiate Changing Expectations

Conflict at midlife often stems from changing expectations. How much time will we spend together? How much money do we want to save? How often do we want to have sex? Resilient couples "surface" problematic expectations, negotiate differences, and find creative ways to blend their expectations. As noted in chapter 7, relocation decisions often bring different expectations to the surface.

4. Find a Common Voice

When faced with a crises or challenge, resilient couples speak as much as possible with a common voice. For example, in deciding how to respond to an adult child's request for assistance (chapter 6), they discuss the options and negotiate a common course of action. They avoid the temptation to negotiate "side deals" with family members, and they support each other in conversations with family and friends.

5. Maintain an External System of Support

Resilient couples build supportive relationships outside the marriage. They tend to nurture relationships with friends and often find support in their family relationships. Connections with external groups (volunteer organizations, religious communities, recreational groups) are important when individual and relational identities are revised (chapter 4). In addition, external support systems are a source of distraction and strength during times of crisis. They provide and an unending source of meaningful conversation and joint action during the normal periods.

6. Develop the Habit of Dialogue

Dialogue is the kind of communication that promotes understanding during times of disagreement (chapter 2). It can be contrasted with debate, which is designed to yield a winner, and even persuasion, which is designed to change opinions. Dialogue fosters cooperation rather than competition, even as it honors real differences of opinion. Partners who engage in dialogue agree to "join the same team" in an effort to better understand a problem and develop a collaborative solution.

7. Sustain Intimacy

Most successful couples actively cultivate emotional and physical closeness. They recognize signs of emotional distancing and talk about them. They respect a partner's need for an "emotional break," but they also expect emotional honesty. Self-disclosure is used freely in many of these marriages. Feelings are acknowledged and explored. When couples describe their partners' strengths, they often mention empathy and understanding. Typically, these couples value their sexual relationship. They talk about sex freely and find ways to keep it fresh. Chapter 2 discusses the communication practices that function to redevelop intimacy.

CONCLUDING THOUGHTS: REMODELING THE EMPTY NEST

Our intention in this chapter has been to introduce the reader to the assumptions and key analytical concepts that guide us as communication educators and lifespan researchers. These ideas inform subsequent chapters and help us organize them. But their main purpose is to help you identify potential explanations for the emotional and relational stresses reported by clients. We find that concepts like resilience, dialectical tensions, and roles, when appropriately adapted by a professional, give clients an enriched relational language—one that helps them move beyond the limiting metaphor of the empty nest.

REFERENCES

Bakhtin, M. M. (1981). *The dialectic imagination: Four essays* (M. Holquist Ed.; C. Emerson & M. Holquist, Trans.). Austin: University of Texas Press.

Baxter, L. A. (2003). A tale of two voices: Relational dialectics theory. *Journal of Family Communication, 4*, 181–192.

Baxter, L. A., & Montgomery, B. M. (1996). *Relating: Dialogues and dialectics.* New York: Guilford Press.

Blumer, H. (1969). *Symbolic interactionism: Theory and method.* Berkeley: University of California Press

Mackey, R., & O'Brien, B. (1995). Lasting marriages: Men and women growing together. *Journal of Marriage and Family, 58*, 527–528.

Park, N., Peterson, C., & Seligman, M. (2004). Strengths of character and well-being. *Journal of Social and Clinical Psychology, 23*, 603–619.

Resilience solutions group. (2008). www.asu.edu/resilience

Szinovacz, M. E., & Davey, A. (2007). *Caregiving contexts: Cultural, familial, and societal implications.* New York: Springer Publishing Company.

Waldron, V., & Kelley, D. (2008). *Communicating forgiveness.* Thousand Oaks, CA: Sage Publications.

Waldron, V., Gitelson, R., & Kelley, D. (2005). Gender differences in social adaptation to a retirement community: Longitudinal changes and the role of mediated communication. *Journal of Applied Gerontology, 24*, 283–298.

Wilmot, W. W., & Hocker, J. (2007). *Interpersonal conflict* (7th ed.). New York: McGraw-Hill.

Recoupling: Optimizing Relational Processes

2 Improving Communication

After 26 years of relative stability, Meg and Don find themselves hip deep in change. Three of their four children have left home and the couple's oldest daughter is getting married. At Don's suggestion, they recently left a familiar religious community for a new one that aligns more closely with their political commitments. After years of working for a large firm, Meg is filing the papers to launch her own small business. Natural optimism and their shared sense of humor have helped the partners adapt to these changes. Gradually, they have become aware of shifts in their communication. Meg says they no longer act like two individuals cooperating to beat the odds as parents, providers, and lovers. Now they feel more like a team preparing for a promising new season. Don and Meg are realizing that some of their most familiar patterns of interaction are no longer relevant, no longer work, or, in some cases, never worked in the first place. As their old life fades from view and their marriage moves to centerstage, Meg and Don are taking stock. When pressed, Don describes them as more flexible and forgiving. He is making adjustments and finding ways to support Meg's need for change. For her part, Meg is letting go of grudges and talking out conflicts, sure signs for her that the marriage is growing more resilient. Having eased up on a decades-long effort to change each other, this veteran couple is now communicating in a manner that is more flexible, supportive, and accepting of difference.

Communication is consistently placed in the list of top three reasons couples divorce. At midlife, smoldering resentments and destructive communication practices sometimes become intolerable. Inability to manage conflict, lack of emotional closeness, and an absence of supportive communication are among the numerous relational complaints that surface at this time of married life (Waldron & Kelley, 2008). Yet, as we learned from Don and Meg, midlife changes in external circumstances can be the catalyst for increased flexibility and insight. Grounded in our interviews with resilient couples, this chapter focuses on communication practices that help couples adapt to the unique challenges of centerstage marriage.

Early in our research, we assumed that middle-aged partners would have settled into reasonably constructive communication patterns and that destructive behaviors would be weeded out over decades of marriage. Certainly, this is the case for many marriage veterans. But in lengthy interviews, couples often described this period of life as a time of reassessment. For some, the passing of time had served to habituate poor patterns of communication and harden feelings of resentment. The end of active parenting was perceived to be a "make or break" turning point for less satisfied couples. More satisfied ones, those like Don and Meg, saw it as a time to optimize an already strong partnership. Both kinds of couples surprised us with descriptions of substantive change. And quite a few sought guidance from counselors, religious advisors, or close friends as they assessed and adjusted the communication patterns that had defined the marriage for so long.

REASSESSING FAMILIAR PATTERNS

The pressure to make relational adjustments came from a variety of sources. One of those was career change; illustrated by a couple we call Sandra and Carlos. For years, he held an executive office in the financial division of a well-known international conglomerate. But after weathering a series of mergers and culture changes, Carlos was "burned out." He accepted an early retirement buyout at the age of 54. Sandra was in a much different place at the age of 47—eager to resume a public service career that had been delayed by a long stint as a stay-at-home parent. When we talked to them, the couple was in the midst of negotiating new roles and communication patterns. Carlos had assumed the responsibilities of cook, grocery shopper, and housecleaner. Sandra had just transitioned from a volunteer position to a paid leadership role at her favorite nonprofit. They both claimed to be happier, but they were struggling with new patterns of communication, which seemed oddly "reversed" for this traditional couple. Why couldn't Sandra warn him if she would be late for dinner, Carlos wanted to know? And why did she insist that he accompany her to the many fundraising events that her nonprofit hosted each year? Sandra was frustrated by Carlos' need for structure and predictability at this point in their lives. She asked him to "lighten up" and be more supportive as she reestablished herself professionally.

A second source of change is the role relaxation that accompanies the end of active parenting. Even the most flexible of married couples tend to allocate roles during the busy early years of parenting. In the interests of efficiency and improved coordination, specialization often replaces negotiation and joint decision making. Autocracy is encouraged within certain realms of domestic life because it just too exhausting to share trivial decisions. For example, in a traditional family, Mom decides how much money is appropriate to spend on tennis shoes or school supplies. Dad may specialize in other financial decisions, such as those involving car repair or college savings. Once the kids are gone, some of these often implicit agreements can become obsolete and they need to be renegotiated. Couples who fail to do so may feel stuck in old patterns. Partners may feel disadvantaged by old arrangements, which (for example) limit their influence on how the couple's shared financial resources are used.

Pressure to change communication patterns comes from a third source—the family relationship challenges that often arise at midlife. These challenges are the topic of chapter 6, but we note here that couples in our studies often reported difficult conversations about the challenges of adult children and aging parents. These conversations can surface old tensions about money and family obligations, as couples decide how to support an aging parent, how much financial support to provide adult offspring, and how to respond to boomerang children. The communication skills of some couples will be taxed by the high stakes and emotional intensity of these conflicts, which require inventive, collaborative, and patient forms of interaction. As Tim and Lori illustrate for us, these discussions can be particularly trying in blended families, with their complicated family histories and relational commitments.

Tim and Lori had been married 12 years, and both had two children from a previous marriage. All four kids were off to college now; two of them, Brandon and Mitch (Tim's children), were living together. After a major sibling conflict,

Mitch moved out even though he lacked the financial resources to live on his own for very long. Without consulting Lori, Tim agreed to "rescue" Mitch with a loan. Lori strongly preferred that Mitch make peace with his brother, and she worried that the other kids would perceive Tim's financial help as favoritism. They had struggled for years to be even-handed in their dealings with four step-siblings. The couple's early discussions about this matter were marked by accusations and defensiveness. Eventually, though, the couple negotiated a mutually acceptable response, one which not only honored their parenting commitments to Mitch and the other adult children but also renewed their commitment to marital consultation and solidarity. Tim admitted that he had overreacted to his son's distress, something he was prone to do. Lori acknowledged his concern but asked that they jointly develop a solution to address the concerns of the whole family. They ended up providing short-term financial assistance to Tim but insisted that the brothers negotiate an acceptable living arrangement within a month.

Finally, midlife couples feel pressured to change their communication when confronted with the reality that old patterns simply are not working. One or both partners recognize that the marriage is failing to meet its potential. Faced with the prospect of decades of dissatisfaction, some couples seek counseling for the first time or simply approach counseling sessions with a new sense of urgency. As one counseling colleague shared with us, this is the "make or break" period for some of her female clients. We heard from midlife partners who lost (or never developed) the ability to communicate without really noticing . . . until the kids were gone. Fundamentally, poor communication practices had been obscured behind years of ritualized interactions about work demands, the kid's braces, and school activities. During the active parenting years, the marriage seemed okay, because the family business was running relatively smooth. At midlife, relational needs and expectations change, distractions diminish, and time spent together increases. All of these trends combine to expose a couples' communicative weaknesses.

BUILDING COMMUNICATION CAPACITY

The running family joke, according to Ross and Dena (married 24 years) was that they would kill each other when the kids moved out. As they described it, their sometimes tumultuous relationship was held together by the most tenuous of threads. For most of it Ross had traveled 3 to

5 days a week selling medical equipment. When he was home, the kids kept the couple engaged and distracted from the personality differences that sparked their frequent arguments. Friends kidded that the marriage worked only because Ross was gone most of the time and, of course, the kids were so cute! Fortunately, Dena and Ross realized they had some hard work to do—some of it involved simply accepting their differences. But they also realized that the success of their relationship would turn on their capacity to communicate more effectively. The couple learned to adjust their conflict management tactics, toning down the competitive approach that came so naturally. They recognized that, no matter what the topic, their conflicts were nearly always about control and winning. The prospect of a lifelong war was ultimately unappealing, so the mercurial couple pledged to be less verbally aggressive, more collaborative, and ultimately more mindful about the communication practices they used.

In this chapter, we explore communication problems that surface most frequently when veteran couples recount the challenges of the centerstage of married life. Of course, poor communication is a pervasive cause of distress at every stage of marriage and some of the solutions are basic; for example, better listening, fewer hurtful comments, more compliments, and supportive messages. Some midlife couples simply need assistance in diagnosing and (finally) confronting these most fundamental building blocks of healthy communication. Others grapple with communication challenges that really do seem unique to, or at least amplified by, their development position in the life course. In the following pages, we help you serve the needs of both kinds of clients.

SOURCES OF DISTRESS

Although there are many communicative sources of distress, we organize them around these major categories: (1) inequitable relationship maintenance practices, (2) rigidity of communication practices and perceptions, (3) skill deficits, and (4) physiological effects of aging.

Inadequate Relationship Maintenance Practices

Although researchers and clinicians often focus on marital conflicts, it has become increasingly obvious that it is the routine communication practice of couples that require our attention. It turns out that resiliency in marriage has a lot to do with *relationship maintaining* communication (Canary & Dainton, 2003). From this increasingly prominent point of

view, marriages fail for the same reasons that automobiles break down—
occasionally they crash and burn, but more commonly they succumb
to poor maintenance practices. After years of neglect, key components
wear down, points of friction wear thin, and the complex synchronization
required to keep the system running becomes increasingly out of balance.

The maintenance of a healthy marriage requires regular and conscientious communicative investments by both partners. A marriage withers
when the contribution of one or both partners lag, but the deficit may
become obvious only at midlife. At least five different maintenance practices are required for marriages to thrive.

BOX 2.1 FIVE KEY RELATIONSHIP MAINTENANCE PRACTICES

1 Sharing tasks
2 Offering assurances
3 Maintaining openness
4 Communicating positivity
5 Maintaining social networks

Task Sharing

Successful relationships are characterized by a subjective sense of *equity*.
That is, each individual contributes a roughly equal amount of "relational
work" to sustaining the marriage and the larger family. Relationship work
includes childraising, home maintenance, paid employment, arranging
social activities, planning family vacations, maintaining relationships with
extended family, and countless other tasks. Partners often perform different kinds of tasks, particularly in traditional marriages. Of course, some
tasks are shared and others are delegated to one of the partners based on
ability, interest, availability, and other criteria.

Task sharing is a means by which partners maintain equity—the
subjective perception of fairness. Feelings of inequity often surface at
midlife. Partners feel *under benefited* when the relational work they are
performing outweighs the benefits they are receiving. It arises from a
sense that one's partner is contributing less but receiving more benefit. Of course, it is quite typical for marriages to experience periods of
significant inequity. For a period of time, one partner may be too ill to
contribute materially or even emotionally to the relationship. Or, a job

layoff may leave one partner carrying the financial burden for an extended period. In healthy relationships, the partners accept these inequities and make necessary adjustments. They tend to calculate equity over the long term and often view their capacity to weather periods of inequity as a sign of relationship strength.

Nonetheless, unequal task sharing can be a source of distress in centerstage marriages, largely because previously negotiated task arrangements were unfair, or seem so now. Marcy described how this became a problem in her marriage with Randy.

For years, I had done most of the domestic work at our house: cooking, cleaning, and getting the kids to and from school. That kind of thing. Randy was at his job all day, and it seemed like the right way to balance things. But the kids got older and I started working, at first just part time. But I was still doing all of the other stuff. No one helped me cook dinner or do the laundry. I started to feel more and more stressed and resentful. When the kids moved out and things didn't change, I became frustrated, like I was going to explode. I told Randy he needed to pitch in more or he was going to have a very unhappy home life.

Marcy experienced what psychologist Marie Hochschild (1993) described as the *second shift* phenomena, a tendency for women to retain responsibility for a disproportionate amount of domestic work, over and above their work outside the home. To establish equitable task sharing, partners must honestly inventory the work they are each contributing to the household. Some couples will need assistance in defining what counts as work. For example, some men (and some women) do not recognize that tasks like meal planning, cooking, and arranging family relationships take considerable effort. Maintaining the family vehicles and keeping track of finances are other forms of work. All of these are important relationship maintenance tasks. Next, the couple will need to negotiate task assignments with an eye to reestablishing equity. This step may result in new arrangements, as partners accept new tasks, learn to share others, and sometimes "contract out" certain kinds of work.

Communicating Assurance

Research suggests that even long-time spouses need to hear assurances from their partners. This is particularly true during times of uncertainty or significant change. As we have suggested, middle-stage marriage inevitably brings some uncertainty. Partners may wonder if their bond can be sustained without the glue of childrearing. As bodies age, sexual insecurity may become a concern. New experiences like the loss of a job or a return to school may surface long dormant insecurities. Assurances come in multiple forms, but they all tend to affirm the future of the relationship and love for the partner. Here are some concrete examples, reported by midlife couples:

- "We talked about how much fun we will have when we retire, traveling and being together all of the time."
- "She tells me I look 'sexy' with gray hair."
- "When I get cranky, I wonder how he puts up with it. But he tells me he married me 'forever.'"
- "Sometimes we sit down and look at our old pictures and it helps us remember why we have stayed together and how good we have been together. And that keeps us going even during the tough times."

Resilient couples communicate assurance by engaging in what researchers call *marriage rituals*—repeated and predictable sequences of events that, when performed, affirm the relationship's past and signal a commitment to the future. Maintaining these rituals becomes particularly important during times of uncertainty or stress. One couple described their escape to a mountain cabin every January. In addition to enjoying each other's uninterrupted company, they review the "state of their union" and plan for the coming year.

Maintaining Openness

A frequent complaint of couples is inequity in the sharing of personal feelings or the willingness to discuss difficult topics like sex or money. Openness of this type is a defining feature of intimacy, but it does entail a certain amount of vulnerability. Some partners grow weary of their mate's reluctance to be open. They resent having to always do the sometimes hard work of surfacing unspoken emotions, initiating difficult conversations, or probing for the cause of relational tension.

Communicating Positivity

A durable contribution of the pioneering work of psychologist John Gottman (1994) is the *positivity ratio*, a notion that resurfaces in discussions of relationship maintenance practices. The idea is simple: By creating more positive than negative experiences for one another, romantic partners maintain satisfying relationships. A close examination of the communication practices of unsatisfied midlife couples is often revealing. Many can easily recall the negative communication behaviors that characterize their daily interactions: criticisms, unsupportive comments, insults, inattentive behavior, rudeness, grumpiness, slothfulness, failure to offer help, and so on. Positive experiences are a less common feature of their ordinary interactions, but this ratio can be improved when partners cultivate positivity through compliments, acknowledgments of success, sharing warm memories, expressions of affection, gifts, invitations, gratitude, discussing plans for the future, expressions of solidarity, and the use of humor.

Maintaining Social Networks

Most married couples find companionship, social support, and new conversational topics through their connections to common friends and family members. Finding and keeping these connections is an important relationship maintenance task. In some marriages, the responsibility for maintaining social connections falls to one partner (in traditional marriages, it is often treated as women's work). At midlife, a time of changing social networks, this allocation of responsibility may need to be reassessed and shared more equitably.

Rigidity in Communication Practices and Perceptions

Centerstage clients are typically advantaged by long experience, but there are downsides too. As one husband told us, the passing of time can bring a kind of "hardening of the relational arteries." Communication becomes more habitual and mindless, rigid routines replace spontaneity and flexibility, and partners become inattentive to the relational meanings implied by their messages.

Mindless Behavior

Psychologist Ellen Langer (1990) coined the term *mindlessness* to describe a state of consciousness that governs habitual behavior. Mindless behavior is different from that which is subconscious because it can be brought to awareness through the choice and efforts of the actor. To use a simple example, walking is largely a mindless endeavor. Leaving the couch and walking to the refrigerator requires little or no conscious processing. However, if an unexpected object is encountered on the way, a discarded toy or a sleeping dog, walking becomes a conscious effort to deal with a novel set of circumstances. Researchers estimate that the *majority* of complex human behavior and, specifically, communication behavior, is mindless. The percentage increases with experience. The implications for midlife clients are obvious. First, much of their marital communication is mindless. Second, dysfunctional patterns of mindless behavior are likely to be noticed only when novel conditions are encountered (as they often are at midlife) or through the assistance of a counselor.

Although it is inherently resistant to self-discovery, mindless behavior can be brought under conscious control. A husband who habitually uses a sarcastic tone of voice can change the tone if he can become aware of its use. The reality, of course, is that in conversation, vocal tone is almost always mindless. The sarcastic husband catches himself only after the damage is done, sometimes with the help of his wife. Insight about these mindless patterns might prompt the husband to apologize and repair the damage. As explained in more detail below, counselors can help clients learn to anticipate mindless behavior, by attending to internal and external cues (including rising levels of arousal). A first step is to look for signs that mindlessness is driving marital distress.

BOX 2.2 WHAT YOU MIGHT HEAR FROM CLIENTS: SIGNS OF MINDLESS COMMUNICATION PATTERNS

- Recurring conflicts and arguments
- Repeated use of hurtful behavior despite pledges to stop
- Frustration at the difficulty of changing one's own behavior
- Limited awareness about the causes of marital conflict
- Reports that certain kinds of interactions trigger emotional reactions or "push buttons"
- Frustration that interactions seem to get out of hand, despite good intentions

---

Obsolete Expectations

Clients experience distress when their partners fail to communicate in a way that meets expectations. This experience is common at midlife when partners and circumstances inevitably change, but a client's expectations remain rigid. Outdated expectations were probably quite functional when they were developed, so letting them go can be difficult. Familiar ways of thinking and behaving provide comfort, predictability, and control in a changing world. It is not surprising that midlife couples often lament the partner's failure to conform to expectations.

BOX 2.3 WHAT YOU MIGHT HEAR FROM CLIENTS: UNMET EXPECTATIONS

- We used to go to church together every Sunday. I miss that.
- When she stayed home with the kids, the pace of life seemed more relaxed.
- We used to do everything together; now he has his own interests.
- I want a bigger part in our financial decisions now.
- He still wants me to "play housewife," but that isn't me anymore.
- She wants the kids home every weekend; I say let them spread their wings.

The client who changes the expectations she has for herself, her partner, or her family, admits a new uncertainty into her world. Some clients fear a "domino effect" with one treasured expectation falling after another. For example, the traditional husband who expects to make financial decisions in his household may wonder what will follow when he relaxes that expectation. He risks changing expectations for himself ("Maybe I need to be less controlling") and how the marriage should operate ("Maybe we need to be more democratic in decision making"). As this example suggests, resistance to change sometimes stems from an (often unconscious) desire to preserve a privileged position in a relationship.

In counseling, clients reveal rigid expectations when they express frustration over what *should* be happening in the marriage, but is not. You can help clients identify outdated expectations, unrealistic expectations, and differences in expectation. Resilient couples adjust their expectations and helping them do so may be a goal of therapy.

Relational Messages

Successful marital communication requires the partners to attend to the relational implications of their messages. Recurring conflicts are rarely about topics (Should we move?) and more frequently about the relational implications (You are forcing me to move!). Even experienced couples need help in surfacing the relational implication of their messages. In fact, the relational sensitivity of veteran couples may be dulled by decades-long habits of interaction.

Many couples never learn the difference between content and relationship levels of communication. And yet, this critical distinction in meaning shapes perception during interactions and results in most significant conflicts in marriage. Some couples find their way to divorce still believing that what they are fighting about is money, the kids, or some other tangible issue.

The content of a message is the denotative meanings of its words. However, any given utterance imposes a definition of the relationship. Relational meanings are often signaled and accepted mindlessly and they address such key relational qualities as trust, respect, power, inclusion, intimacy, and liking.

BOX 2.4 DIMENSIONS OF RELATIONAL MESSAGES

Trust: Can you be counted on?
Respect: Do I hold you in high regard? Are you an equal?
Power: Who is in charge of this conversation? This relationship?
Inclusion: Am I being invited to participate, consulted, or rejected?
Intimacy: How emotionally close do we want to be right now?
Liking: Do I feel liking or contempt for you right now?

When a couple argues over finances, money is the apparent topic. However, at the relational level, the issue is, for example, that he or she did not adhere to the guidelines that they had agreed on. Respect and trust are the relational issues driving the conflict. Lisa and Samuel, a veteran couple interviewed for our previous book on forgiveness (Waldron & Kelley, 2008), recounted how Lisa secretly overspent their budget, placing them in deep financial peril—twice. Sam told us:

She got us into big trouble. I had to forgive her for not confiding in me, not for getting us into financial trouble. Any kind of forgiveness I had to do was to forgive her for not confiding in me.

In Sam's mind, the content (overspending) was not the main problem. He could accept the fact that Lisa was a poor money manager. The bigger problem was the relational meaning embedded in Lisa's decision to hide the problem from her husband. Her failure to reveal this information signaled a lack of trust and intimacy that deeply bothered Sam. Clients need help in identifying relationship messages. Often, they waste time and energy arguing over content rather than addressing the underlying relational concern. If left unresolved, the relational issues resurface later, disguised as another content issue.

Deficits in Communication Skills

A significant source of distress for couples is the lack of basic communication skill. This is sometimes surprising to counselors for whom communication often comes "naturally." It is easy to overestimate a veteran couple's capacity for productive communication because the assumption is that long experience should yield improved skill. But in our research, we have been struck by the number of couples who felt compelled to make midlife adjustments in communication practices, often because they recognized that communication deficits were the root cause of recurring problems. Here we identify just a few of the most common communication problems reported by midlife couples. For additional detail on helping couples remedy communication difficulties, see *Working with Clients*.

Poor Conflict Management Practices

Constructive conflict management practices help couples negotiate the inevitable differences in goals that arise at midlife. The most common problems are the failure to attend to relational messages (see previous discussion) and the habitual use of competitive (win/lose) or avoidant conflict styles. Clients often need assistance in recognizing mindless destructive responses to conflict, such as a tendency to become defensive when questioned or a propensity to keep legitimate concerns quiet to avoid "a scene." The counselor can help couples spot communication behaviors (stonewalling, intimidation through shouting) that make conflicts dysfunctional. He or she can help them appreciate that conflict is to be expected at midlife. In counseling, couples can explore the underlying concerns that drive the conflict and devise creative responses that better meet the goals of both partners. Increased flexibility and creativity at key points in the life span, in contrast to the usual head butting over narrowly defined differences, is a common theme in the narratives of resilient couples.

Failure to Listen

Poor listening is so commonly cited as a source of marital distress that it has become a cliché. Nonetheless, most people have only a rudimentary understanding of listening in its various forms. Counseling can help partners identify the behaviors that enhance (open-ended questions) or inhibit (interruptions) listening. They should know that different kinds of listening are appropriate for different purposes (see *Working with Clients*).

Unchecked Arousal

Poor listening and conflict management practices often stem from an underlying failure to control arousal. In lay understanding, arousal is associated with sexuality. However, in a more general application, arousal is the "fight-or-flight" response. Physiological arousal is the body's focusing agent. When threatened, the body goes on alert, focuses on survival, filters out extraneous noise and activity, and puts all of its resources into fighting or fleeing for survival. Moderate arousal is beneficial. In conflict situations, it helps participants focus, process the multiple potential meanings of complex messages, and construct creative and adaptive responses.

Arousal becomes problematic at higher levels because it focuses attention too narrowly on a perceived threat and limits response options to a few fight-or-flight options. John Gottman's (1982) detailed observations of marital conflicts suggest that many husbands find increased arousal—particularly when associated with negative emotion—psychologically uncomfortable. As such, as a way of managing their discomfort, they may withdraw from the interaction or attack and then withdraw.

High arousal promotes the kind of mindless, instinctual responses, which are needed in highly threatening situations (e.g., quickly locking the car doors at the unexpected appearance of a masked person in a parking garage). These automatic reactions are less functional in marital conflicts where rising arousal levels "trigger" defensive responses, which are often reciprocated by a highly aroused partner. The result is an escalating spiral of attack-defend moves. In therapy, clients can learn to control arousal levels by (1) responding mindfully to arousal cues and (2) replacing simplistic fight-or-flight responses with more adaptive communication behaviors (see later discussion).

BOX 2.4 CASE STUDY: HIGH AROUSAL UNDERMINES COMMUNICATION

Kevin and Patti are in their second marriage—married 15 years. Patti's son, Ryan, resented Kevin's parenting efforts, and as a teenager, he frequently rebelled. Ryan graduated early from high school so he could "get out of this house" and head for college. In his first year, Ryan's grades suffered, and in Kevin's opinion, "He blew through enough money to live comfortably for 2 years." Kevin was highly agitated by what he perceived to be a waste of resources, and he accused Patti of coddling Kevin. She was stung by his criticism and leapt to his defense. She attacked Kevin for "valuing money more than my son." He had no right to pick on Ryan, who "is still young and learning to manage his money." Patti's attacking response was driven in part by her fear that Ryan would turn to his dad (Patti's ex-husband), whom Patti believed was a bad influence. The couple traded insults and their voices rose, but their basic disagreement about how to parent was never really addressed

Patti and Kevin found a counselor who helped them improve their listening and problem-solving skills. But these lessons were often discarded in the midst of heated conflicts where familiar attack-defend patterns quickly resurfaced. The couple's inability to control rising levels of arousal continued to undermine their relationship.

Inability to Engage in Dialogue

We reserve the term *dialogue* for communication designed to promote understanding. Dialogue is a process in which communicators abandon efforts to persuade or argue. Instead, the purpose is to fully explore problems and define as many perspectives as possible. The participants eschew ownership of any given position so ego involvement is minimized. They work together to locate points of similarity and difference and avoid the temptation to minimize differences. Dialogue proceeds under the assumption that understanding is in itself a worthwhile relational accomplishment. It assumes that decision-making is improved when options and contingencies are fully explored. Partners who reach decisions through dialogue typically feel more respected and relationally connected than those who make decisions through debate.

Clients are often unfamiliar with the process of dialogue, largely due to cultural assumptions in the United States, which favor persuasion, debate, and winning. In counseling, these assumptions often need to be surfaced. The sometimes overwhelming urge to argue or win must be checked. Dialogue is a particularly important skill at midlife, when couples face complicated decisions. Will we move or stay in our current home? Is a career change a good idea? How do we prepare for the end of our working years? How do we respond to the needs of elderly parents?

Physiological Effects of Aging

At midlife, clients begin to experience age-related changes in physiology, some of which affect marital communication. These are sometimes overlooked or discounted as sources of marital distress. You can help clients recognize the effects on themselves (or their partners) and encourage them to make appropriate adaptations. Perhaps the most obvious of physical changes stem from chronic or acute illness. This topic is addressed in chapter 8. Other physical changes that affect communication are inevitable declines in vision and hearing. It is easy for couples to fail to recognize the impact that hearing and sight loss may have on stress levels in their home and, subsequently, their communication with one another. But research on midlife couples confirms that they may need assistance in confronting and adapting to physiological challenges. For example, one study reported emotionally distressed family members with acquired profound hearing loss (APHL) were likely to cope through potentially ineffective strategies such as avoidance, self-blame, and wishful thinking (Hallam, Ashton, Sherbourne, Gailey, & Courney, 2007). You can refer clients to organizations that teach family members to cope with more constructive communication practices and by using communication technologies.

Changes in physical attractiveness also influence communication. As couples age into their mid-40s and 50s, they often experience weight gain, hair loss and graying, and changes in skin quality. These changes may affect perceptions of attractiveness and sometimes prompt increases in criticism, defensiveness, and withdrawal. Loss of self-confidence, depression, desire to spend money on physical enhancement, or renewed interest in "eating right" and "working out" may all be sources of conflict in a midlife marriage. These concerns may affect one or both partners' sexual desire, which may, in turn, undermine the closeness and security of the relationship.

Physical changes also may include shifts in metabolism resulting in lower energy and reduced activity. For couples used to being "on the go," these changes might precipitate corresponding changes in how they spend time together. A couple who loved to hike may find less energy for it until after retirement. Similarly, menopause (and perimenopause) has the potential to impact the relationship as the wife potentially experiences changes in her physical appearance, sleep patterns, mood stability, sexual appetite, and fatigue.

In counseling, some midlife partners confront unrealistic expectations about aging, beauty, and sexuality. Clients sometimes need an opportunity to voice aging-related insecurities as a first step in establishing realistic standards for health and beauty. Spousal criticism of appearance (e.g., Aren't you gaining some weight? Shouldn't you be going to the gym more often?) can be devastating. Counselors can sometimes help critical spouses understand why this kind of communication is hurtful and suggest more encouraging forms of communication. Counselors may help the couple repair the damage through a process of forgiveness (see chapter 3). In addition, midlife couples need encouragement for their efforts to maintain physical vigor and health. Although it is often associated with slowed metabolism and weight gain, the centerstage of marriage often brings more time for exercise and self-care. It may be easier than ever to eat well. Couples often find that shared commitments to exercise and healthy living become integral parts of their evolving relational identity.

ANALYTICAL TOOLS

The analytical frameworks introduced in chapter 1 can be helpful in interpreting clients' descriptions of the communication challenges and opportunities they encounter during the centerstage of married life.

Applying the Dialectical Framework

Several dialectical tensions are prominent in the relational narratives of midlife couples. One common theme involves *autonomy* and *interdependence*. Couples who have been particularly family- or child-focused may seek greater autonomy in new careers, hobbies, and organizations. These new pursuits may result in lower levels of collaboration and discussion, which can be disconcerting for some partners. Alternatively, some couples who played highly specialized parenting roles may find themselves collaborating more closely and talking more. This, too, can be disconcerting.

Openness and *closedness* are related dialectical tensions. As partners become more autonomous, they may also feel increased insecurity. Increased information sharing helps partners manage feelings of unpredictability. The husband who supports his spouse's decision to complete an unfinished college degree may feel assured by her efforts to keep him in the loop as she takes new classes, meets new people, and considers new career goals. Increases in autonomy often promote open communication because the partners have more differentiated experiences to discuss. With children out of the house, they may find themselves with more time to sit and talk. One of the busy couples we interviewed built "listening time" into their daily routine. Each evening, they would have a drink together, sit out on the patio, and listen to each other.

Another prominent dialectical tension is *judgment versus acceptance*. Some spouses postpone difficult discussions in an effort to keep the family functioning smoothly. After the kids moved out, Stacey, married 34 years, told her husband Dave that during most of their marriage she had simply agreed with him to "keep the peace." Then, more specifically, she stated, "And I'm not going to just agree for peace any longer." For 34 years, Dave experienced the acceptance side of this dialectic. Today, they are learning how to negotiate a better balance between accepting one another and offering critique (judgment).

Christina, married 43 years, confided to us that, after the kids were gone, she was rather surprised to discover who she had actually married. Careers and kids had kept Von and her so busy that she had not really taken time to ponder what their lives would be like as a couple when the kids were gone. Von was fun to date and a good father to their children, but Christina found herself irritated by him once the children had moved out. This resulted in a barrage of things she needed to "fix" in him (judgment). Only now, 5 years later, is she learning to balance her constructive criticism with words of encouragement and validation.

BOX 2.5 HOW DO I USE IT? MANAGING DIALECTICAL TENSIONS

- Help clients focus on neglected poles of each dialectic (e.g., if autonomy is prominent help them conceptualize interdependence)
- Identify the interrelatedness of dialectics. When "bored" partners agree to increase autonomy, their individual pursuits yield more conversational topics (opportunities for *openness*).

- Help clients accept what feels like an overemphasis on one end of the continuum (e.g., during a partner's illness increased in interdependence may be needed).
- Help clients reframe dialectical tensions (e.g., what initially seems to be personal criticism or "excessive judging" to one partner may be reframed as an honest critique intended to assure long-term success).

Applying the Resiliency Framework

The resiliency characteristics of optimism and flexibility are often mentioned by couples who participate in our studies. Optimism is closely related to the positivity ratio introduced earlier. A dearth of encouraging communication leads to despair or hopelessness in the face of marital challenges, whereas resilient couples seem to cultivate hope through the conscious use of assurances, compliments, and positive assessments. These couples are not unrealistic; they simply maintain a healthy ratio of positive to negative experiences. Flexibility, or adaptability, is a hallmark of competent communication. Research demonstrates that unhappy couples produce rigid (predictable) patterns of communication (see Gottman, 1994), including attack-defend sequences. Satisfied partners are more adaptive, adjusting their communicative responses to contingencies of the present moment, rather than simply "executing" stock responses.

Applying the Roles Framework

Roles are both created by communication patterns and help create communication patterns. Role loss and role ambivalence are common experiences at midlife and they tend to intensify relational uncertainty. Uncertainty can be uncomfortable. Couples cannot eliminate it, but they can manage uncertainty by increasing self-disclosure, collaborative planning, discussing hypothetical outcomes, and communicating assurances. Uncertainty can be exacerbated by avoidant communication.

Another role consideration regards gender. The role differentiation that often takes place with the advent of children sometimes reproduces traditional gender expectations associated with fatherhood and motherhood (Mackey & O'Brien, 1995). As the children leave, these parental roles are less powerful and may need to be reworked. In some families, mothers are expected to be relationally focused, others oriented, peacemakers. As women leave that role behind, they may become more task-focused, self-oriented, and assertive. These changes may be confusing or threatening to family members, including her husband. Of course, the end of active fatherhood may stimulate changes in men. Couples should be cognizant of these role changes and flexible enough to welcome them.

WORKING WITH CLIENTS

This section provides a streamlined set of counseling tasks that we hope will be useful in helping centerstage couples improve their communication practices.

Inventory Relationship Maintenance Practices

Encourage clients to inventory their use of five types of relationship maintenance communication described earlier: sharing tasks, offering assurances, maintaining openness, communicating positivity, managing social work. In counseling, clients can list and even practice behaviors that will address deficiencies in these areas. Issues of equity should be discussed and possibilities for reallocating relationship maintenance responsibilities can be explored. Some other practical suggestions for counseling sessions:

- Recognize that resentful clients are sometimes *under-benefited*. They perceive inequities in the performance of maintenance.
- Look for the *second-shift* phenomenon, an indicator of gender inequity.
- Help clients value and expand their relationship maintenance activities.
- Prompt clients to invent new task sharing arrangements.
- Encourage clients to improve their positivity ratio.
- Suggest ways for both partners to expand and maintain the social network.

Change Mindless Behavior

You can help clients control mindless behavior in a three-step process. First, clients must be made aware of the destructive elements of their communication behavior. Clients are rarely aware of the sarcastic tone of voice they use during conflicts or the intimidating gestures they use when emotionally aroused. The counselor can provide useful feedback in this regard. The partner may need to provide clear, nonevaluative descriptions of the behaviors they observe at home. A second step is to substitute alternate behavior. As with many habitual (and addictive) behaviors, it is often beneficial to spend less time trying to extinguish a behavior than it is to practice a constructive replacement. For example, a spouse who habitually uses "cutting" humor could substitute humor that validates the partner. A third step is to help clients manage arousal (see later discussion) because, at high levels, it is associated with mindless behavior.

We suggest that couples work together to change deeply ingrained patterns. One approach is to schedule periodic couple meetings during times of low arousal. During this time, couples focus on changing patterns of behavior and avoid the fixing of blame. Individuals give permission to their partner to help them identify and change mindless communication behaviors. Each partner should *ask* how he or she can best help the mate change undesired behavior. The resultant discussion should be behaviorally specific. Statements such as, "I want to be more encouraging," are seldom helpful in actually changing behavior. In contrast, "When I come home at night, I want the first thing I say to you to be something positive" is specific. Finally, couples should be instructed to engage these tasks with a sense that they offer hope for the future of a valued relationship. Their willingness to working together is a harbinger of success.

BOX 2.6 PARTNERS WORKING TOGETHER TO CHANGE MINDLESS BEHAVIORS

- Schedule a couple meeting
- Talk openly as a couple about behaviors that need to be changed
- Avoid blaming
- Give the partner permission to help change behavior
- Ask how to help the partner recognize and change mindless behavior
- Be behaviorally specific
- Be affirming and hopeful

Keep Arousal in Check

Keeping arousal at a moderate level keeps conflicts from spiraling out of control and facilitates more creative and constructive communication.

General stress reduction is the first step in managing arousal. Couples who are constantly harried find it virtually impossible to interact well at home. Discuss the negative effects of sleep deprivation and encourage partners to find down time together. A second technique is to help clients plan responses to situations that typically elevate their arousal levels. Veteran couples can predict conflict situations with confidence. Help clients identify "triggering" behaviors such as conversational interruptions, critical comments, or failure to complete household tasks. Help them design highly specific, constructive responses. For example, rather than "exploding" when being interrupted in conversation, a spouse might say something like, "I want to hear what you have to say, but feel frustrated when I can't complete my thought." Arousal is driven in part by negative rumination, obsessive thinking about the injustice they experience in the relationship or the spouse's negative qualities. Clients need help with the task of replacing nonproductive rumination (e.g., "I can't believe how unfair this is") with less inflammatory thoughts ("I know he doesn't mean to hurt me. We can improve our communication").

Finally, because arousal is a physiological response, it can be reduced by physical action. Physical release of the arousal helps clients prepare for more mindful, creative, and productive responses. See Box 2.7 for examples.

BOX 2.7 PHYSICAL RESPONSES THAT REDUCE AROUSAL

- Deep breathing
- "Vent" with a friend before talking with spouse
- Prearrange that either partner can ask for a 10 minute break in conversation
- Run, kick box, or garden (exert energy)
- Move the conversation to a new or more relaxing environment
- Walk together while talking

Expand the Listening Repertoire

Relational problems are often the result of poor listening. However, it is important to recognize that listening is a relational process, not an individual one. Good listening not only requires individual concentration, but it also evolves through a series of constructive interactions. Queries, explanations, clarification, reframings—all of these are used in a cooperative way to work around potential misunderstandings and probe possible meanings. Good listening promotes a positive cycle of reciprocation and it reduces arousal.

Typically, clients will complain that their partner is not listening because their partner is not agreeing with them or did not understand them. Often, the partner is listening; he or she is using a different listening mode.

BOX 2.8 HELPING CLIENTS IDENTIFY DIFFERENT MODES OF LISTENING

- *Empathetic listening* involves understanding the speaker's emotional state and attitudes. Clients who listen empathetically can be so attuned to emotions that they miss content details, giving the impression of nonlistening.
- *Deliberative listening* involves critical assessment. The listener evaluates and assesses the speaker's reasoning. Clients whose primary listening mode is deliberative may be accused of missing the (emotional) point of the message or of being "critical" when the partner was hoping for support.
- *Listening to learn* involves a search for the facts and ideas presented by a speaker. Clients who primarily listen to learn may be so focused on "facts" that they lose sight of the bigger picture or miss the underlying relational messages.
- *Active listening* helps the speaker clarify his or her thoughts through a process of rephrasing or questioning. Active listeners' use of "strategies" such as paraphrasing and questioning, which, when misused, seem inauthentic or controlling.

Redevelop Intimacy

Some couples lose their sense of intimacy during the child-raising years. Regaining it is a priority of some of the centerstage couples who seek counseling. Intimacy is redeveloped along several dimensions of access. Over years of marriage, partners may intentionally or accidentally create barriers to social, informational, emotional, and physical access. Social access can be increased by encouraging clients to plan time together and experience joint activities. Informational access is frequently developed through small talk. Often individuals take this seemingly shallow form of communication for granted, but research indicates that happy couples who share the little things are better able to talk when serious relational issues confront them. A willingness to share dreams, insecurities, emotions, and concerns is the definition of psychological access. Finally, for many couples, physical access increases in response to increases in the other types of access. It includes not only sexual intimacy, but also holding hands or snuggling on the couch while watching a movie.

Use Metacommunication to Disrupt Reciprocity

Metacommunication occurs when couples talk about how they are communicating. Reciprocity is the tendency of communicators to match the behavior patterns of the partner. Expressions of affection are often reciprocated. The response to, "I love you," is usually, "I love you too." But hostility is reciprocated as well, particularly in conflict situations. If Larry criticizes Deanne for her poor eating habits, she may match the negativity she finds in his message. "Well who are you to talk? Didn't you tell me just last week that your new pants were getting tight?" Although negative patterns of reciprocation are common, they are not inevitable. Partners can learn to respond with behaviors that call attention to potentially destructive patterns and reframe them. Deanne might say something like, "Your comment about my weight makes me feel defensive. Can we talk about what you really meant when you said that?" Increasing this type of *metacommunication* is the goal of some of the educational exercises we use with students and couples (see the *Exercises* at the end of this chapter).

Reconceptualize Conflict

For many couples, conflict has a strictly negative connotation. The metaphors they use to describe it are jarring and unpleasant—battles, fights, relationship breakdowns—but conflicts are inevitable in marriage and they can be positive. Constructive conflicts have the effect of surfacing unspoken assumptions, prompting reflection, motivating change, and cultivating respect among the parties. One goal of counseling is to help couples build the communication practices that make conflict more productive. We have suggested couple meetings as a way to remedy the mindlessness that often drives destructive conflict behavior. Controlling arousal, expanded listening skills, and increased use of metacommunication were suggested as well (see *Exercises* for additional ideas).

Another goal of counseling may be to help couples adopt positive, or at least neutral, metaphors for conflict. By doing so, couples see that conflict does not need to involve winning and losing. Conflicts can help couples "air out" a relationship that is becoming stale. They can be the means by which couples confront the relatively few noxious weeds that have invaded the highly cultivated garden that is their relationship. Conflicts are brief detours on a long and rewarding journey, the spice of life, or the spark which reignites passion. Earlier, we suggested the metaphor of the dialogue, a team-based approach to developing a deeper understanding of differences and similarities. Indeed, reimagining conflict may help your married clients redefine their relationship as they move beyond the empty nest.

CONCLUDING THOUGHTS

This chapter covers just some of the many communication issues that challenge couples during the centerstage of marriage. Because communication is central to nearly every aspect of married life, you will find it discussed in each chapter of this book. For more detailed analyses of the role of communication behaviors in marital conflict, see the references included below, particularly the work of John Gottman. For your clients' reading, we have referenced a variety of highly regarded but highly accessible books and Web sites in Appendix A. Finally, activities that have proved helpful to us in teaching communication practices are described in the *Exercises* section at the end of the chapter. You may find them helpful in your own counseling sessions or workshops.

QUESTIONS FOR CLIENTS

1 Do your conversations with your spouse sometimes differ from what you expect? In what ways?
2 Do you observe mindless reactions in your communication that might be causing difficulties in your relationship?
3 Does heightened arousal cause your conflicts to "get away" from you?

4   Do you have more time to sit and talk at this stage of your marriage or less time?

5   Is talking and sharing your feelings easy? Awkward? Rewarding? When is it easiest?

6   Are there rituals that help hold your relationship together? (e.g., always reading before going to bed, summer vacation at the lake, coffee and the paper in the morning.)

7   Do you receive and offer social support in your marriage? Can you give examples?

8   What is the ratio of negative to positive comments in your conversations with your spouse?

9   Are you familiar with the notion of dialogue? When you have disagreements, it is possible to be on the "same team" as you consider possible solutions?

10 What relational messages do you typically send to your spouse? Do you signal respect? Trust? Inclusion in important decisions?

EXERCISES

Exercise 2.1 Changing Negative Mindless Behaviors

The goals of this exercise are to become aware of negative behavior and change unwanted habits.

1   Become *mindful* of negative mindless behavior.
    a   Get feedback from friends.
    b   Get feedback from spouse about possible *triggering behavior* (give your spouse permission to *gently* point out times when you engage in the negative behavior).
    c   Keep a journal in which you record your own behavior and possible triggers (the behavior that precedes and "sets off" the unwanted behavior).
    d   Record an interaction and watch yourself.
    e   Focus on specific behavior, not general attitudes ("I use sarcasm when asked questions" as opposed to "I need to be less negative").
2   Replace negative behavior with positive.
    a   Identify specific situations in which you would like to replace negative behavior.

    b Plan specific behavior (actual phrases or nonverbal elements) you would like to use to replace negative behavior.

3 Monitor arousal levels.

    a Replace negative rumination with positive constructive thoughts.

    b Use various physical strategies to reduce arousal (deep breathing, taking a walk, or postponing a conversation).

    c Work as a team (allow your partner to signal you when you are becoming highly aroused).

    d Work on changing one behavior at a time.

Exercise 2.2 Building Rituals

The goal of this exercise is to build positive patterns of relational behavior.

Go to your favorite coffee spot and spend an hour talking about what new rituals you'd like to create to keep your marriage strong. Focus on experiences that will help strengthen areas of your relationship that are important to you. Maybe it's Friday happy hour for half price appetizers and catching up on the week's activities, or a monthly hike in the mountains, or, like friends of ours, brushing your teeth and racing to bed!

Exercise 2.3 Relationship Maintenance

The goal of this exercise is to become more conscious of positive behaviors that will help maintain a healthy marriage.

Keep a journal over the next week making note of each time you engage in one of the following maintenance activities. Record specific descriptions of the interactions.

- Sharing tasks both inside and outside the house
- Offering assurances or commitments about the relationship
- Maintaining openness both verbally and nonverbally
- Communicating positivity, compliments, and enjoyment
- Maintaining social networks of friends and family

Exercise 2.4 Using Relational Dialectics

The goal of this exercise is to focus on relational dialectics that may need adjustment during your current life transition.

1   First, each partner should place a mark on each of the following communication dialectic continua to indicate their current disposition.

Autonomy————————————————Interdependence
Openness————————————————Closedness
Novelty—————————————————Predictability
Judgment————————————————Acceptance

2   Next, discuss if each dialectical position feels right at this time. If adjustments need to be made, discuss if:
- One dialectical pole needs to be emphasized over another.
- Dialectical poles can be alternated, emphasizing one and then switching to the other when appropriate.
- Each dialectical pole needs to be emphasized
- One or both dialectical poles need to be reframed (e.g. autonomy can be reframed from "separateness" to "spurring individual growth.")

Exercise 2.5 Conducting a Conflict Assessment Meeting

The goal of this exercise is to determine what works for you as a couple when managing conflict.

Basic Assumptions

- You are not to fix any current problems; you are to discuss how you *do* conflict and problem solving together.
- You are not to blame; each person is to take responsibility for their own actions.
- There is no right or wrong. The focus is on finding *what works*.

Guidelines for Creating the Meeting

- Schedule a time to meet without distractions.
- If one partner is hesitant about the meeting, create appropriate time limits.
- Do not meet in an environment where you typically have conflict.
- Discuss what has or has not "worked" in past conflicts (draw from conflicts where emotional hostilities have cooled).
- Highlight why certain behaviors worked for you.

- Highlight why certain behaviors did not work for you.
  - Ask clarifying questions ("Help me better understand how I could have said that better.")
  - Offer clarifying information ("It would help me if you could give me a concrete example when we're talking about our relationship.")
- Summarize what works.
- Make specific goals as to what you are going to try to implement in your next minor conflict or disagreement. (Do not try to change too much, too fast).
- Schedule a follow-up session within the near future that is focused on the following questions:
  - What is working?
  - What needs adjustment?
- Schedule a second follow-up session, followed by other follow-up sessions periodically (think of this like getting the oil changed in you car).

REFERENCES

Canary, D., & Dainton, M. (Eds.). (2003). *Maintaining relationships through communication: Relational, contextual, and cultural variations*. Mahwah, NJ: Lawrence Erlbaum Associates.

Gottman, J. (1982). Emotional responsiveness in marital conversation. *Journal of Communication, 32,* 108–120.

Gottman, J. (1994). *What predicts divorce?*. Hillsdale, NJ: Lawrence Erlbaum Publishers.

Hallam, R. S., Ashton, P., Sherbourne, K., Gailey, L., & Corney, R. (2007). Coping, conversation tactics and marital interaction in persons with acquired profound hearling loss (APHL): Correlates of distress. *Audiological Medicine, 5*(2), 103–111.

Hochschild, A. (1993). *The second shift.* New York: Penguin Books.

Langer, E. (1990). *Mindfulness*. Cambridge, MA: Decapo Press.

Mackey, R., & O'Brien, B. (1995). Lasting marriages: Men and women growing together. *Journal of Marriage and Family, 58,* 527–528.

Waldron, V., & Kelley, D. (2008). *Communicating forgiveness*. Los Angeles, CA: Sage Publications.

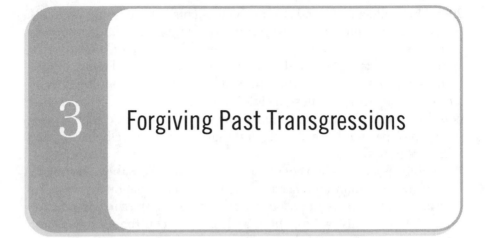

3 Forgiving Past Transgressions

Years ago, when the kids were young, Judd made a hard decision. He left his fast-paced job as a supervisor at a major construction company to manage a small business owned by the family of his wife Amanda. In those days, Judd routinely worked 70-hour weeks. The money was good, and he thrived on the responsibility the company invested in him. But home by herself with the kids at least 6 days a week, Amanda felt isolated and emotionally exhausted. She appreciated the material goods that Judd's high salary brought to the household, but she also resented the long hours. She worried about the marriage and wanted the kids to know their father. Eventually, Amanda grew depressed. Judd knew a change was needed. The family business kept him closer to home and the hours were reasonable and more flexible. He made a good living. But years later, Judd is bored and longing for the excitement of his old job. He feels restless and often resentful. Judd is frequently short with Amanda. He knows it isn't fair, but Judd secretly blames her for holding him back all those years ago. Now that the kids have moved on, the couple argues more frequently for reasons they don't completely understand.

Judd and Amanda are not unusual. Our many interviews with long-term romantic partners convinced us that almost every centerstage couple has confronted some kind of relational crisis—an emotionally trying time when the health of the relationship was put at risk (Waldron & Kelley,

2008). For Judd and Amanda the problem seems to be long-held and unresolved resentment. Others struggle with the lingering relational residue that follows a serious transgression committed in the past, such as infidelity, a major deception, authoritarian behavior, or verbal abuse. Some mates struggle to make sense of traumatic life events such as the loss of a business, a partner's illness, a child's wayward behavior. Although imposed primarily by external circumstances, these traumatic experiences sometimes spawn relational stress and trigger maladaptive behavior that is later regretted.

Midlife is a time when couples tally up the sacrifices they have made for the good of family and marriage. Sometimes calculation leaves them wanting, and they feel compelled to set things right before moving ahead. As first steps in this process, Judd and Amanda confronted feelings of blame and acknowledged the resulting patterns of dysfunctional communication. By doing so, they eventually reestablished the intimacy that defined the earlier stages of their relationship. We recall another case in which a husband insisted that his young family relocate to a distant city so he could accept a new job. With close friends and family nearby, his spouse was reluctant, but she eventually agreed under duress. Now, more than 2 decades later, she still looks back with a feeling of loss for the life they might have had. And she is *still* struggling to forgive her husband's autocratic decision.

For these and many other clients, the centerstage of marriage is a time when old wounds are reopened. They may have "made peace" in the past, but having failed to really forgive, their intimacy has been compromised. As Vic, married 27 years, told us about his wife's affair 10 years before, "We made peace a long time ago, but I realize now that I never really forgave her for the affair." Indeed, midlife is a time when unresolved doubts are expressed. Buried hurts are exhumed. Silent grudges are verbalized. The economic and family constraints that kept these issues submerged may be loosened now, and your clients may find them bobbing persistently to the surface. These are potentially important openings—opportunities to reestablish an authentic and intimate relationship—to return the marriage to centerstage.

As suggested by our opening narrative, Judd appears to harbor lingering resentment toward his wife Amanda. He may have been unable (or unwilling) to express these feeling in the past, and he may not fully understand them now. Nonetheless, Judd's unresolved grudge is a constant relational irritant, one that Amanda likely senses with feelings of confusion, resentment, guilt, and fear. In any case, unresolved issues from the past color this couple's present interactions and may cloud their future together.

In this chapter, we focus on the therapist's role in guiding the potentially powerful practice of *forgiveness*. Building on the work of other researchers and clinicians (Enright, 2001; Luskin, 2002; Worthington, 2005), we conceptualize forgiveness to be a relational negotiation as well as an individual decision.

DEFINING FORGIVENESS AS RELATIONAL NEGOTIATION

BOX 3.1 COMMUNICATIVE TASKS OF FORGIVENESS

Forgiveness is a relational process whereby harmful conduct is acknowledged by one or both partners; the harmed partner extends undeserved mercy to the perceived transgressor; one or both partners experience a transformation from negative to positive states, and the meaning of the relationship is renegotiated, with the possibility of reconciliation. *(Waldron & Kelley, 2008, p. 5)*

With the guidance of a counselor, clients can complete seven "forgiveness tasks," including explicit acknowledgment of the harm they have caused and the emotions they feel. Through a process of sensemaking and forgiveness-seeking, clients create possibilities for constructive rather than vengeful responses to their hurt. Forgiveness is not always possible or even advisable, but an authentic forgiveness process prompts partners to renegotiate relationships in ways that leave them feeling more honest and satisfied. These communication tasks take time and work, but we think the benefits of forgiveness are worth the effort. So do numerous clinicians, researchers, and spiritual leaders (see *References* at the end of the chapter). Indeed, forgiveness can be a hopeful and positive alternative to the alienation, grudge-holding, and vengefulness we find in some centerstage marriages.

WHY FORGIVE?

A client who has been seriously hurt may decide to forgive for any number of reasons. First, they may do it to improve their own sense of wellness.

Holding a grudge has been shown to have damaging psychological (and perhaps even physical) effects (Luskin, 2002) and most clients will sense this intuitively. They may be looking for a way to put things in the past and to get over their anger and hurt. Second, some clients feel compelled to forgive by religious traditions or spiritual commitments. They may be motivated by scripture or the guidance of moral leaders. Third, forgiveness is linked to client beliefs about relational justice. From this perspective, seeking and granting forgiveness may be inhibited or facilitated by clients' perspectives on restoring respect, fairness, and dignity.

BOX 3.2 WHY ARE CLIENTS WILLING TO FORGIVE?

- To improve psychological and physical well being
- Out of compassion for the partner
- To be consistent with religious commitments
- To restore relational justice
- As a first step toward reconciliation

WHAT FORGIVENESS IS NOT

Of course, for many clients, forgiveness is associated with reconciliation—the desire to repair a broken relationship. However, reconciliation is not always the goal of forgiveness processes, and probably should not be in some abusive relationships. Given its potential benefits, forgiveness may be desirable in its own right. But in so many cases, distressed partners must negotiate a meaningful and just forgiveness before they can experience renewed intimacy.

In our work as researchers and teachers, we sometimes hear objections to the very concept of forgiveness. Some of your clients will see forgiveness as a "weak" response to relational transgressions—an invitation to further wrongdoing. Some of these are simply bent on revenge. They cannot let go of an often very understandable need to "get even." But most objectors simply mistake forgiveness for other less powerful concepts. So, let's be clear. Forgiving does not mean denying, excusing, or pardoning bad behavior. It does not mean forgetting hurtful incidents or simply letting "bygones be bygones." Forgiveness is not forbearance, and as we noted above, it does not require reconciliation.

You can help clients understand that forgiveness does mean a full acknowledgment that they have been harmed (or harmed someone else). It does mean holding one's self and one's partner accountable to moral standards. It is a process of asking for, granting, and sometimes negotiating an improved understanding. Forgiveness does ask the victim(s) to begin a process of releasing bitterness, even as it acknowledges their "right" to feel bitter or vengeful about the harm they have experienced. The process creates the possibility for positive psychological states, such as hope, self-respect, empathy, and relief, to replace negative ones. In many cases, forgiveness requires the parties to negotiate a different and sometimes more respectful relationship.

SOURCES OF DISTRESS

An important role for counselors is to help clients articulate the reasons for their distress: What needs forgiving? We have pursued this basic question in our research.

Listening to Midlife Couples: What Needs Forgiving?

Of course, minor disagreements and misunderstandings rarely require a counselor-assisted forgiveness process. Experienced couples manage these without assistance. Forgiveness is reserved for serious transgressions—relationship threatening incidents with long-lasting impact. Below, we present a list of the most common kinds of "forgiveness-requiring" relational incidents, as reported to us by long-term married couples (Harvey, 2004; Waldron & Kelley, 2008).

- *Financial transgressions,* including business failures, deceptions, mistakes, bad habits
- *Parenting disagreements,* over values, discipline, education, and stepchildren
- *Infidelity,* emotional or physical affairs by one or both partners
- *Alcoholism and drug dependence*, and associated neglect, abuse, or deception
- *Health-related challenges*, especially when poor habits contributed to the illness
- *Anger and verbal aggression,* including volatile or intimidating behavior

- *Extended family*, including interference from in-laws and divided loyalties
- *Neglect*, including excessive work and emotional disengagement
- *Abuse of power*, including unilateral decision making and disrespectful behavior
- *Moral transgressions*, such as cheating on taxes or use of pornography
- *Harbored resentment*, such as unplanned pregnancy, or career sacrifices

Some items on this list are familiar to any therapist, including infidelity or financial mismanagement. And, of course, most of these incidents could occur at any time in the life course. But some of these issues caught our attention because (1) they are most likely to affect marriages during the centerstage of life or (2) they in some way are surprising that they would require forgiveness.

Health-related challenges are connected to forgiveness in several ways. We heard centerstage couples describe how health problems that could be ignored or managed in their younger years, caught up with them later, often in their 50s. These stories involved heart attack, stroke, diabetes, breast and prostate cancers, and other conditions and often contained negative emotion associated with a partner's choices not to live a healthy lifestyle. Serious illnesses like these also can cause role stress, as one partner becomes a caretaker and the other a dependent. Prolonged periods of caretaking can spawn feelings of frustration, exhaustion, and hopelessness. The caretaker may feel resentment if the illness has been precipitated by the partner's poor health habits, including overeating, drinking, or unwillingness to exercise. Other centerstage marriages were stressed by the burdens of caring for ill children or aging parents. The circumstances sometimes lead to ill-tempered conflicts and lasting bitterness. Finally, as Jake's story suggests, family members' dysfunctional reactions to health problems are sometimes the issue.

Jake was a caring father and a "can do" guy, unwilling to accept that his adult daughter's persistent intestinal ailments could not be quickly "cured." He researched the internet and constantly queried his daughter about her health status. Jake insisted that she try new dietary regimens and was frustrated by what he perceived to be her passive approach to the disease. Jake's controlling approach caused friction in the parenting relationship and tension in his marriage.

Ultimately, Jake saw that his need to control uncertainty made him overlook an important relational responsibility—to express empathy and concern for his daughter's pain and his wife's distress. He ended up apologizing and trying to make amends.

Parenting disagreements may be the root cause of distress reported by some of your midlife clients. Parenting is characterized by heavy emotional investments and strong identification with childrearing practices of the parents' own families. For these reasons, parenting conflicts can leave lasting scars and resentments, which simmer long after the children leave home.

Cindi and Matt (aged 42 and 44) were typical in this regard. Ten years ago, when their 11-year-old son Jalen was struggling in math class, Cindi believed the problem was a lack of personal discipline. She wanted Jalen to experience more consequences for his poor performance. Remembering his own school challenges, Matt disagreed, arguing that the teacher wasn't adapting to Jalen's learning style. He felt Jalen would be more motivated if he could see how school "related to real life." Jalen needed more encouragement for the strengths he displayed in school. The disagreement came to a head when Jalen's report card showed a "D" in math. Cindi reacted by grounding him on the spot, without consulting Matt. The incident exploded into a heated argument fueled by bitter complaints and screaming insults. The memory of this ugly incident pains the couple. Now they view it as a symptom of their different childhood experiences and their need to communicate more constructively about them.

COMPLICATING CONDITIONS: HELPING CLIENTS JUDGE THE SERIOUSNESS OF TRANSGRESSIONS

We have argued that forgiveness is only required for the more serious of relational challenges. But what counts as serious? This issue is often a point of contention in distressed couples. Some have difficulty identifying the source of distress and some simply disagree about the seriousness of the problem. In some cases, the "offending partner" minimizes the problem. Wounded partners do this as well in an effort to protect the spouse or avoid confronting difficult topics. Counselors can help clients make sense of their situation and develop a language for describing what happened to them. The list of incidents presented above and the questions provided below may help with this sense-making process.

Was the Transgression Intentional?

Transgressions perceived to be willful or intentional are usually more hurtful. Those who choose to hurt others are expected to account for their actions and seek forgiveness. When external circumstances fully explain the offender's behavior, forgiveness is typically not called for. Of course, many relational incidents involve a mix of intended and unintended consequences.

The counselor or therapist can help clients address the complex issue of intentionality. In doing so, they should be aware of the tendency of victims to assume that hurtful behavior is intentional. Offenders exhibit the opposite tendency, emphasizing external circumstances as the cause. However, harmed partners will sometimes minimize the offense: "He/she didn't mean to hurt me." This conversational move is sometimes an effort to avoid the difficult tasks of confronting wrongdoing and negotiating forgiveness. It resembles excusing or pardoning. The forgiveness process is short-circuited; this likely leads to rumination.

BOX 3.3 HOW DO I USE IT? HELPING CLIENTS JUDGE THE SERIOUSNESS OF TRANSGRESSIONS

1   Was the transgression intentional?
2   Has it been forgiven previously? Is it likely to be repeated?
3   Is the problem chronic or a single incident?
4   Who is the "audience" and how do they matter?
5   Is responsibility shared?
6   Is the transgression "unforgivable?" If so, why?

Has the Offense Been Forgiven Previously? Is It Likely to be Repeated?

For many clients, the decision to forgive is based on the assumption that a transgression will not reoccur. The process of forgiveness is typically predicated on the remorse expressed by the offender and a sense that he or she "gets" the seriousness of the transgression. A willingness to be accountable may restore predictability to the future. It assures the wounded partner and rebuilds psychological safety. Of course, therapists can help clients realistically assess the chance of a reoccurrence. Repeated violations obviously change the forgiveness equation. In response to repeated offenses some clients adopt a "conditional forgiveness" strategy (see below) in which compliance with explicit requirements is a preliminary step in a relationship rebuilding process.

Is the Transgression a Chronic Pattern or a Single Traumatic Event?

In long-term relationships, partners are called to forgive extended patterns of hurtful behavior in addition to isolated instances of harm. In therapy, or through personal revelation, clients realize that long-lived patterns of dysfunctional behavior are the source of current dissatisfaction. They may "discover" that, for years, their partner has been disrespectful, not listening, nonconsultative, or selfish. These patterns are interpreted differently now due to increased education, changing peer groups, religious experiences, or modified cultural norms. In such cases, clients often need assistance with *sense-making* (see *Working With Clients* below), as they define the harm they have experienced, the behavioral patterns that sustain it, and the ways in which the partners might share responsibility for a longstanding pattern. Maureen and Clint needed that kind of assistance.

Maureen and Clint vowed early in their marriage to keep close relations with extended family. But insensitive comments from Clint's mother made that commitment hard to keep. "You would be pretty if you weren't so heavy," she told Maureen. She also felt compelled to critique Maureen's housekeeping, parenting style, and even her character. Maureen rarely felt supported by Clint when she defended herself from his mother's criticisms. As the years passed, this problem became a source of chronic tension. Looking back over 2 decades, Clint explains his passivity by noting Maureen was "feisty" and "thick skinned." She could defend herself, he thought. In addition, Clint was reluctant to hurt his mom's feelings. Clint sees now that his persistent avoidance only compounded the problem and contributed to Maureen's current feelings of resentment and futility. His willingness to take responsibility was crucial to Maureen, making it easier to forgive him.

How Does the "Audience" Complicate Matters?

The effects of transgressions are complicated and magnified by the presence of an audience. Clients obtain status from their identity as a happy couple. This perception is sustained and "performed" through interactions with children, extended family, friends, and community group members. Transgressions observed by one or more of these publics are often viewed as forgiveness-requiring acts. A husband who told us his inebriated wife was unacceptably "flirty" at a party was all the more chagrined by the presence of coworkers and mutual friends. When marital problems become public, as when lingering tensions erupt in a loud argument at a family gathering, part of the subsequent "repair work" involves the restoration of the couple's public identity and, perhaps, acknowledgment that external perceptions were inaccurate. Therapists can help clients identify the magnifying effects of external audiences and help them devise strategies for communicating a new and more authentic public identity.

Is Responsibility Shared?

When clients perceive that they share responsibility for a harmful incident, they are sometimes more amenable to forgiveness. In fact, in many of our relational narratives, partners acknowledge shared responsibility. We see shared responsibility in the case of Cindi and Matt (above), the parents who disagreed over their son's schooling. Of course, clients are often blind to their own contributions. The therapist can help them develop clearer self-perceptions and increased empathy for their partner. At the same time, it is not uncommon for one partner to be primarily responsible.

Is the Offense "Unforgivable?" Why?

Counselors can help clients question their assumptions about unforgivable offenses. In our work with younger couples, it is not uncommon to hear about "unforgivable" offenses. Typically, sexual infidelity is the offense they have in mind. Of course, certain partners do choose to forgive this painful transgression. Some want to preserve the large investment they made in a marriage; some hold a strong belief in the value of marriage. We interviewed some survivors of infidelity. Not surprisingly, they told us it took years to heal the hurt and restore trust. For most recovering couples, even those that report high levels of satisfaction, the emotional scars remain. In addition to completing forgiveness tasks (described below), some of these couples truly started over, rebuilding their relationship from scratch with new ground rules and revitalized commitments. Some even "courted" all over again. Survivors rarely evidenced a "forgive and forget" attitude. Instead, they were determined to learn from the mistakes of the past. They were inclined to "forgive and remember."

We hasten to add that forgiveness is not always possible, or even desirable. This is particularly true in abusive relationships, where apparently sincere apologies and heartfelt offers of forgiveness are repeated in a dysfunctional cycle. Forgiveness is sometimes "demanded" by abusers who use guilt and manipulation to extract it. This pattern merely minimizes consequences for abusive acts and enables further violations. Of course, this co-optation of the concept bears no resemblance to authentic forgiveness, which above all holds violators accountable and empowers those who have been harmed. Nonetheless, therapists help clients distinguish real forgiveness (as defined above) from its pretenders. Victims of abuse may be forgiving for any number of reasons, but therapists must be cautious in suggesting it. This may be particularly true for female victims of the domestic abuse cycle.

ANALYTICAL TOOLS

Counselors can help clients discover a language to expresses their feelings about past transgressions. From chapter 1, we use the notions of dialectical tensions and resilience to help with this task.

Applying the Dialectical Framework

Dialectical theory reminds us that the joining of individuals in close relationships inevitably gives rise to "tensions" that are expressed and managed through discourse. As clients struggle to forgive transgressions from the past, they will likely give voice to several dialectical tensions. The first of these involves competing desires for justice and mercy. On one hand, clients who have been hurt want justice. They may lament a lack of fairness, demand accountability, and express indignation—a "moral emotion" elicited by perceptions of unfair treatment. At the same time, wounded partners may feel compelled by love or obligation to be merciful. That is, to be generous, compassionate, or understanding of "extenuating circumstances." To be merciful is to eschew revenge, an understandable impulse under the circumstances. A merciful person has "a right" to retribution, but chooses not to exercise it.

In therapy, clients explore these contradictory positions, affirm the validity of both desires, and explore ways to manage these oppositional forces. For example, some clients will be helped by reading material on restorative justice, and others might be motivated through reading scriptures or religious commentaries that explore the roles of both mercy and justice within religious tradition. Our forgiveness model takes a "sequencing" approach, suggesting that issues of accountability must be resolved before mercy can be extended. A therapist was helpful in helping Gloria and Ed manage the justice versus mercy dialectic.

Gloria was stunned when a police officer arrived at their home to arrest her husband Ed for embezzlement. She hoped it was all a terrible mistake, but she was shattered to learn that her husband of 17 years had indeed committed a serious crime. As the shock wore off, Gloria took stock of the damage. Ed had sabotaged their future. Their only source of income was lost, attorney fees were draining their savings, and their home would soon be sold. In addition to the financial costs were public humiliation and the sudden uprooting of the children. Gloria felt deeply betrayed. In her view, Ed deserved to suffer for causing his family so much pain and loss. Her first impulse was to punish him by leaving the marriage and taking the four kids with her. But, with time, she realized that shame, regret, and self-criticism were ravaging Ed. In therapy, Ed apologized and Gloria reminded herself that Ed had been a dedicated husband, son, friend, father, and volunteer. The seeds of mercy were planted and forgiveness became a possibility.

A second dialectic is *rumination versus release*. Before starting therapy, clients may have spent considerable time ruminating about past offenses. Thinking and rethinking can be exhausting, but it also sustains feelings of indignation, an emotion clients may feel entitled to under the circumstances. Rumination sustains a grudge. At the same time, errors in logic remain unquestioned as they might be if the grievance was explored through verbal interaction. Negative rumination, the continual fueling of negative feelings, is often in tension with a need to put the offense in the past, to "let go" of a legitimate but psychologically draining desire for retribution. Therapists can help clients become aware of, verbalize, and manage the tension between rumination and release. This dialectic may be partly resolved as clients learn to articulate their conflicting needs to themselves and their partners.

Trusting versus protecting is a third dialectical tension expressed by clients.

Teri developed a habit of undermining her husband Gary's parenting authority. In front of their children, she frequently disagreed with his parenting decisions. The result was a decades-long rift between Teri and Gary. The boys are young adults now, but Gary thinks they respect him less due to their mother's history of "undermining" behavior. Gary is defensive, distant, and even vengeful at family gatherings. At the urging of their children, the couple finally sought counseling. Teri admits that her practices hurt Gary and pledged to change. She wants Gary to ease up on her, but he is having a difficult time trusting Teri, "Will she keep her end of the bargain?"

Clients like Gary may *want* to trust again, but at the same time, they desire protection against future pain. This trusting versus protecting dialectic is sometimes managed through "reframing," in which clients convince themselves that the harm was unintentional—the result of an *accident* unlikely to repeat itself. In such instances, trust can be rebuilt relatively easily. But when the act *was intentional*, it simply cannot be, and should not be, explained away. Faced with this reality, some clients choose the protecting side of the dialectic in an effort to minimize the risk of further emotional pain. Guarded, defensive, indignant, or distant styles of interaction are used for this purpose, and clients may "nurse a grudge." Counselors can help clients like Gary recognize their conflicting impulses to trust and protect.

Another approach, "choosing," is used by clients who are too willing to accept superficial repairs to a damaged relationship. These clients choose trust over protection, failing to take sensible steps to guard against a continuation of the problem. A case in point is "cheap forgiveness," in which offenders are offered mercy before they acknowledge the harm they have caused, the rules they have violated, or the relational values they have flouted (also see Enright, 2001; Worthington, 2005). Such behavior invites repeated transgressions. The victimized partner risks becoming a "doormat," suffers a decline in self-respect, and recommits to a partner who may not fully "get" the serious consequences of their behavior.

Using the Dialectical Framework

As a therapeutic intervention, a guided forgiveness process (see *Working With Clients* below) helps partners acknowledge and manage dialectical tensions—to practice *both* justice and mercy, to be thoughtful even as they release the tendency to ruminate, and to rebuild trust in a manner that feels less risky (also see Worthington, 2005). Consider the trusting versus protecting dialectic: To encourage trust-building the offender is given the opportunity to acknowledge wrongdoing and recommit to relational values and standards of conduct. To protect the wounded partner, new relational safeguards may be devised. In addition, forgiving is often a contingent and continuing process, predicated on compliance by the partner with certain conditions. This process cultivates trust and protection and increases chances for reconciliation.

BOX 3.4 HOW DO I USE IT? THREE APPROACHES TO MANAGING FORGIVENESS DIALECTICS

Choosing: Embracing one side of the dialectic, for example, by replacing rumination with a verbalized request for an apology.

Sequencing: Seeking accountability first, then working on being merciful.

Reframing: Redefining the transgression as an "understandable accident;" developing empathy for the offender

---

Applying the Resilience Framework

Recall that resilience theory encourages clients to exploit resources and strengths. Our own research suggests that forgiveness is a characteristic of resilient marriages. At midlife, connections between forgiveness and resilience can be fostered in several ways.

Triumphant Memories Motivate Forgiveness

Nearly all midlife couples have overcome challenges and many have forgiven before. Recalling past triumphs helps wounded couples gain a sense of perspective and builds confidence in the restorative powers of forgiveness. These memories can foster hope and give clients the motivation to forgive. Therapists help couples mine the past for lessons that can be applied now. Katherine felt deeply depressed when her husband James lost his job and remained unemployed for many months. She tried hard to be supportive, but eventually became resentful and critical of his job-seeking efforts. James became defensive and the couple quarreled frequently. However, as Katherine reported, they found the motivation to forgive current hostilities by revisiting past triumphs.

We were dirt poor when we got married. When the kids were little, we ate hot dogs and called it "steak." Only James had a job then, but we managed to save a little bit of money. And we had a lot of fun, we really did. So I know we can do it again if we have to, even if we have to move to a smaller house and give up some things. I think that is our strength right now, remembering that we have been through worse times together.

Empathetic Capacity Makes Forgiveness Feasible

Empathy is a resource that helps clients think differently about the harmful acts of others. Psychologist and researcher Everett Worthington (2005) makes a convincing case that a key to healing relationships is developing empathy for those who have hurt us. Our interviews with resilient couples generally support this idea. A capacity for empathy makes it easier to forgive. Empathetic people do not excuse bad behavior, but they try to understand its larger context. They evaluate the transgressions of others in light of their own history of human fallibility: "Why did this happen and could I have behaved similarly under the circumstances?" Clients may recall their own feelings of guilt and shame for the harmful acts they committed, and they may remember their own desire to be forgiven for these acts. Through these activities counselors help clients "rehumanize" the offender, making forgiveness seem more feasible.

Reconnecting With Spiritual Values

For many clients, religious traditions and faith communities are important sources of strength during times of crisis. For Christian clients, the motivation to forgive might come from familiar biblical passages such as: "Forgive us our debts as we forgive debtors" (Mathew 6:12) and "Father forgive them, for they know not what they do" (Luke 23:34). However, most faith traditions have similar precepts. Therapists who are familiar with important texts and the teachings of inspirational religious leaders may be particularly helpful to these clients. After experiencing a serious relational transgression, many clients will find it helpful to seek counsel from a rabbi, pastor, priest, or religious elder. These discussions may yield deeper understanding, comfort, hope, and the affirmation that comes from membership in a supportive community.

Forgiveness Yields Hope for an Improved Relational Future

Resilient couples tend to be hopeful. They are *not* unrealistic, but they find evidence in the present that supports the potential for positive future outcomes. Forgiveness is a process that helps them put bad feelings in the past and start focusing on opportunities for an improved future. Therapists cultivate hope by helping clients identify positive role models—people who have forgiven and experienced positive relational outcomes. During the process, they help clients find realistic signs of improvement and provide alternative readings of unrealistically gloomy assessments. Couples can be encouraged to form new bonds with hopeful and positive people and limit contact with those persons who stimulate negative thoughts and past-oriented thinking.

WORKING WITH CLIENTS

Clinicians use several forgiveness-based models with clients. For example, Worthington (1998) suggests five forgiveness steps. First, they must do the emotional work of *recalling the hurt* they experienced due to the actions of the offender. The second step involves the development *of empathy*—coming to understand the transgressor's feelings and perspective and (perhaps), even developing some compassion for him or her. Developing of empathy, the most important of the steps, rehumanizes the offender. Third is an altruistic decision to *give a gift*. Although feelings of bitterness or revenge are justified, the wounded party chooses to be merciful and forgiving instead.

BOX 3.5 GIVING THE GIFT OF FORGIVENESS

Based on Worthington's (1998) work, it appears that the decision to forgive turns on the client's answer to these three questions:

1 Can I describe my own past transgressions, including feelings of guilt I might have experienced?
2 Can I recall the positive feelings I had when forgiven for these transgressions, such as relief and gratitude?
3 Would I like to help the offender experience these feelings by giving a gift of forgiveness?

The fourth step reinforces this decision with a *public commitment* to forgiveness. This can be expressed in conversations with friends, shared in therapy groups, or even written in journals. These recorded assertions sustain the forgiver when the will waivers. Reviewing them is a way to replace negative rumination with more constructive thoughts. During the final step, *holding on to forgiveness*, the therapist helps the client build support systems, manage the negative feelings that will periodically return, and provides assurance and encouragement.

The Communicative Tasks of Forgiveness Model

Building on the pioneering earlier work of Worthington, and Enright (and many others), we have recently proposed the *Communicative Tasks of Forgiveness* (CTF) model (Waldron & Kelley, 2008). It acknowledges the importance of such psychological processes as empathy and focuses on the communicative behaviors that clients use when enacting them (Fig. 3.1).

The model assumes that the acknowledgment of harm is a high-priority task for both partners, but the forgiveness process is a gradual and iterative one, defined by seven relational tasks. Each task, to a greater or lesser extent, requires communication from both parties. Counselors can guide clients through the tasks. The tasks do not need to be performed in order (although in practice they often are). Steps are sometimes skipped. For example, forgiveness is not *always* sought explicitly, rules are not

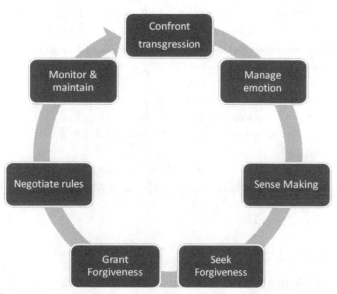

Figure 3.1 Communicative Tasks of Forgiveness (Waldron and Kelley, 2008)

always negotiated. Clients may cycle between steps for long periods of time, and some tasks (e.g., emotion management) will be repeated. Counselors can help clients identify the communication behaviors that help or hinder completion of each task.

Task 1: Confronting the Transgression

The clients recognize that wrongdoing has been committed and at least one partner has been badly hurt. Minor relational annoyances call for forbearance, negotiation, or understanding, but they rarely require forgiveness. So a critical role for the therapist is helping clients *explicitly acknowledge* significant harm, by putting it into words.

Behaviors that help clients: describing offensive behavior, labeling hurt and harm, making suspicions explicit, confessing, truth telling, identifying violated expectations, and self-disclosing.

Behaviors that hinder clients: denying responsibility, minimizing harm, justifying, and evading.

Task 2: Managing Emotion

Reactions to serious transgressions are emotional, although the emotion is sometimes suppressed or misdirected. Eventually (perhaps not immediately), emotions must be acknowledged (preferably by victim and offender), expressed, and absorbed. This process takes time. Emotions like anger, fear, frustration, outrage, resentment, bitterness, and hopelessness are commonly experienced. Clients may need assistance in recognizing and expressing them. Eventually emotion must be deintensified, channeled, and explored for meaning.

Behaviors that help clients: voicing, labeling, accepting, listening to, and legitimizing emotions; helping offenders listen to and accept emotional responses; allowing emotions to vent and "cool off"; and finding words to communicate emotions.

Behaviors that hinder clients: silencing, denying, delegitimizing, or sanitizing authentic emotion; interrupting, reciprocating, or belittling emotional displays; defensiveness in response to emotional displays; and inability to detect emotion.

Task 3: Sense-Making

Transgressions disrupt relationships. They cause confusion and uncertainty and prompt reflection about relational rules and values.

Sense-making is the process of deriving the meaning of a disruptive episode. Ideally, it proceeds after the most intense emotions have dissipated and clients can exchange information about questions such as the following. Why did this happen? Which rules and values have been violated? How serious is this situation? Is the act forgivable? Why or why not? How will it affect me (and us) in the future? The therapist helps clients ask and answer these and other questions. Clients may need assistance in managing the *rumination versus release* dialectic and in developing empathy (see above). Helping clients develop a sense of perspective—How can this episode be viewed within the larger relationship narrative?—is another potentially important contribution. Sense-making helps a distressed couple honestly assess the damage, and it facilitates a more informed kind of forgiveness.

Behaviors that help clients: exchanging information about motives and reasons, constructive questions, honest explanations, listening, paraphrasing, perspective taking, and expressions of empathy.

Behaviors that hinder clients: defensiveness, accusations, evasive answers, overgeneralizations, reticence, false attributions, and deceptions.

Task 4: Seeking Forgiveness

Having acknowledged harm, managed the emotions, and explored the possible meanings of the transgression, the couple may be ready to forgive. Forgiveness is a process of both seeking and granting. Table 3.1 presents some of the more *common* forgiveness-seeking tactics we have

Table 3.1

FORGIVENESS-SEEKING TACTICS

STRATEGY	SAMPLE BEHAVIORS
Explicit acknowledgement*	admissions, apologies, expressions of remorse or regret
Nonverbal Assurances*	eye contact, head nods, touches, hugs
Compensation*	promises, offers, gifts, repeated assurances
Explanation	openness, disclosures, reasons, information exchanges
Humor	self deprecation, teasing, laughing

*Associated with positive partner responses

observed in "forgiveness episodes" reported by romantic couples (Waldron & Kelley, 2005; Kelley & Waldron, 2005). Partners reported more positive relational consequences when forgiveness seekers explicitly acknowledged harm and expressed remorse or regret ("I am truly sorry that I hurt you and I wish I could take it back."). Wounded mates also looked to the nonverbal behavior of the forgiveness seeker for signs of sincerity (or insincerity). They sought assurance that offending partners fully understand the seriousness of the relational offense and were unlikely to repeat it. The combination of explicitly acknowledging responsibility along with nonverbal sincerity was powerful. We also found that offers of compensation ("I will work extra hard to keep this from happening again") were sometimes viewed positively. Typically, it is not the compensation itself that is desired. Instead, it is the commitment to repair the relationship.

Our research indicates that no positive effect is gained when offenders simply offer "explanations." And, although some offenders try to "lighten the mood" with humor, this tactic is typically unsuccessful and unappreciated. An exception would be self-deprecating humor, which had positive effects for some couples.

In addition to these communication tactics used by offenders, we discovered more elaborate forgiveness practices, which were jointly enacted by couples. In some cases, the key was a willingness to seek outside assistance. In such cases, forgiveness was predicated on a willingness of one or both partners to attend a counseling session or seek treatment for drug dependence. Letting time pass was another approach, as some wounded partners need to let their emotions cool and thoughts clear before trying to forgive. Resuming relational rituals was a third approach. Some couples try to enact familiar routines, like going out to dinner or attending family events, before they engage the more complicated process of negotiating forgiveness.

Behaviors that help clients: apologies, expressions of remorse and regret, offers of compensation, and nonverbal signs of sincerity.

Behaviors that hurt clients: hedging, nonverbal signs of insincerity, superfluous explanation, underestimation of harm, lack of remorse, and humor.

Task 5: Granting/Accepting Forgiveness

When clients negotiate forgiveness, they experience at least a temporary shift in relational power, from seeker to grantor. The process will not move forward until the victimized partner allows it to do so.

Table 3.2

FORGIVENESS-GRANTING TACTICS	
STRATEGY	**SAMPLE BEHAVIORS**
Explicit Statements*	"Yes. I forgive you."
Engagement*	Willingness to discuss the situation
Minimization	"It is no big deal", "It doesn't matter"
Conditional	"I will forgive you only if . . ."
Nonverbal displays*	Touching the offender, eye contact

*Associated with positive partner responses

Nonetheless, forgiveness-granting tactics vary in their relational effects (Table 3.2). Perhaps the *least* effective tactic is the minimization ("no big deal") approach. The victim denies the significance of the offense. Forgiveness seems unnecessary. On occasion, forgiveness negotiations reveal that a perceived problem was a misunderstanding. Minimization, a "mercy-only" response may be appropriate under these circumstances. But it is rarely effective in serious situations, in part because the need for justice is ignored—the offender is not held accountable and the victim's relational rights are denied.

Our surveys of married and dating couples indicate that (1) explicit statements of forgiveness and (2) a willingness to engage with the offender in meaningful discussion yielded the most positive outcomes. This combination of strategies allows the victimized client to exercise his or her power to be forgiving (merciful) without minimizing the seriousness of the matter. It is a hopeful approach in that it signals a willingness to engage, and it creates the possibility of a better future (if not full reconciliation). Many forgiveness seekers report finding hope and assurance in nonverbal behaviors (e.g., eye gaze, touch) of the grantor. These behaviors seem to reinforce the sincerity of the forgiving message.

Many clients will prefer a *conditional* ("I will forgive you if . . . ") approach. Often these conditions are new communication rules ("If you call home when you will be late from work") or prohibitions on repeated transgressions ("if you promise not to hurt me this way ever again"). They reduce the victimized partner's feelings of vulnerability and uncertainty (see the *trusting versus protecting* dialectic above). Conditional forgiveness may be an interim step in a larger forgiveness process—a way to rebuild trust (and, perhaps, impose a penalty) and wait to see if a fuller forgiveness is possible. Theorists and theologians debate whether or not conditional forgiveness is actually forgiveness at all, but it is commonly practiced. In our research, those who use the conditional approach sometimes report negative relational consequences. However, we observed that conditional forgiveness is used most often when the transgression is severe. Conditional forgiveness may be perceived as the only viable option when the need for protection is high.

Behaviors that help clients: explicit forgiveness, affirming nonverbal behaviors, openness to discussion, and conditional forgiveness (when risk reduction is tantamount).

Behaviors that hurt clients: minimization, unwillingness to discuss, and conditional forgiveness (conditions may signal lack of trust, but see above).

Task 6: Renegotiating Rules and Values

Forgiveness negotiations have the effect of reaffirming existing relational values and agreements. But relational renegotiation is also common. Clients might negotiate new practices to make recurrence of the transgression unlikely. For example, one couple pledged to start "weekly dates" as a check against their tendency to lose track of the marriage in the rush of their busy careers. A wife whose husband had committed adultery insisted that they "start over from the very beginning" by courting each other and "rechoosing" the marriage. Another couple, plagued by recurring financial mismanagement, pledged to consult before spending more than $100 on any new purchase.

These steps can build confidence in a recovering relationship. And they hold the partners accountable for improved behavior. In helping clients design new rules and practices, the therapist extends the forgiveness process into the future, making it easier to release the past. These agreements increase predictability and modulate emotional turbulence. They preserve some elements of a wounded relationship but others are changed for the better.

Behaviors that help clients: clarify existing communication rules, affirm core relational values for the future, propose new rules to increase predictability and decrease chances of a recurrent transgression, engage in mutual planning, explore hypothetical scenarios and challenges, and reimagine a positive relational future.

Behaviors that hinder clients: focusing on past failures, ignoring positive aspects of the existing relationship, making unrealistic or vague plans for improvement, resuming old patterns, and failing to anticipate potential challenges.

Task 7: Monitoring and Maintaining

As clients transition out of the forgiveness process therapists can help them honor new commitments. At times, clients will need to reaffirm their decision to forgive and the reasons for it. They may revisit earlier tasks (e.g., emotion management) as new challenges arise or painful episodes are relived. Clients will need to monitor their progress and negotiate adjustments. Another source of difficulty may be communication with extended family members, friends, and other "audiences." For example, how (if it all) does a couple want to explain their response to an affair? How can friends and family be enlisted as sources of support? How might they hinder the couple's efforts to forgive?

Behaviors that help clients: seek regular "checkups" from counselors or other support providers; identify and look for signs of success; identity warning signs; reaffirm forgiveness decision and rationale; repeat earlier forgiveness tasks as needed; develop and implement a communication strategy for various audiences; develop and maintain social support systems.

Behaviors that hinder clients: failing to seek continued support from therapists; failing to monitor success; ignoring signs of success and failure; stressful interactions with family, friends, and other "audiences;" lack of social support.

BOX 3.6 DOES FORGIVENESS MATTER? A STUDY OF RELATIONAL OUTCOMES

We surveyed 187 romantic partners who had experienced serious relational transgressions which required them to request or grant forgiveness (Waldron & Kelley, 2005; Kelley & Waldron, 2005). The quality of the relationship was rated (in terms of its intimacy, openness, stability, and overall satisfaction) before the transgression, immediately after forgiveness was granted, and at the current time (on average, 2 years later). Results showed that forgiveness tactics were correlated with positive and negative relational change, even when transgression severity was controlled for. In short, the communicative approach used by clients to seek and grant forgiveness may have long-term relational significance.

CONCLUDING THOUGHTS

We began this chapter by referencing our interviews with long-term married couples. Although there were a few lucky exceptions, nearly every veteran couple we talked with could recount serious relational challenges. A significant number of these occurred during the years of centerstage marriage, the subject of this book. Despite the fact that nearly every respondent had been deeply hurt by their partner in marriage, these relationships survived and often prospered for decades. Of course, many marriages do not survive and some possibly should not. But this chapter focused on the lessons we have learned from the survivors—lessons of resilience and forgiveness.

Forgiveness is by no means a cure all. Some transgressions will seem unforgivable; some partners unrepentant; some relationships unsalvageable. But as we define it, forgiveness is a potent blend of justice and mercy. It is a starting place for midlife partners who are wounded but hoping for a better relational future. Real forgiveness can be a lengthy and daunting process for individuals and couples. As we hope this chapter makes clear, the therapist can provide crucial guidance as clients work through its cognitive, emotional, and behavioral challenges.

Given that so much of our work on forgiveness has been shaped by our interactions with veteran couples, it is only fitting that we end with a distillation of their collective advice. Here are eight lessons we deduced from interviews with veteran couples (most married more than 40 years) on how to forgive serious relational transgressions. They may be helpful to your clients as they repair a wounded centerstage marriage.

1 Acknowledge wrongdoing: Recognize that you did wrong (or were wronged).
2 Apologize sincerely: Don't say it if you don't mean it.
3 Address emotion explicitly: Put your feelings into words. Don't stew over it.
4 Request assistance: Don't hesitate to talk with a therapist, spiritual advisor, or friend.
5 Forgive and remember: Learn your lesson but release the pain and bitterness.
6 Use time to your advantage: Be patient. Real forgiveness takes months, years, and even decades.
7 Invoke spiritual values: Transcend current circumstances.

8 Flex roles and rules: Adapt, drop unrealistic expectations, and adjust communication practices.

QUESTIONS FOR CLIENTS

1 Does forgiveness signify strength or weakness to you?

2 Is forgiveness important in your spiritual traditions or personal values?

3 Have you previously misunderstood forgiveness as excusing, denying, or forgetting?

4 Have you had the experience of reconciling without really forgiving?

5 Have you ever offered forgiveness too quickly, only to realize later that you harbor resentment or hard feelings regarding the incident?

6 Do you currently hold a grudge? How does it affect you?

7 Do you consider certain acts unforgivable? What are those?

8 What is making it hard for you to forgive? (Consider intentionality, fear of repeat offenses, lack of partner remorse)

9 Are you experiencing conflicting needs? (Consider justice versus mercy, rumination versus release, trusting versus protecting.)

10 What would help you forgive your partner?

11 Have you ever needed to be forgiven for your actions?

12 Which of the seven forgiveness tasks have you completed/not completed?

13 Have you sought the assistance of a third party (clergy, counselor, therapist) to help navigate a forgiveness incident with your partner? Did this help? And, if so, why?

EXERCISES

Exercise 3.1 Movie Night

The goal of this exercise is to think about forgiveness by watching a film that shows positive and/or negative examples of the forgiveness process.

Watch a film (see suggestions below) with a forgiveness theme. Take notes on what you think are the most important forgiveness concepts. Discuss with your partner.

- Which acts required forgiveness? Describe the harm or wrong-doing.
- Did the "offenders" acknowledge the harm and express remorse?
- Were the "victims" able to forgive? Was forgiveness authentic or "cheap?"
- Did you see evidence of grudge holding, excusing, or denying?
- How was forgiveness sought?
- How was forgiveness granted?
- How did forgiveness contribute to, or hinder, the characters' relationship?

Recommended Films:

- An Unfinished Life (Multiple characters struggle to forgive)
- Antwone Fisher (Forgiveness as liberation from an abusive past)
- Cry My Beloved Country (Forgiving the personal and political)
- Husbands and Wives (Midlife couple separates, forgives, and reconciles)
- Playing By Heart (Forgiving a "near affair")

Exercise 3.2 Case Analysis

The goal of this exercise is to review the case of Ed and Gloria (reprinted below) to stimulate conversation about the role of empathy and compassion in forgiveness.

Gloria was stunned when a police officer arrived at her home to arrest her husband Ed for embezzlement. She hoped it was all a terrible mistake, but she was shattered to learn that her husband of 17 years had indeed committed a serious crime. As the shock wore off, Gloria took stock of the damage. Ed had sabotaged their future. Their only source of income was lost, attorney fees were draining their savings, and their home would soon be sold. In addition to the financial costs were public humiliation and the sudden uprooting of the children. Gloria felt deeply betrayed. In her view, Ed deserved to suffer for causing his family so much pain and loss. Her first impulse was to punish him by leaving the marriage and taking the four kids with her. But, with time, she realized that shame, regret, and self-criticism were ravaging Ed. In therapy, Ed apologized and Gloria reminded herself that Ed had been a dedicated husband, son, friend, father, and volunteer. The seeds of mercy were planted and forgiveness became a possibility.

■ Discuss what Gloria might have been feeling. How would you have reacted?

■ Discuss what Ed might have been feeling. How would you have reacted?

■ Why did Gloria become more forgiving?

■ Share an incident when you exhibited compassion for your partner or someone else. What motivated you to be compassionate? Are those motivations still present? Why or why not?

■ Share an incident when you received compassion from your partner or someone else. How did you feel? Could you create that feeling in others?

Exercise 3.3 Build on Past Successes

The goal of this exercise is to learn how to handle current forgiveness issues by reviewing what you have done successfully in the past.

1   Compile a list of the relational challenges that you have overcome in the past.
2   To what extent was forgiveness a useful part of the process?
3   What behaviors or attitudes helped you work through these forgiveness issues?
4   What specific ways can you apply your forgiveness successes to your current situation?

Exercise 3.4 Forgiving Climate

The goal of this exercise is to look at the environment in which you live and determine how it may encourage or discourage attitudes of forgiveness.

1   Think about and discuss your network of friends and family. To what extent would you describe them as "forgiving people?"
2   How do they exhibit genuine forgiveness?
3   Do you also find evidence of unforgiving attitudes and grudge holding? What has been its effect on family/friend relationships?
4   Based on what you have seen, describe how you would like to best approach forgiveness in your family relationships?

REFERENCES

Enright, R. D. (2001). *Forgiveness is a choice: A step-by-step process for resolving anger and restoring hope*. Washinton, DC: American Psychological Association.

Harvey, J. (2004). *Trauma and recovery strategies across the lifespan of long-term married couples*. Tempe, AZ: Arizona State University.

Kelley, D., & Waldron, V. R. (2005). An investigation of forgiveness-seeking communication and relational outcomes. *Communication Quarterly*, 53, 339–358.

Luskin, F. (2002). *Forgive for good: A proven prescription for health and happiness*. New York: Harper Collins.

Waldron, V. R., & Kelley, D. (2005). Forgiveness as a response to relational transgression. *Journal of Social and Personal Relationships*, 22, 723–742.

Waldron, V. R., & Kelley, D. (2008). *Communicating forgiveness*. Los Angeles, CA: Sage Publications.

Worthington, E. L. (Ed.). (1998). *Handbook of forgiveness*. New York: Routledge.

Worthington, E. L. (2005). *The power of forgiving*. Philadelphia: Templeton Foundation Press.

4

Finding New and Meaningful Activities

Joanie works as a teacher at the local junior high, but she says her "real job" was raising her three sons. For more than 2 decades, she and her husband Rod structured their lives around the boys' activities. Rod coached their baseball teams until they were in high school, and he organized youth activities at their synagogue. Joanie served as a Cub Scout leader for each of her sons. She volunteered with the parent teacher association at their local elementary school and then the high school booster club. For years the couple faithfully attended sports events and band concerts. Three or four weekday evenings, they would gather in the bleachers with the other parents, rooting for the kids and sharing the latest family and neighborhood news. Rod and Joanie made time for the occasional movie date or weekend trip, but most of their social life revolved around the kids. With other parents, they arranged campouts, sports banquets, and synagogue-sponsored community service projects. Family vacations were fitted between sports commitments and often included side trips to investigate colleges that the boys might someday attend. When the children were old enough to drive, Joanie and Rod began to realize how much their own friendships were based on short conversations when dropping the kids off at friends' houses. This year, the couples' youngest son, Glen, left home for college. Joanie has been dreading this moment for years. She feels disoriented in her quiet house and depressed by the loss of daily contact with her sons. Rod misses the routine of attending sports events. He reports that their contacts with other parents have started to dwindle despite his efforts to organize several social gatherings. Joanie and Rod feel that they "should" be enjoying their new freedom. In reality, they feel lonely, out of touch with their friends, and sometimes struggle to find conversational topics over dinner. Life has lost some of its meaning.

This chapter focuses on a fundamental factor affecting marital satisfaction at midlife—how partners spend their time. Studies suggest that couples like Joanie and Rod spend less time together and report fewer sources of mutual pleasure than their older and younger counterparts report. In therapy, they report lower levels of satisfaction with shared recreational activities (Norris, Snyder, & Rice, 1997). Although the picture is oversimplified, marriage researchers portray middle-aged partners as so stressed, distracted, and conflicted over the process of "launching" their children that they can find little time to share other kinds of meaningful activity (Levensen, Carstensen, & Gottman, 1993). Given these observations, it is not surprising that for many couples marital satisfaction appears to hit a low point during the middle years (Gagnon, Hersen, Kabacoff, & Van Hasselt, 1999).

Fortunately, there is hope for couples like Joanie and Rod, who have devoted themselves to childrearing, but now find themselves adrift. The cessation of active childrearing frees up resources which can be invested in personal and relational development. Indeed, as couples age, the development of new and meaningful shared activity is a key to improving satisfaction. The period after the children leave home can be a time of personal and relational renewal, characterized by new social engagements, the discovery of latent capacities, and the development of more rewarding and flexible kinds of collaboration.

As the time and energy devoted to in-home parenting subsides, you may be asked to help married clients answer a series of questions (see Box 4.1). You may find that clients express mixed reactions to the gradual abating of childrearing activities. Some will be exhilarated or overwhelmed by the pursuit or rediscovery of latent interests and the possible onslaught of new activity. Others will feel disoriented, even frightened, by the loss of parenting activities and the identity affirmation that comes with them. Joanie and Rod felt this way for months. Faced with a new surplus of unstructured time, some clients will report relational boredom and others will be exasperated by spouses who cling to the past, unwilling to try new activities and roles. Finally, a challenge for some couples is negotiating the extent to which new activities will be shared or pursued individually.

**BOX 4.1 WHAT YOU MIGHT HEAR FROM CLIENTS:
WHAT DO WE DO NOW?**

How will we spend the time we formerly devoted to parenting?

How will we find new sources of meaning and fulfillment?

We feel like we do not have much in common anymore.

Is it okay to pursue my own activities?

How do we know when we are spending too much time together, or too little?

Where will we find new friends? How do we restart old friendships?

What will we talk about?

Do we change the roles and routines that have served us so well?

In the pages that follow, we first examine how the activities of a married couple are structured by the demands of child raising and how they change as parenting requirements diminish. Next, we consider the kinds of distress clients are likely to report as they seek new patterns of meaningful activity. Third, we apply the analytical frameworks (from chapter 1) to interpret client experiences. Fourth, we offer suggestions for helping clients work through this important life transition. The chapter ends with questions for clients and therapeutic exercises.

CONSTRAINTS ON ACTIVITY DURING CHILDREARING

Childrearing imposes certain constraints on the way couples spend their time. Compared to earlier and later periods of the relationship, the childrearing phase is characterized by the following characteristics.

Structured Activity

The lives of parents are structured by the schedules of their children. During the early years, children's need for feeding, bathing, and sleeping determines what caretakers will be doing at a given time of the day or night. Later, structure is imposed by school calendars, extracurricular activities such as music or sports practices, and the need to transport children to and from various social engagements, doctor's appointments, and other appointments. When added to the demands of work outside the home, these commitments make for a highly planned, sometimes harried existence. Typical parents report few periods of "down time" and little freedom to control their own lives.

Sanctioned Activity

Parenting is generally a positively sanctioned behavior in our culture, so parents feel confident that time spent on parenting is the "right" thing to do. For some clients, parenting provides a built-in reason for avoiding certain kinds of activities that may have been common in the past, but feel "wrong" now. These might include drug and alcohol use, nights "out on the town," or spontaneous trips with friends. Other constraints on activity include wanting to be a role model for children, shifts in personal values that come with parental responsibility, and not wanting to disadvantage one's partner (e.g., by leaving him or her disproportionately responsible for watching over the children on weekends).

Identity-Affirming Activity

Parenting lends a person a clearly demarcated social identity as a mom or dad. Other roles may follow: Girl Scout leader, sports coach, car pool driver, Sunday school teacher, PTA member. It is relatively easy for parents to know who they are during this stage of life because society offers well-structured roles which parents often feel compelled to fill.

Shared Social Activity

Parents often report difficulty in maintaining friendships with childless friends. Indeed, parenting immerses them in a competing and sometimes all-consuming social network. It feels "natural" to form bonds with the parents of their children's friends, who are likely to live nearby, attend many of the same activities, and share a compelling interest in the well-being of children. Indeed, parenting provides the common topics of discussion and interdependencies that foster relationship development. Unfortunately, for some couples, when the children are gone, they realize that their friendships have been constrained to a fairly narrow set of commonalities, many of which diminished as the children grew older.

Coordinated Activity

Childrearing is a complex undertaking that requires planning, cooperation, coordination, monitoring, compromise, and continuing adjustment. Even spouses who have fairly differentiated roles must use these roles to work together toward a common goal—successfully raising a child from infancy to adulthood. In short, parents spend considerable time collaborating in "running" the family. Successful collaboration yields a sense of fulfillment and fosters a shared identity. For this reason, some couples who report unsatisfying marriages still manage to find gratification in their parenting partnership. The motivation to collaborate may be lessened when parenting responsibilities ease and focus is shifted back to the neglected relationship.

Together these five types of activity create a sense of predictability, comfort, and general "busyness" in the lives of new parents. After an initial period of negotiation over domestic tasks and responsibilities, most adopt activity routines that endure through the childrearing years. When partners do make adjustments in this routine, they typically respond to external requirements, such as a child changing schools, rather than their own desires. Vacations and other leisure activities are often structured around the needs of the children. As time passes, the energy and time required by parenting can impede efforts to maintain the marital relationship through shared activity (see chapter 2). It is not surprising then that the cessation of active parenting leaves some couple with feelings of uncertainty, disconnectedness, and purposelessness.

MIDLIFE TRANSITIONS: FINDING FULFILLMENT IN NEW PATTERNS OF ACTIVITY

As the effort devoted to parenting lessens, clients necessarily experience changes in activity patterns, some of which are disconcerting (see *Sources of Distress* below). However, midlife can be a time of optimism, as couples find new and meaningful ways to spend their time, together and apart. Our studies of long-term marriages confirm that finding pleasurable shared activities is a key to longevity. Successful couples often laid the groundwork for shared activity long before the kids left home. Box 4.2 shares some of these steps, which may be useful as you help clients prepare for this transition.

BOX 4.2 PREPARING FOR MIDLIFE CHANGES IN ACTIVITY: STEPS TO TAKE DURING THE CHILD-RAISING YEARS

- Continue to nurture early interests and hobbies (e.g., keep playing the piano)
- Join a club (even if the commitment is minimal in the short term)
- Continue to take trips and make dates "as a couple"
- Cultivate friendships with people who are not parents of kids' friends
- Invest effort in maintaining old friendships (that may be parents of kids' friends)
- Develop the habit of learning and discussing new things with your mate
- Maintain a small but meaningful service role in a community or religious organization (unconnected to youth)

Clients who are ill-prepared for centerstage marriage may need help in finding an "upside" when the parenting mission fades (see *Working With Clients* below). You can also steer them to a variety of helpful organizations and resources. We reviewed our interviews with midlife couples looking at changes in how they spent their time after the kids left home. Many of their reports were uplifting. Here is a summary of positive themes that may be heartening to distressed clients.

Increased Spontaneity

Having spent years in a highly scheduled environment, some couples relished the opportunity to be spontaneous. They made last minute decisions to go out for dinner or take in a movie and enjoyed the freedom to launch weekend trips or gather with friends on short notice. These couples welcomed unpredictability into their lives and approached their activities with flexibility and creativity.

Self-Fulfillment

Midlife can be a time to refocus on the needs and desires of the self. After years of relative selflessness, clients can spend their time on activities that meet their own needs, rather than those of their children. In interviews, we heard from those who rekindled old pursuits (e.g., playing the piano), started new ones (e.g., learning new cooking techniques), and invested in their own well-being (e.g., joining a health club). Having invested heavily in the well-being of their offspring, these women and men found the time and energy to take care of themselves.

New Directions

With the responsibilities of parenting receding, some couples felt free to make long-term changes, some of which had been delayed for years. For some, this meant finding a more rewarding line of work. A longtime teacher took early retirement and started a new career as a realtor. A health care supply manager returned to school to pursue a career as a nurse. A stay-at-home mom took the opportunity to complete her college degree.

These changes in direction were often cited as positive turning points in marriages. Three reasons were cited for the positive effects, all related to how the respondents wanted to spend their time. First, so much time is devoted to work that a change in that activity has monumental effects on the daily lives of workers and their spouses. These participants changed careers so they could spend more time doing things they like and less time engaged in activities that cause stress and unhappiness.

Second, some career changes were made to gain flexibility and control over time. Two examples come to mind. By becoming a nurse practitioner, Ron could work three 12-hour shifts each week, freeing more time for the weekend hobbies he shared with his wife Debbie. By leaving her job as a retail manager and starting her own interior design business, Laura gained control over her work schedule (which remained demanding). She could more closely synchronize her schedule with that of her husband who worked as a pilot for a major airline. Third, some career changers sought an increase in income, which, among other things, made it possible for them to afford the travel and recreational activities they now had time to pursue with their spouse.

More Time for Intimacy

Many couples described the post-parenting years as a time of increased closeness and sexual intimacy. More of their time could be devoted to "just talking." Their sex lives were no longer curtailed by the presence of children in the house and the distractions of parenting. The health of the marriage moved up the priority list.

Easy Companionship

Couples took pleasure in the time they had to simply "hang out" together. Many described an easy companionship that developed around such routine tasks as grocery shopping, cooking, and exercising. Sharing such tasks as meal preparation fostered a spirit of collaboration and created time for unhurried conversation. During the child-rearing years, for reasons of efficiency and coordination, these activities had been delegated to one partner.

Time for Reflection and Mutual Planning

After adjusting to the relative quiet of a child-free home, couples enjoyed the opportunities for contemplation and reflection provided by a less harried lifestyle. Some spent more time thinking, talking, and listening. Compared to younger couples, they spent more time assessing their current circumstances and planning future events such as vacations, retirement, or changes in family obligations (e.g., grandparenting). In general, midlife offers the opportunity to be more deliberate in decision making and less pressed for time.

SOURCES OF DISTRESS

Most centerstage couples adopt new and rewarding patterns of activity. But it is not uncommon for them to struggle for months or even years to find their footing. In recalling this period of life, veteran couples describe multiple types of distress. Anticipating these problems can better help clients negotiate what is sometimes a difficult transition.

The "Too Quiet" House

Although many parents look forward to the day when their house becomes a quiet sanctuary, the reality can be disturbing. Children are often conversational partners for parents. The comings and goings of the kids and their friends brings certain vitality to some households, a steady stream of social energy and conversational topics. Some parents relish being at the center, or even the periphery, of this whirl of social motion. The "too quiet" house may be one that lacks distraction, novelty, and opportunities for social connection. New activities, both outside and inside the home (e.g., homeowners association meetings are now held at the couples' house), can gratify these needs, which in the past have been met by children at home.

Loss of Identity

Many women and men are highly invested in their identities as parents. The loss of traditional parenting activities, even mundane ones like driving the carpool or monitoring homework, makes it impossible to maintain a valued identity. Clients may report feelings of loss and meaningless. Some will cling too strongly to their parenting identity. Possible outcomes include excessive meddling in the lives of their adult children, an unwillingness to entertain new roles, and a fixation on the past at the expense of the future.

Parents like Arturo (see below) need help in recognizing how their identities have been expressed, and possibly constrained, by their investment in parenting activities. In such cases, development of new and meaningful forms of identity expression is crucial.

Arturo was a successful and popular "jock" in high school, quarterback of the football team, and varsity baseball player. Much to his disappointment, Arturo's sports career ended before he wanted it to. Colleges expressed little interest due to his small size, and none offered the athletic scholarship he coveted. As do so many parents, Arturo transferred his sports ambitions to his son, Palo. Arturo coached Palo's teams at every level of competition. Father and son practiced together constantly, and Palo spent many summer weeks at the best sports camps. During Palo's high school years, Arturo attended every game, constantly consulted with the coaches, and volunteered to "scout" the competition. He protested when Palo's playing time was limited and urged the boy to work harder to increase his chances of a college scholarship. Arturo spent many hours on the family computer, researching colleges and contacting athletic programs on behalf of his son. Eventually, Palo accepted a modest scholarship from a small out-of-state college, partly to escape the scrutiny of his father. After a year, Palo decided he'd "had enough" sports and dedicated himself to his pre-med studies. Arturo finds himself at a loss these days, unsure of how to spend his after work hours, and unsure of what the future holds for him.

Arturo eventually realized that his commitment to Palo's sports career was driven largely by his own unmet ambitions. The over-the-top involvement in Palo's success distracted Arturo from an unrewarding career as a salesman. But it also placed undue pressure on their relationship. A career change may be in his future, but for now, Arturo is expanding his activities in a way that preserves both his interest in sport and his relationship with Palo. He is training to be an umpire for youth sports, an activity that should keep him happily engaged for many years.

Relational Boredom

Having spent years jointly engaged in parenting activities, some couples simply do not know how to spend their time together once the kids are gone. This problem is most acute for those who have neglected their non-parenting interests. The most obvious symptom is an acute lack of conversational topics. Some clients will mistake this lack of common interest as severe marriage difficulty. Other couples have sufficient common interests but have neglected the art of communication for too long and only now are experiencing the consequences. In either case, it is important these couples reevaluate their relational communication practices (see chapter 2). Couples who succeed in adopting new activities or joining new social groups will find more to talk about. You can help them inventory their interests and explore new ways to expand their engagements with the larger world (see *Exercises* at the end of this chapter).

Social Isolation

Parents tend to socialize with other parents. Proximity and the common activities of their kids make it easy for parents to develop friendships. Determined to expose their children to a broad range of developmental experiences, many parents increase their involvement in schools, recreational organizations, and religious communities. These engagements put them in contact with other adults of similar values and life circumstances. In short, parenting drives social integration. Some of these social engagements will last, but others wither as the kids grow older and disperse. As a result, midlife couples sometimes feel socially isolated. In response, one or both partners may become more reliant on the marriage for social gratification.

This dependence can be problematic. Research suggests that multiple and varied social connections foster psychological resilience in individuals and marriages (Bryant & Conger, 1995; Waldron, Gitelson, & Kelley, 2005). For some long-term couples, marital satisfaction increases when the individual partners find some of their social and leisure activities outside of the marriage. These outside activities are a vital source

of new conversational topics. Moreover, even the most dedicated partner will be hard pressed to meet all of the emotional and social needs
of a spouse. Friends and leisure companions are vital sources of emotional support and identity affirmation, and they provide a sympathetic
audience for complaints. These outside connections can be an emotional
safety valve, releasing pressures that inevitably build in a marriage.

Socially isolated clients need tools and encouragement to pursue new
kinds of social engagements in addition to redefining and revitalizing
the friendships they have developed through their parenting activities.
Highly dependent spouses may be a challenge for some. These clients
need assistance in negotiating mutually beneficial social arrangements
with their partners.

Uncertainty and Fear

Midlife may offer opportunities for career change, a return to school, and
other radical changes in familiar routines. These decisions have sweeping
implications for how individuals and couples spend their time. Clients
contemplating significant life changes may need assistance in imagining
a new future, identifying realistic and unrealistic expectations, managing uncertainty, overcoming fear of the unknown, and negotiating new
domestic agreements with a spouse.

Mardy had been working part-time as a receptionist at her children's
elementary school for many years. As a parent of three children, she
appreciated the flexibility of part-time work and the opportunity to interact with
other adults on a daily basis. But her youngest would soon be graduating from
high school, and Mardy was ready to launch her long-delayed teaching career.
First, she would need to return to college to complete her college degree.

Mardy was excited by the prospects of a rewarding career and increased
income, but she knew herself to be a creature of habit. She valued
predictability and enjoyed the easy routines of the life she shared with her
husband Sergio. Mardy had a hard time imagining what life would be like at
college in a classroom full of younger students. It had been nearly 20 years
since she left school. What if she failed her courses? Mardy also worried about
the effects on her traditionally inclined husband. What would he think about
sharing some of the domestic tasks, such as preparing dinner, which she had
performed for so many years? Would the demands of full-time coursework cut
into the plans she and Sergio had made for travel? Other uncertainties

bothered her as well. Would she still have time for the regular gatherings with friends that she had come to cherish?

With the help of her therapist, Mardy addressed these concerns in several concrete ways. Before quitting her job, she enrolled for a single class at the local college. She consulted with academic advisors and members of the adult students club. The interactions were positive and convinced Mardy that her fears were unrealistic. She felt more confidence in her ability to do college-level work. However, Mardy decided that a full-time schedule would be too disruptive to her marriage, so she eased into her education, enrolling half-time that first year. At first, Sergio was disappointed that their postparenting plans would need to change. He had been looking forward to a less hectic, more autonomous lifestyle. But Mardy stood firm, and Sergio agreed that their traditional marriage could stand some updating. He would pitch in by assuming most of the cooking chores. Also, Mardy cautioned Sergio that she would be unavailable on some nights and weekends. He would need to become more skilled at planning activities with friends.

The result of this process was a gradual but rewarding change in the daily activities of both Mardy and Sergio. Mardy found considerable fulfillment in her school activities, and she developed interesting new relationships at the college. Sergio spent more time with his friends and took considerable pride in Mardy's academic accomplishments. Both partners spoke positively about the new flexibility in their relationship.

Relationship Stresses

Mardy and Sergio were mostly successful in managing her return to school, but not all couples are so satisfied with midlife changes in familiar patterns of activity. For example, Karen grew increasingly resentful of the time her husband Pat devoted to competitive chess. He had always enjoyed the game, but once the kids were gone, Pat started traveling to distant tournaments on weekends. He enjoyed the steep competition and the companionship of fellow enthusiasts.

Melanie reported a different kind of frustration. Her husband John depended on her almost completely to meet his social needs. Especially once the kids left home, he insisted that nearly all of their leisure time be spent together. Unlike Melanie, John had little need to spend time with same-sex friends. He pursued no independent hobbies. John was threatened by his wife's desire to spend some of her time on her own.

Melanie loved her husband and enjoyed his company, but she felt stifled by a lack of independent activity.

Van was close to his family, all of whom lived in the vicinity of the home he shared with Jackie. Van's relatives and their children gathered regularly for social occasions, which Van generally enjoyed and Jackie typically dreaded. She felt like an outsider at these gatherings and grew weary of hearing the same old stories and inside jokes. When the children were young, Jackie faithfully attended the various parties and picnics "to keep the family peace" and assure that her kids "knew their cousins." Now the kids are gone, and Jackie refuses to attend most of Van's family events. He is annoyed and perplexed, but Jackie feels that she "paid her dues" a long time ago. She wants to spend more time with her husband and with their mutual friends.

Helping couples like Pat and Karen, Melanie and John, and Jackie and Van as they work out new and mutually acceptable patterns of activity often means reassessing and discussing their expectations for postparenting life. They may require help in understanding the connection between activity patterns and marital satisfaction. In counseling sessions, clients can be encouraged to confront activity-limiting assumptions, expand their social engagements, and become more flexible. Specifically, encourage their efforts to build a larger repertoire of shared and individual interests.

ANALYTICAL TOOLS

The following analytic framework discussions are specifically tailored for application to helping clients make sense of their feelings and experiences when creating new and meaningful activities.

Applying the Dialectical Framework

As midlife couples contemplate how to fill the "activity gap" once filled by active parenting, they sometimes express ambivalent or opposing feelings. Identifying pertinent dialectical tensions can help clients recognize and articulate underlying conflicts that may be causing them distress.

Stability versus Change (and Past versus Future)

The shift to centerstage marriage provides a unique opportunity to make significant lifestyle changes. These may be expressed as a willingness to loosen ties with children and a future-oriented desire to seek new social involvements, hobbies, and travel. At the same time, one or both partners may value familiar patterns of activity; reenacting valued roles and preserving family rituals remain priorities for them. This approach is expressed in efforts to maintain ties with adult children, schedule familiar kinds of family gatherings, and by voicing reservations about proposed changes. These competing visions are often experienced simultaneously by an individual partner, creating a sense of ambivalence or uncertainty about one's goals and desires. Alternatively, when couples emphasize different poles of this dialectical tension (one wants change, the other wants stability), often partners feel as though their desires are being overlooked. In such cases, integrative approaches are useful to manage the discrepancy. For example, the partners may pursue a mix of activities that allows them to preserve continuity with the past (stability) while opening up possibilities for a different future (change).

BOX 4.3 HOW DO I USE IT? MANAGING THE STABILITY VERSUS CHANGE AND PAST VERSUS FUTURE DIALECTICS

- *Maintain stability and honor the past*: Develop family scrapbooks; plan occasional family reunions; continue familiar activities (coaching; volunteering at a school); maintain a Facebook account for family members; share stories; actively maintain friendships with parents of children's friends.
- *Embrace change and look to the future:* Plan trips to new destinations; join a health club together; take community education classes; talk to adult children less frequently; invite new friends to new restaurants; share plans for the future.
- *Balance change and stability:* Schedule fewer family gatherings, but the times the family does get together should be "special"; move into a new home but have one room designated for family guests (especially, children and grandchildren); maintain family rituals but have someone else plan and be responsible for them.

Applying the Resilience Framework

The resilience framework directs our attention to the strengths and resources that help couples replace active parenting with other meaningful activities. Encourage clients to consider these possibilities.

Tapping Latent Capacity

Through reflection at midlife, persons sometimes discover untapped talents. Individuals may discover that they have the capacity to learn a foreign language, ride a mountain bike, organize an on-line discussion group, or thrive in a college classroom. Couples may find that that they can collaborate in new ways, by becoming active in local politics, starting a small business, actively managing their financial resources, or remodeling their house. By tapping latent talents, middle-aged people add energy, novelty, and fulfillment to their lives and their relationships.

Deepening Existing Commitments

Some clients have the resources to develop and deepen their involvement in existing commitments. Here are two examples.

Example 1: Cecilia and Anthony. Having nurtured her fascination with aviation for years through reading and visits to museums, Cecilia finally pursued her pilot's license at 52 years of age. Her kids' tuition bills were mostly paid and Cecilia now had the time and money to nurture her hobby. Her husband Anthony sang in the church choir for years. Recently, he accepted a part-time leadership position at their church, as director of the youth music ministry. The new position kept Anthony busy several nights a week, and he enjoyed the opportunity to work closely with the other adults on the music staff.

Example 2: Lucy and Domingo. Lucy and her husband Domingo had always shared an interest in cooking and food. After the kids left home, they invested in an upgraded kitchen and enrolled in several classes at a local culinary institute. Recently, they invited a group of friends and coworkers to join them in a "cooking collaborative." Members of the group take turns preparing a meal each month. The group gathers to eat, socialize, and share cooking tips.

As indicated by these examples, midlife clients can fill the activity gap by leveraging their existing enthusiasms, experience, and social connections. The result can be a richer life characterized by new forms of collaboration, learning, and leadership.

Developing Flexibility and Trust

Changes to familiar activity patterns can be threatening to individuals and relationships. It is not uncommon for a spouse to feel neglect, jealousy, or fear when a partner becomes deeply engaged in a new activity. These emotional reactions are linked to troubling questions, some of which may be unexpressed. Am I now less important to my spouse? What will it mean if we spend more time doing things apart and less time doing things together? How do I feel about my partner forming new relationships that exclude me? Will I be left behind as my partner develops in new directions? Denise asked some of these questions when her husband Jamal wanted to quit his sales job and enroll in a demanding software engineering program at the local university. She worried about the short-term effects on their finances and feared that the demanding academic schedule would leave little time for her. Denise admitted to feelings of envy because she had yet to complete her own college degree and hoped to do some day.

Clients like Denise need assurance from their partners and their therapists. Resilient couples draw on reserves of trust that have been developed over years of marriage. They also exhibit flexibility in the face of changing circumstances, but they often need help. Ask couples who need to develop trust the following questions:

- What valued aspects of the relationship are threatened by this new activity?
- How does this new activity raise uncertainty for the partners? What can you do to reduce uncertainty? What kinds of uncertainty can be tolerated?
- What benefits to one or both partners will flow from this change?
- What relational routines and roles will need to change to make this new activity possible?
- What enduring relational values must be honored, even if we make these changes?
- What can we learn from changes we have made in the past?

Denise and Jamal ultimately decided that they could manage the impact of Jamal's return to school. She felt assured by his pledge to continue some of their shared activities, including their participation in a local running club. Although it would take a year longer to complete his degree, Jamal would attend school half-time and continue to work part-time. This move reduced Denise's financial anxieties. The couple drew strength from their previous success in making adjustments, including the time when Denise quit her job to stay at home with their young children.

Applying the Roles Framework

Activities clients engage in on a daily basis define and affirm their identities. Therefore, it is not surprising that role theory provides a useful language for describing clients' reactions to changes in the way they spend their time. Here we consider just two of the most obvious applications.

Role Loss

Clients may struggle with a reality faced by most parents. Their role dramatically diminishes as their children become adults. You can help clients (1) label and acknowledge the experience of role loss, (2) celebrate their successes in the parent role, (3) define a revised and appropriately-bounded role to play in the lives of adult children, and (4) define new and fulfilling nonparenting roles.

Role Sharing

A common experience of midlife couples, one that is generally associated with marital satisfaction, is increased sharing of some relational activities. Role sharing facilitates the personal growth of the individual partners, adds flexibility to their relationship, and often leads to increased empathy and communication. From our conversations with veteran couples, here are some examples of activities that are increasingly shared as marriage progresses into midlife.

- The production of financial income
- Cooking, house cleaning, and other domestic chores
- Maintaining relationships with extended family members
- Financial and retirement planning
- Arranging social activities with friends
- Initiating sexual relations
- Planning trips and vacations
- Initiating health maintenance and exercise activities

WORKING WITH CLIENTS

In this section, we offer specific suggestions for assisting clients with the project of establishing new and meaningful activities as their parenting commitments diminish. In doing so, we supplement the material introduced earlier in the chapter. We begin with six foundational tasks to complete in your work with clients, and then proceed to specific suggestions for helping clients establish new and fulfilling engagements.

Seeking Meaningful Activity: Six Foundational Steps

Assess Expectations

Some of the distress experienced by midlife couples comes from unrealistic expectations. Parents overestimate the extent to which their college-aged offspring need or want parental involvement. Of course, children vary considerably in maturity and independence, but parents who expect that their lives will continue to revolve around the children are often disappointed. These inaccurate expectations may lead to frustration on the part of parents and their offspring. They certainly make it possible for parents to put off the sometimes unwelcome task of finding new sources of fulfilling activity.

Another problem involves partners with differing expectations. For example, one may be looking forward to finding a new home, closer to restaurants and social activities that he or she enjoys. The other may be reluctant to leave the home in the suburbs that connects the couple so clearly to their past. Partners may be vaguely aware of these differences in expectations, but therapy may provide the opportunity to confront them. You can help them find points of agreement and negotiate on points of difference.

Identify Limiting Assumptions

Opportunities to pursue a different and perhaps richer set of activities are sometimes obscured by self-limiting assumptions and tacit agreements. These implicit understandings may have been valid when children lived in the home, but may no longer apply. For example, to avoid family disruption, the couple may have agreed to live in the same city for many years, but relocation to a more agreeable climate may now be an option. Couples sometimes need convincing that it is "OK" to spend money on their own recreational interests. Another issue: Do the partners want to spend all of their vacations privately or are they open to occasionally vacationing with friends? In addition, old restrictions may be lifted because the partners now have more time, money, or energy. Activities like travel, dancing lessons, or attending the theater may be viable now. The point is to help couples locate and remove unnecessary barriers to an enriched life.

Assess Current Activities and Social Connections

Encourage the couple to list the activities in which they participate, the groups to which they belong, the friends with whom they socialize. Are they happy with the status quo? Should some old activities be dropped? New ones added? Would life be richer if they pursued more kinds of activities with different kinds of people? If so, encourage them to develop a plan of action that can be enacted one small step at a time.

Inventory Interests, Talents, and Strengths

As suggested previously (see *Applying the Resilience Framework* above), you can encourage clients to inventory their neglected interests, develop latent talents, and deepen existing involvements. In some cases, you can help clients assess the risk of trying something new and the costs of failing to try. Some merely need to give themselves permission to pursue their passions. Donna encouraged her children as they became talented jazz musicians in the school music program. As a girl, she had dabbled in the piano, but had never benefited from lessons. At midlife, she retained a strong desire to create music, but feared she was "too old to learn." It was only with the encouragement of her closest friend that she finally engaged a piano teacher. Only at her husband's insistence would she agree to spend the funds necessary to buy a good-quality piano of her very own.

Locate Guidance and Support

Midlife couples find themselves in "learning mode" confronting unfamiliar circumstances and contemplating new courses of action. Returning to school, starting a fitness regimen, becoming active in community service, accepting new leadership roles—these can be major leaps into uncharted waters. You can encourage clients to seek advice and support from those who have experienced these transitions. Of course, you can be an important source of support during times of change and decision making, but other kinds of expertise can be helpful at midlife. Jane sought the help of a personal trainer when she recommitted to a fitness regimen. Kyle consulted with a senior work colleague before agreeing to join the advisory board for a local charity. She helped him gauge the time commitments and politics of the volunteer post. Francesca established a mentoring relationship with the director of the women's resource center at her local community college. The advice and emotional support she received helped her persevere during that first challenging semester. Although they may be experiencing temporary distress, many of your midlife clients will be experienced, independent, and successful in career or family life. Asking for guidance is a skill in and of itself. When necessary help clients plan concrete steps to find help.

Make and Maintain Relational Adjustments

We have argued that individuals and couples often make significant changes in activity as their parenting commitments diminish. In either case, the relational status quo is likely to be disrupted and adjustments in relational practices must be negotiated. Clients may need your assistance with the communication practices that facilitate major change. We mentioned some of these earlier in this chapter and others appear in chapter 2. Box 4.4 presents a comprehensive list of communication behaviors that may be useful to midlife couples as they negotiate changes in the activities that they will pursue alone and together.

BOX 4.4 HELPFUL RELATIONSHIP PRACTICES FOR COUPLES NEGOTIATING CHANGES IN ACTIVITY

1 Exploring partner and self-expectations about post-parenting activities
2 Affirming core relational values and commitments
3 Revealing and acknowledging concerns, uncertainties, and emotional reactions to change
4 Offering more flexibility in relationship roles and routines
5 Expressing support for the personal development of the partner
6 Offering relational resources like time, money, and emotional support to facilitate change
7 Providing messages of assurance to the partner
8 Editing messages which increase defensiveness and insecurity, undermine your partner's sense of confidence, or impugn his or her motives for seeking meaningful activities

---

EMERGING OPPORTUNITIES FOR MEANINGFUL ENGAGEMENT: EXAMPLES FOR CLIENTS

Countless opportunities are available to midlife couples who are seeking new and meaningful forms of engagement with the world around them. Following is a sampler of ideas that may be helpful with clients who are struggling to find activities that "fit." We emphasize ideas that are somewhat novel or gaining in popularity and those that are proving popular with baby boomers, the generation currently experiencing the challenges and opportunities of midlife. More information can be found under resources.

Significant Service

In contrast to traditional volunteerism, the "significant service" movement involves midlife volunteers with service opportunities designed to tap and develop their skills. Charitable and government organizations gain substantive help in addressing technical, creative, research, and managerial challenges. Volunteers gain satisfaction, personal development, and sometimes, partial compensation for their efforts. The emphasis is on deriving measurable and potentially transformative benefits for service organizations and their communities.

Lifelong Learning Programs

Once a bastion for senior citizens seeking classes in arts and crafts, lifelong learning programs are now more likely to offer challenging college-level learning opportunities in a variety of formats, including small group discussion and on-line instruction. Programs are targeting younger students. They often provide opportunities to share expertise as well as learn. Offered at numerous universities and colleges, these programs also offer a chance for midlife couples to form relationships with learning-oriented peers in a stimulating environment.

Civic Engagement

Under the civic engagement label, a variety of organizations train citizens for leadership positions in their own communities and neighborhood. The goal is to improve the quality of local governance and to provide high quality training to those who are willing to make a difference in their communities.

Green Volunteerism

Increasing concerns about environmental sustainability have spawned a plethora of young organizations, which need help from experienced citizens. Couples and individuals will find numerous opportunities to become involved in wildlife protection, land conservation, recycling, and renewable resources, among many other causes. Many of these opportunities will be local, whereas others can be combined with personal travel plans.

Mentorship Programs

Mentoring is an increasingly common activity for midlife couples, who often enjoy the opportunities to share their experiences as parents, employees, or simply as functional and caring adults. Midlife couples serve as formal or informal mentors to younger couples in programs organized by synagogues or churches. Particularly in areas where families are stressed, school districts seek adult mentors for at-risk students. Other programs are sponsored by local governments, charities, and business organizations.

Entrepreneurship

Entrepreneurs are noted for their creative spark, energy, and success in starting new ventures. An emerging movement seeks to transplant the spirit of entrepreneurship from the for-profit to the nonprofit and community service sectors of the economy. At midlife, some employees are ready to put aside predictable jobs in favor of a new adventure. Of course, some have no choice due to economic changes and layoffs. The opportunity to create a new business or social service model will appeal to some midlife clients.

CONCLUDING THOUGHTS

The gradual diminishment of parenting activity is disconcerting to some parents and welcomed by others. It is not uncommon for conscientious parents to feel disoriented at this stage of life. In this chapter, we have articulated some of the forces that contribute to their distress. We have also argued that resilient couples develop new and meaningful patterns of activity during this period of life. Their success is attributable to such factors as flexibility, creativity, communication, and the willingness to seek assistance from others. The resources presented in *Appendix A* and exercises presented at the end of this chapter were designed to provide concrete assistance to you and your centerstage clients. We hope you will find them useful as you guide clients during this time of transition.

QUESTIONS FOR CLIENTS

1   How satisfied are you with the way you spent time as a couple during the childrearing years? How will it be different now?

2   If money and time were no objects, how would you describe a perfect week together as a couple? What would be the perfect weekend? How about the perfect day? Can the two of you find a way to make it happen?

3   Now that the kids are gone, which activities would you like to do more often?

4   Think of the activities you enjoyed during the parenting years. Do you want to retain some of those? How could you stay involved in them?

5   What latent talents do you have that have yet to be developed? How can your spouse help you develop them?

6   Do you know how to pursue the new activities you are interested in? (See *Appendix A* for ideas.)

7   What are the interests you hold in common as a couple? What activities would help you pursue them?

8   Do you expect to spend more or less time together in the coming years? Is it ok for partners to pursue individual interests? Are there limits that should apply?

EXERCISES

Exercise 4.1 Evaluating Constraints of the Childrearing Years

The goal of this exercise is to think about choices you made when childrearing and their influence on your current situation (post-live-in children).

1   Structured Activity
    a   What percentage of your activities as a couple was "kid based"?
    b   What were your favorite activities when the children were still in the house?
    c   How have you filled the gap that was left when your kids grew older?
2   Sanctioned Activity
    a   How did your activities as a couple change when you went from young couple to young family?
    b   How are your activities changing again, now that the children are gone?
3   Identity Affirming Activity
    a   To what extent is your identity shaped by being "mom" or "dad"?
    b   To what extent is your identity shaped by being a "wife" or "husband"?
    c   How will these identities be supported or changed in coming years?
4   Structured Social Activity
    Make a list of the friends you had when your oldest child was a sophomore in high school. How many of those people do you still do things with on a monthly basis? Write down something you can do this week to reconnect with friends you have not seen in more than a month.
5   Collaborative Activity
    a   Identify three ways you had to work together as a couple during the childrearing years.
    b   Now, look at the decisions you have made as couple in the last three months. Do your more recent decisions need to be made differently?

Exercise 4.2 Taking Steps Now to Create New Activities

The goal of this exercise is to begin making changes for more *couple activity* while children are still in the house.

1   Identify spheres of activity where you could be more independent and less involved. (For example, could your 16-year-old son drive himself to and from work, freeing up time for you to be alone in the house?)

2 Think of something fun the two of you seldom get to do together.
3 Periodically block out time for activity discussed at *Step 2*. (Be diligent in planning or ingrained habits will override your desire to find some couple time.)

Exercise 4.3 Rediscovering Common Interests

The goal of this exercise is to bolster your relationship by rediscovering common interests.

1 First, on a large sheet of paper, brainstorm activities that you used to enjoy as a couple, but have somehow lost along the way (e.g., playing cards or having a little wine and cheese time before dinner.) Put this list of activities in the middle of the paper.
2 Next, brainstorm activities that you always wanted to pursue, "if you ever had the time." If you agree on the activity, put it in the middle of the page with the previous activities. If the activity is something only one of you is interested in, list it on the side of the paper (wife's on one side of the paper, husband's on the other).
3 After you have generated the list of behaviors use a colored marker (one color for the wife and a separate color for the husband) to circle the highest priority ideas. (Note: They do not have to be big ideas to get circled. Taking an evening stroll most nights may be as fun as skydiving.)
4 Finally, for each idea that you agree upon as a couple (you both circled it), make a plan when and how it will be incorporated into your week, month, or year. (Not everything needs to be done at once!) For the items that only one spouse circled, discuss how you can support him or her. For example, I may not want to skydive, but I am willing to go and take pictures or to create a "memories book" of each place you do skydive.

Exercise 4.4 Stability or Change? Past or Present?

The goal of this exercise is to identify how personality differences contribute to dialectical tensions in your relationship.

Stability versus Change

1   As a couple, identify two challenges your family had to confront during the childrearing years (e.g., short-term financial problem, Grandma moving in, needing to purchase additional transportation as the children got older).
2   For each of these challenges identify whether your (and your spouse's) initial preference was for change or stability (e.g., "lets go look for a new car" versus "lets find a way to make our existing vehicles work for all of us").
3   To what extent are the responses to these two challenges typical of how you and your spouse manage transition?

Past versus Future

1   Identify as many of your activities as possible (from the last month) that are *past-oriented* activities or *future-oriented* activities. Past-oriented activities could include making photo albums, maintaining family rituals, constructing genealogies. Future-oriented activities could include planning for retirement, turning the kids' room into a workout room, remodeling the kitchen.
2   Which of these activities does each partner prefer?
3   Do these preferences reflect a general tendency in how you make decisions together?

Exercise 4.5 Building Resilience

The goal of this exercise is to examine characteristics that keep your marriage resilient during centerstage marriage.

1   Have a cup of coffee or tea together and talk about all the things you loved to do in high school and college (or during the post high school years). Remember your watercolor class or playing the guitar?
  a   Talk about whether you each might begin to pursue one of your old talents/interests.
  b   Maybe it's time to take another water color class or pull your guitar out from under the bed.
2   Pull out your calendar and make a list of commitments each of you had over the last month.

3 Are there certain current commitments that you could be giving more to? (For example, once a month you help at the local food bank. Maybe it's time for a weekly commitment.)

4 Are there certain commitments that you would like to become more of a defining part of your life?

5 During the conversations suggested above, take time to ask one another, "If we (I) pursue this new activity, how can I make sure that you know that you are my number one priority?"

Exercise 4.6 Time Together Pie Chart

The goal of this exercise is to foster agreement about how much time to spend together.

1 Individually, each of you draw a pie chart showing how much of your leisure time you spend with your spouse and alone.

2 Compare your charts.

   a Did you come close to agreeing on how much time you spend together?

   b Do you want to change the amount of time together?

3 Brainstorm three ways that time together can be increased this month.

REFERENCES

Bryant, C., & Conger, R. D. (1999). Marital success and domains of social support in long-term relationships. Does the influence of network members ever end? *Journal of Marriage & the Family, 61*, 437–451.

Goldsmith, D. J. (2004). *Communicating social support*. Cambridge, UK: Cambridge University Press.

Waldron, V., Gitelson, R., & Kelley, D. (2005). Gender differences in social adaptation to a retirement community: Longitudinal changes and the role of mediated communication. *Journal of Applied Gerontology, 24*, 283–298.

Waldron, V., & Kelley, D. (2008). *Communicating forgiveness*. Newbury Park, CA: Sage Publications.

Retooling: Adapting to Midlife Events

PART
II

5

New Career Directions: Coping with Job Loss and Returning to School

Mia worked for a national chain of department stores for 18 years. She and her husband Andy relocated several times during that period in response to company requests and promotions. Accustomed to long workdays and frequent buying trips, Mia was thankful that Andy's work as a computer consultant was less time-consuming and more flexible. Over the years, it had been Andy who provided much of the daily supervision for their two girls, now 19- and 21-years-old. A promotion to a senior buyer position left Mia feeling that her commitment was finally paying off. The generous salary would come in handy as the girls' tuition bills mounted. Before long, the couple would start investing larger sums in their retirement fund. Against this bright background of career accomplishment, Mia detected some troubling shadows. Her sector of the retail economy was changing rapidly due to mergers and increased competition. The venerable company for whom she worked had begun closing unprofitable stores and upgrading its product lines. A new vice president had been hired with the primary objective of improving efficiencies and cutting costs. In the hopes of making herself "lay-off proof," Mia had been contemplating a return to college to complete her business degree. But she and Andy worried that the combination of her demanding job and night time classes would deplete their already limited time together, even if Mia went part-time. Despite her suspicions, Mia was devastated when the new vice president delivered the bad news in a private meeting. In an effort to cut costs, one whole tier of senior

managers, including Mia, would be let go immediately. A 6-month severance
package was intended to soften the blow. Numb, Mia was asked to gather her
personal belongings and was quickly escorted to the door by a security officer.

Most transitions experienced by centerstage couples involve gradual
adjustments in course. One or two variables change, but the general trajectory of the marriage is unaffected. Launching children into adulthood
is one of those incremental changes. Partners know that the children
must leave eventually and they have time to prepare. Wide-sweeping
disruption can be avoided by sticking with the same house, friends, and
jobs. In short, major changes in direction often can be avoided if the
couples want it that way. In contrast, despite the telltale warning signs,
Mia and Andy were largely caught off guard. Her job loss was imposed
by outside circumstances, not chosen. Having enjoyed stability for years,
the pair must now contemplate a major change in direction.

In this chapter, we consider two of these direction-altering experiences, ones that are increasingly affecting the lives of centerstage couples:
The loss of a job and a return to school. As we will explain, these relationship changing transitions are both similar and different. In fact, they
may be two elements in a larger process of midlife "recareering." Mia
and Andy illustrate this point. They are now weighing the advantages of
Mia returning to school full-time. Would she be better off in the long
run with a college degree? Should she use this unfortunate experience
as motivation to retool and change careers? Of course, spouses like Andy
will be disoriented by a partner's job loss and/or return to college. Andy
may feel pressure to increase his earning potential and, with Mia around
the house more, he will experience some changes in his parenting role
and relational routines. Not surprisingly, clients like Mia and Andy often
need assistance as they explore the personal and relational implications
of these major changes.

JOB LOSS

Job loss is becoming a common experience at midlife. Middle-aged men
are most vulnerable. Alex, the 47-year-old man featured in the story below, may be typical of some male clients, but since the 1990s, women
like Mia have been forced out of the labor market in increasing numbers
(Malen & Stroh, 1998). Indeed, the number of midlife clients distressed
by the loss of work is likely to increase. According to the U.S. Department
of Labor Statistics (2008), roughly 3 million Americans are unemployed

at the time of this writing. An analysis conducted by the Bloomberg financial organization in April of 2008 suggests that layoff trends are accelerating. More than 80,000 workers were dropped from payrolls in March 2008 (Schlisserman, 2008), the third consecutive monthly reduction in employment numbers, and the largest in 5 years.

BOX 5.1 "I DIDN'T WANT TO BE A MIDDLE-AGED MAN LOOKING FOR A JOB"

"I didn't want to be a middle-aged man looking for a job"

As reported by the Dayton Daily News (Cummings, 2007), Alex Whillock had labored for an auto styling business for almost two decades. Nonetheless, with business plummeting, the company recently laid him off. In a story becoming too familiar in the United States, Whillock received a pink slip with his paycheck, having received, "no warning or anything." At age 47, Alex is one of many veteran workers who now find themselves unexpectedly on the job market. In Dayton, large and small businesses have been shedding jobs or leaving town completely in recent years. Unemployed and middle-aged men and women are launching often futile job searches in an increasingly unpromising local market.

"I didn't want to be a middle-aged man looking for a job, but that's the way it turned out," Whillock noted in comments to the newspaper reporter, who also interviewed Delores Woodall, a counselor at Montgomery County's Job Placement office. Ms. Woodall, who has advised job seekers for decades, noted that many recent clients held the same job for 10 to 20 years. For most, unemployment is a bewildering experience. Woodall's middle-aged clients expect to find a new job quickly. They exhibit high levels of motivation, but they underestimate the difficulty of finding a similar job and have much to learn about the search process.

As Whillock soon discovered, losing a job at midlife can undermine self esteem. Alex was discouraged when he couldn't find work in his area of expertise which involves car upholstery. He soon was forced to file for unemployment. The payments covered his mortgage, but Alex relied on his spouse's salary for nearly everything else. "I basically became a house husband for a while," he explained. To keep himself from going stir crazy during the lengthy job search, Whillock busied himself with domestic tasks, such as preparing dinner and organizing the family garage. In time Alex reluctantly concluded that he wouldn't find a job comparable to his old one. Recently, determined to control his own fate, he abandoned his job search and started a custom upholstery company of his own.

Job loss is not a "normative developmental event" like the launching of children, so a couple is rarely well prepared to cope with it. Like so many others, Alex was caught by surprise. A unique feature of job loss is its imposition by outside forces—it is not a choice. Its victims experience a troubling loss of control and a heightened sense of uncertainty. In addition, for those who have held their jobs for long periods, like both Mia and Alex, unanticipated termination affects personal identity and self-esteem. Mia was heavily invested in her identity as a successful executive and breadwinner for her family, but given the general decline of her industry, Mia worried about finding a similar executive-level position. She felt a sense of failure and disorientation, a loss of her working self, the largest part of her personal identity.

Clients experiencing the stress of job loss report a variety of other negative consequences, including anxiety, depression, and susceptibility to illness (Hobdy, Hayslip, Kaminski, Crowley, Riggs, York, 2007). Loss of hope, lowered self-esteem, and marital stresses are common when the period of unemployment is extended. Clients may lose confidence in their employment prospects. Some wonder if they are "too old to learn" new skills. Fortunately, interventions at the individual and relational level can improve psychosocial functioning, positive marital functioning, and job-seeking skills.

RETURNING TO SCHOOL

A second kind of change is more likely to be chosen, rather than imposed by external events. We refer here to midlife clients who choose to enter or return to college, although, of course, clients like Mia are prompted in part by external factors like job loss and dimming professional prospects.

Nontraditional or "reentry" students report a variety of educational motives (see Box 5.2). For some, the cessation of active parenting is a natural "pause" in a busy life—one that allows them to complete an unfinished degree. At American universities and community colleges, a large percentage of traditional 18- to 22-year-old students (well over 50%) do not complete degrees on their first attempt. So it is not surprising that many return years later, encouraged by changes in personal maturity, financial resources, or family responsibilities.

Individuals also return to school because the same economic trends that force workers, like Alex, out of the job market are encouraging them to retool through education at local colleges and universities. The emerging "knowledge-based" economy increasingly requires workers to possess the reasoning and communication skills associated with college-level training.

Midlife students are a diverse group. They include stay-at-home parents preparing for a first career, those who have been displaced by job loss, and employees simply seeking to update their skills. The large majority of these career-oriented workers begin their studies at a community college (Taniguchi & Kaufman, 2007), although some enroll directly or eventually transfer to a university. Other learning motives cited by midlife learners, include self-fulfillment, the desire to be a role model for children or grandchildren, and the satisfaction of unmet intellectual needs (Gearon, 2008).

BOX 5.2 WHY THEY LEARN: MOTIVES OF NONTRADITIONAL STUDENTS

- Preparing for a career
- Career switching and "retooling"
- Economic necessity
- Intrinsic motivation to learn
- Staying current with new technology and trends
- Gaining personal satisfaction from achieving educational goals
- Completing "unfinished business" from the past
- Serving as a role model for children or grandchildren

As with job loss, more of your clients will find their lives and relationships affected by an educational transition. Based on U.S. Census data from 2003, the government counts some 6.1 million "nontraditional" college students in U.S. colleges and universities, composing approximately 37% of all college students (American Council on Education, 2008) and nearly half of those seeking a degree. What do we know about them? The report suggests that clients affected by educational transition are more likely to be female. Of those over 35 years of age, nearly *two thirds* of nontraditional students are women. These students are beset by a variety of challenges, some of which you will recognize in your counseling sessions. (See *Box* 5.3 for one recent congressional analysis of the trends and trials of these students.) Both male and female returnees are likely to be married. The impact on the marriage and the support of the partner are major sources of concern for this group (Quimby & O' Brien, 2006). We know that many of these students do not complete their educational objective. Yet, those who do often credit the support of the spouse and other family members, or at least report relatively low levels of relational distress. Given these observations, many clients need assistance in managing the personal and marital challenges that accompany a return to school.

BOX 5.3 CHALLENGES FACING NONTRADITIONAL STUDENTS: A CONGRESSIONAL ANALYSIS

Nontraditional students are slowly becoming the norm; the percentage of nontraditional students on college campuses—excluding those participating in adult education that will not lead to a credential or degree—has increased to 47% in 2001 from 34% in 1991. These undergraduates are more likely to be balancing school with work (40% work full-time, up from just one-fourth) and parenting (27% have children, up from 20%) than they were 15 years ago.

Unfortunately, nontraditional students are much less likely to attain a degree than their traditional counterparts. Among students seeking a bachelor's degree, half the number of highly nontraditional students left college within the first 3 years, compared with just 12% of traditional students. Similarly, among those seeking an associate's degree, 62% of highly nontraditional students left without any degree, compared with 19% of traditional students. This trend has a disproportionate impact on minority communities. Over 80% of both black and Hispanic undergraduate students are nontraditional in some way. Nearly two thirds of black students are financially independent and are almost three times as likely to be single parents. Hispanic and black students are also especially likely to be first generation college students (57% and 47%, respectively). (Statement issued by The Office of Senator Hilary Clinton, 2008)

SOURCES OF DISTRESS

Job loss and a return to school cause distress for some of the same reasons, but they are also different in important ways. We consider them individually, and then discuss unique factors.

Distress From Job Loss

Clients facing a job loss express the following kinds of concerns.

Identity Threat

For many midlife clients the work role is a major component of identity. That was certainly true for Mia, whose story opened this chapter, although Mia also valued her roles as mother and wife. Nonetheless, Mia was deeply distressed by the turn of events at work. As with many clients, her distress is attributable to role centrality—the relative importance of a role in defining the self. In traditional American culture, male identity is linked strongly to the work role. In conventional families, males receive considerable approval from the spouse and other influential persons for their performance of work roles and their earning of income. For this reason, traditional males may be deeply disoriented by the loss of a job and traditional couples may experience increased relational tension.

Early research suggested that females, even those who worked outside the home, suffered less acute psychological effects from job loss. One explanation was the tendency of females to identify with multiple roles simultaneously (wife/parent/employee). In addition, their capacity to cultivate social support after a loss was thought to be advantageous. However, more recent work indicates that women like Mia, those for whom work is a central component of identity, are just as negatively impacted as men. The upshot for centerstage marriage is the need to diversify identities after a job loss and subsequently renegotiate aspects of the relationship. This is particularly important when the period of employment has been lengthy or job loss is likely to be repeated due to poor economic conditions.

Financial Worries

The loss of income and the accompanying uncertainty it raises are obvious sources of distress. Some midlife couples have accumulated considerable resources and, due to saving and planning, may weather an extended period of unemployment. However, many others will experience financial distress almost immediately. Clients may experience a variety of challenges, ranging from mild (a long-awaited vacation must be delayed) to serious (falling behind on house payments). Some will express guilt at the failure to meet obligations. Mia and Andy worried about failing to pay the full costs of college tuition, as they had promised their children. Of course, financial stresses are a common contributor to marital discord, but couples need to understand that financial stressors may be fueling their marital strife. You can help clients negotiate their financial priorities during this time of scarcity and make them aware of opportunities to negotiate financial relief (from banks, creditors, or the IRS). See *Appendix A* for specific ideas.

Insecure Attachment

Attachment theory, first developed by Bowlby (1988) to explain children's relationships with caretakers, has proven useful in explaining some kinds of adult behavior, particularly in response to stressful life events. Attachment styles reflect a person's internal working model of self-other relationships. Secure adults report strong emotional bonds with others. They are confident and trusting in their close relationships—neither overly dependent on them, nor excessively self-reliant. Securely attached persons believe that others will be there to help during a crisis, including a job loss (Hobdy et al., 2007). Those with insecure social connections tend be more distressed by job loss and less able to mobilize the kinds of social support that prove useful in such situations. Therapy can be helpful in identifying enduring patterns of attachment and their debilitating or facilitating effects on responses to job loss. Tendencies to be avoidant or excessively self-reliant can be exacerbated by a job loss. These orientations may be underlying sources of marital distress.

Lost Relationships

For many people the workplace is a source of camaraderie, communication, and friendship. A client's most frequent conversational partners may be the coworker in the next cubicle or the customers he or she visits on a regular basis. Job loss can deal a crushing blow to a client's social support network. The regular and sustaining communication shared by even casual workers is disrupted. Maintaining these connections is simply more difficult when coworkers are no longer in close proximity. Of course, many work associations are "blended"—the participants are friends as well as coworkers. In such cases, the loss may be even more profound. In some cases, posttermination relationships are complicated by survivor's guilt or the loss of common work goals. The loss will be most painful for clients who rely heavily on their work for social gratification and for those who leave after many years.

An alternative perspective is worth considering in discussions with clients. Similar to family relationships, workplace relations can be a source of stress, some of which might be alleviated after job loss. Escape from an abusive supervisor or unsupportive coworkers may be the silver lining for a situation that otherwise seems dark.

The Implicit Employment Contract

Work is predicated on a kind of informal psychological contract between employee and employer, although the pact is rapidly fraying in the American economy. In exchange for allegiance and hard work, employees implicitly expect some degree of fairness, loyalty, and security from their employers. Reactions to termination are more extreme when the victim feels the contact was grossly violated. In therapy, clients may need assistance in articulating their violated expectations and describing feelings of bitterness, shock, and betrayal. Their capacity to trust others may be shaken and some will over-generalize this reaction to other relationships. This potential disruption of worldview requires clients to rethink expectations about work and the role it plays in their personal and marital happiness.

Distress Upon Returning to School

Research suggests that returning to school is a source of distress for some middle-aged persons and a source of great satisfaction for others (Quimby & O'Brien, 2006). Of course, many clients will experience both kinds of reactions. The following textbox lists some of the questions and concerns raised by middle-aged persons who are returning to school (see also, Siebert, 2000). In this section, we examine some of their most commonly reported sources of difficulty.

BOX 5.4 WHAT YOU MIGHT HEAR FROM CLIENTS: CONCERNS OF RETURNING STUDENTS

- I haven't written a paper since I was 19! I don't know if I can do it?
- My math skills are out of date. Will that stop me from graduating?
- I feel old! It seems like the other students are looking at me.
- I failed in the past. What if it happens again?
- The kids all know how to use the internet, but I really don't. Help!
- I won't fit in. These students and professors don't live in my world.
- I heard that the professors really don't want older students in class.
- It will take forever to get this degree done. I am not sure I can last!
- I feel guilty for taking time away from my family.
- I should be working instead of spending time and money on school.
- It seems like my husband/wife/relative is threatened by my schooling.

Looking/Feeling Different

Older students often report acute feelings of self-consciousness. They look different than traditional students, have different interests, and may be learning for different reasons. The feeling of "not fitting in" is more acute in settings where other nontraditional students are scarce and academic services are designed for younger students. Mia expressed this concern. In imagining what college might be like, she envisioned classrooms full of young and carefree kids; a dramatic contrast to her own businesslike approach and heavy sense of responsibility.

Interacting With Fellow Students

Another source of anxiety is social. Some nontraditional students find it difficult to interact with fellow students. Outside of school, they may enjoy a position of respect in family or work relationships, particularly in relation to younger or less experienced persons. At school, status differences are erased. Some nontraditional students report having "nothing in common" with younger students. Some are intimidated in their interactions with faculty, whereas others find it difficult to accept the higher status roles accorded to faculty in a college setting.

Self-Pressure and Unrealistic Expectations

Nontraditional students are often hardworking academic achievers (Sander, 2008), but some undermine their own success with high-pressure expectations. For some, receiving any grade less than an "A" is a devastating blow, as it was to Cary, a 46-year-old returning student (see Box 5.5).

BOX 5.5 A CASE STUDY IN INACCURATE EXPECTATIONS

Much to the disappointment of her parents, Cary dropped out of college after a rocky freshman year. In retrospect, she realized that she simply wasn't mature enough at the age of 18. She was distracted by the college social scene, deeply infatuated with her then-boyfriend Bobby (now her husband), and completely unsure of what she wanted for her future. Cary took a variety of office jobs while Bobby completed his degree in hotel management. Soon after, the pair launched what would be a successful marriage. Their son Steven is now a junior in high school, with plans to study business in college. Inspired in part by her son's plans, Cary returned to school 2 years ago, starting at the local community college, where she received "straight As" and considerable encouragement from her professors. This year, Cary transferred to the university, where most of the students are close to her son's age and the academic workload is noticeably more demanding. Cary stays up late many nights, reading the assigned texts very closely and taking extensive notes. But she struggles to write the lengthy term papers; she never really learned to write "academese."

The paper Cary submitted to her history professor was returned with a "B-" grade and numerous suggestions for improvement. She was devastated. A fear of failure—one she hadn't experienced so acutely since her days as a freshman swept over her. Then, Cary felt resentful, sure that the professor must have singled her out for criticism. After all she was "different," noticeably older than her classmates, and more willing to voice her opinions. After working up some courage, Cary visited the professor during office hours, intending to argue for a higher grade. Her professor was both encouraged and surprised at Cary's emotional reaction to the B- grade. "But I am an A student," Cary argued. "I worked really hard on this assignment."

Cary felt pressure to be a role model for her son, and she felt a need to make up for the academic failures of her youth. Her emotional reaction may also reflect limited exposure to negative feedback in the recent past. Many of her community college peers were not university bound, so Cary was perceived as something of an academic star in that environment. The positive recognition was an invaluable form of encouragement, but the different academic expectations left Cary unprepared for some kinds of university-level academic work. For years, Cary had delayed her own career while supporting that of her husband, so her professional identity is very tied up in being a student. For all of these reasons, Cary had difficulty accepting what was a realistic and generally positive assessment of her performance. Fortunately, many traditional students are resilient enough to overcome these temporary disappointments. With the help of her academic counselor, Cary was able to reevaluate her high-pressure expectations, find help with her writing, and regain her confidence.

Lack of System Support

It is a reality that many institutions of higher education lack services adapted for middle-aged students (Philibert, Allen, & Elleven, 2008), although that is much less true at community colleges and for-profit colleges, which cater to the nontraditional market (Andom, 2007). In our own research, returning university students point to the lack of financial aid, support services, and flexible scheduling. Indeed, despite their growing numbers, returning students may simply "fly under the radar" of campus administrators who are often under great pressure to recruit and retain traditional-aged students. Even worse, the motives of older students are sometimes questioned. Natalie applied for medical school at the age of 55. Her application was met with skepticism. Was she merely interested in an academic challenge, or was she seriously seeking a career in medicine? Of course, the lengthening human life span and changing retirement expectations make it likely that a person of Natalie's age could choose to stay in the workforce for decades. Clients should be prepared for the possibility that the expectations of college admissions officers have yet to catch up with these trends.

Shared Sources of Distress

Although job loss and a return to school represent different kinds of midlife change, research indicates that they can be stressful for at least two common reasons.

Low Self-Efficacy

Self-efficacy is confidence in one's ability to complete tasks, generally, or with reference to a specific domain. Low confidence in one's ability to complete job search tasks hampers clients who have experienced a job loss (Malen & Stroh, 1998). The experience of job loss may in itself be a blow to a client's self-efficacy. Counseling may help these clients enhance feelings of self-efficacy and adopt search strategies that are known to increase chances of reemployment.

Returning students may lack confidence in their ability to meet academic performance requirements. Some studies suggest that females report lower levels of self-efficacy than their male counterparts (Quimby & O'Brien, 2006). Interestingly, this same research suggests that efficacy in *domestic* roles is associated with lower levels of distress reported by female students. One implication is that women will benefit when re-sponsibilities at home are made easier by the help of husbands or other family members. As well, the communication of assurance by friends, family, and college teachers increases the confidence of nontraditional students. You can help distressed returning students by (1) developing efficacious strategies for couple renegotiation of roles and role demands, (2) helping to adjust self- and partner expectations to reasonable levels, and (3) offering encouragement and assurance when their confidence falters.

Lack of Social Support

As suggested above, supportive relationships alleviate stress for clients who have lost a job or returned to school. Those with limited or unsup-portive social networks may be disadvantaged. They may place inordi-nate pressure on their spouses to be "all things." In this situation, it is necessary to help clients develop strategies for enlisting the support of family and friends, regulating contacts with unsupportive people, negoti-ating changed relational expectations, and locating new sources of social support.

ANALYTICAL TOOLS

Applying the Dialectical Framework

Centerstage couples express a variety of ambivalent thoughts and feel-ings when one partner is faced with a job loss or the decision to renew their education. Helping clients make sense of these underlying tensions involves the competing pulls of safety and risk.

Safety versus Risk

Faced with a major life change, like a job loss or return to school, the discussions of midlife couples involve the oppositional themes of safety and risk. One or both partners may agree that "sticking with what we know" is the safest course, even as they recognize that changing circum-stances require them to accept the risk that accompanies a change in careers or return to college. Indeed, failing to make changes in the status quo may be a risky move in itself. Some clients will be "frozen" by the

risk associated with a major change of direction. For example, an unemployed spouse may delay retraining indefinitely, preferring instead to
look for a job similar to the one that was lost to a corporate layoff. In in-
dustries that are rapidly changing or shrinking, this persistence could be
futile.

At the same time, partners who find safety in their marriage may
be more successful in managing risky transitions. As we mentioned
above, returning students who enjoy secure attachments are better able
to adjust to the demands of continued education. In particular, nontraditional female students reported lower levels of distress when they
enjoyed relationships that were safe and secure (Quimby & O'Brien,
2006).

BOX 5.6 HOW DO I USE IT? HELPING CLIENTS MANAGE THE SAFETY VERSUS RISK DIALECTIC

In counseling sessions, help clients with these questions.

- Does our marriage provide a sense of safety to each of us?
- Why does it feel safe or unsafe at this point in time?
- What are the risks associated with making this change in our lives?
- What would happen if we chose not to make the change?
- How could we make the change and still feel as safe as possible?

Applying the Resilience Framework

Resilience comes from both internal (psychological) and external resources. You can help clients exploit and develop both kinds.

Internal Resources

Through therapeutic exercises (see *Exercises* below), you can help develop and make use of existing psychological resources, including:

- *Self-efficacy*: The belief that one has the ability to complete a task.
  It can be developed by inventorying previous successes; offering
  encouragement; questioning unnecessary self-limitations; locating encouraging role models; providing opportunities to practice

communication skills, like interviewing for a job or talking with a professor.

- *Secure attachments:* The perception that one's relationships are close, reliable, supportive, and available when needed. Measures of attachment style assess relationships on dimensions of closeness, dependence, and anxiety. During times of stress, insecure attachments are sources of worry and over- or under-dependence. Insecure relationships may undermine clients during times of resilience. You can help clients exploit secure attachments and manage the anxiety and dependence associated with insecure ones.

- *Skills and competencies:* Job seekers and returning students must assess accurately their work and academic competencies, learn to communicate them to others, and update them as needed. You can help by directing them to assessments of aptitude and career interest (typically administered by the student services component of nearly any college or university). Counseling sessions can be important sites for exploring the results. Some clients will be surprised to learn about their untapped potential. You can help clients (1) explore the fit between their interests and various career options, (2) be open minded in considering new possibilities, and (3) analyze the advantages and disadvantages of various careers.

External Resources

Job seekers and returning students find resilience in some of the same places. You can help them identify and mobilize sources of support.

- *Informal sources of support:* After a job loss, job seekers must identify and use their network of social contacts as they seek job leads, connect with new people and organizations, and gather feedback about career options. Returning students often need encouragement and tangible help from a spouse, children, relatives, and friends.

- *Formal sources of support*: Resilient returning students take advantage of the full range of services made available to them, including academic counseling, study skills assessment and assistance, tutoring in math or writing, and campus mentors. Those who experience job loss exploit opportunities for retraining, employment counseling, and skills assessment.

Applying the Roles Framework

The changes discussed in this chapter have obvious role implications, some of which (e.g., identity threat associated with job loss) have already been addressed. Two role related topics deserve further explanation.

The Positive Effects of Multiple Roles

Prevailing wisdom suggests that returning students are burdened by the addition of their student role to extant roles associated with work or family life. Certainly, many students struggle to balance multiple roles. Many others find satisfaction in the performance of multiple roles. For some, additional roles result in an expanded personal identity. For others, adding the role of student provides hope for a different and perhaps improved future. Moreover, the loss of one role is less consequential for those who play multiple roles. Role strain becomes a factor when a new role substantially interferes with the performance of other important roles. A mother who feels confident in her parenting is more likely to feel comfortable in adding the role of student. You can help clients assess their readiness to expand their role repertoire. The spouse's readiness is a significant factor as well. Encourage couples to discuss and plan before a new role is accepted. Help clients identify the resources needed to make the transition positive.

BOX 5.7 SHOULD CLIENTS ACCEPT A NEW STUDENT ROLE? DISCUSSION POINTS FOR COUNSELING SESSIONS

- Will the new role expand the client's identity in a meaningful way?
- Will the new role affect the relationship with the spouse?
- Will the new role make the client more resilient in the face of change?
- Will the new role replace one that has been lost or is diminishing?
- Is the client performing existing roles competently?
- Does the client really want this role, or is he or she simply responding to the expectations of others?
- Will this new role siphon time and energy away from other roles? Will that leave roles unbalanced in the marriage?
- How will this change affect the relational roles played by the client and his or her spouse or other family and friends?

Roles and Changing Power Dynamics

Some roles are imbued with power. When managers lose their jobs they lose the position power granted to them by an organization. The loss of power and the related ability to exert control over people and circumstances can be humbling and discouraging. Job seekers may find it disconcerting or even degrading to be suddenly dependent on others to provide and approve of their qualifications. Some will "do it alone" rather than ask for help. Research suggests that males are more likely to adopt this approach (Malen & Stroh, 1998). Power dynamics affect a marriage when the unemployed spouse becomes uncomfortably dependent on the working spouse or resentful of the spouses' more influential role. You can help clients assess the extent to which power is an important element of their work and marital roles. Some will need help in differentiating their self-worth from the exercise of power. Others must learn about the benefits of substituting persuasion and communication for power tactics, in both domestic and work relationships.

Power also comes in to play when an adult returns to school. Some adult students have difficulty accepting the status differences that define the professional relationships of faculty member, teacher, and student. This sometimes creates communication difficulties. Because of similarities in age, some older students assume it is acceptable to use informal forms of address, calling the professor by his or her first name. Some professors are uncomfortable with this approach because it implies the student enjoys a kind of relational access that is unavailable to other students. Traditional students view it as an effort to curry favor. This "teacher's pet" perception can lead to resentment and avoidance. The opposite extreme is also observed. Some older students are highly attuned to status differences that permeate some work cultures and are unnecessarily intimidated by their professors. These students can be hypersensitive in their communication, afraid of voicing concerns or raising questions for fear that the professor may be offended.

Finally, marital power dynamics are sometimes upset by a spouse's return to school. Spouses may be highly threatened by the partners' educational plans, with their implications for new ideas, outside relationships, and increased autonomy. It is important to help clients recognize and address efforts to reassert power in these settings, which may be manifested in a lack of support from the spouse, inflexibility, guilt-evoking comments, and undue criticism or through the spouse's own attempts to increase his or her power base by a career switch or taking classes. In some cases, transitions of this kind are a stimulus for constructive relational change. In others, counselors can help the spouse prioritize relational and career goals.

WORKING WITH CLIENTS

Throughout this chapter we have suggested practices that are often useful in working with clients who are negotiating new career directions. We now propose a series of action steps for your work with clients.

Helping Clients Respond to Job Loss

The loss of a job can be a high stress event with effects similar to those experienced after divorce, a death in the family, or a serious illness. Job loss is associated with anxiety, depression, and disruption of family functioning. Obviously, the full range of therapeutic options and service-provider partnerships must be considered when working with highly distressed clients. The steps, outlined hereafter, represent a practical process for helping centerstage couples respond specifically to a job loss.

Step 1. Identify, Evaluate, and Discuss Coping Strategies

A first task is to help clients identify and evaluate the coping strategies they are currently using as they respond to job loss or a return to college. Next, it is important to help clients become more intentional in their use of effective current strategies and, then, appropriate new strategies can be suggested. A general assessment of coping behavior can help focus the discussion. One example is the *Ways of Coping Questionnaire* (Folkman, Lazarus, Dunkel-Schetter, DeLongis, & Gruen, 1986). A measure more focused on job loss is the *Job Loss Coping Behavior* questionnaire (Leana & Feldman, 1992). Table 5.1 describes eight ways of coping. Measures of this type distinguish between problem-focused behaviors (efforts to find employment) and symptom reducing behaviors (efforts to alleviate stress and other adverse responses). Clients will benefit from both kinds of coping, but may find themselves less adept in one or more areas.

Table 5.1

DIMENSIONS OF THE *WAYS OF COPING* QUESTIONNAIRE

1 **Accepting Responsibility**: acknowledges one's own role in the problem with a concomitant theme of trying to put things right.
2 **Confrontive Coping**: describes aggressive efforts to alter the situation and suggests some degree of hostility and risk taking.
3 **Distancing**: describes cognitive efforts to detach oneself and to minimize the significance of the situation.
4 **Escape-Avoidance**: describes wishful thinking and behavioral efforts to escape or avoid the problem. Items on this scale contrast with those on the Distancing scale, which suggest detachment.
5 **Planful Problem Solving**: describes deliberate problem-focused efforts to alter the situation, coupled with an analytic approach to solving the problem.
6 **Positive Reappraisal**: describes efforts to create positive meaning by focusing on personal growth. It also has a religious dimension.
7 **Seeking Social Support:** describes efforts to seek informational support, tangible support, and emotional support.
8 **Self-Controlling**: describes efforts to regulate one's feelings and actions.

Note: For related information, see Folkman et al. (1986). The *Ways of Coping Questionnaire* is available at: http://www.mindgarden.com/products/wayss.htm.

BOX 5.8 PROBLEM-FOCUSED COPING BY CLIENTS: CONSIDER AGE AND GENDER DIFFERENCES

Job seekers who pursue problem-focused coping behavior with higher levels of intensity, may be more successful. In a study of 131 unemployed female and male managers, Malen and Stroh (1998) found that older job seekers and men were more likely than younger job seekers and women to use problem-focused coping. In this particular sample, differences in work experience appeared to be the underlying explanation for age and gender differences. The authors suggest that job seekers who believe they have more career options tend to use a more problem-focused approach. The results suggest that counselors should help clients think more broadly about career options. Depending on their work experience, younger clients and women may need additional assistance in developing problem-focused coping strategies, some of which are listed below.

- Participating in on-line and face-to-face networking
- Seeking and reviewing employment advertisements
- Exploring possibilities for relocation
- Preparing and updating resume and related materials
- Engaging the services of a search firm or employment agency
- Scheduling "informational" interviews to increase job knowledge
- Seeking retraining or education

Step 2. Negotiate Marital Impacts

Job loss can have striking and negative effects on a marriage. At the same time, the support of the spouse will be an important contributor to the job seeker's sense of efficacy. Although centerstage couples are often advantaged by years of experience and commitment, professional assistance is often beneficial for the following tasks:

- Maintaining marital solidarity in the face of difficult financial pressures
- Identifying spousal communication that is *unhelpful* during a job search (e.g., complaining, directing, comparing, criticizing)
- Emphasizing spousal communication that is *helpful* during a job search (e.g., encouraging, assuring, listening, offering help)
- Defining job search tasks that can be shared and those which should not be shared
- Finding sources of shared pleasure to counter feelings of negativity
- Renegotiating domestic roles and routines in response to changing roles
- Finding ways to conserve financial resources
- Explaining changes in work status to family and friends
- Talking through feelings of loss, frustration, resentment, and futility
- Exploring creative responses to job loss, including retraining or recareering
- Finding hope in successful responses to previous challenges

Step 3. Mobilize Social Support

As has been discussed, the couple will need to mobilize the support of adult children, relatives, friends, and advisors. You can help reluctant clients understand the importance of social support in buffering the emotional and physical impact of job loss and increasing chances of success.

Step 4. Use Job Search Tools and Resources

Clients who have been employed for many years may find that their job search skills are rusty. Job search tools and resources have changed dramatically in recent years. Although this realization can be deflating, you can help clients increase their sense of efficacy by steering them toward the appropriate resources, some of which are listed at the end of this chapter. Depending on their circumstances, clients will need to:

- Update their resume to meet contemporary expectations
- Submit materials electronically
- Search for jobs using on-line databases and search engines
- Build and maintain a personal web page
- Participate in on-line communities and networks
- Articulate their qualifications in brief statements and interviews

Step 5. Plan and Persist

The experience of job seeking can be overwhelming and discouraging. You can help clients develop a job search plan with clearly stated tasks, schedules, and goals. Finding a job is much like having a job, in the sense that the qualities of organization, persistence, and time-management are crucial to success. Successful job seekers typically designate a certain number of hours per day to their quest. Use periodic counseling sessions as opportunities for clients to report on their activities, evaluate results, and make adjustments in strategy.

Helping Returning Students

When contemplating and executing a return to school, midlife clients will need help with self-assessment, preparation, and relationship negotiation, among other things. You can help them complete the following tasks.

Imagine the Future

Hope for the future sustains motivation. It is a crucial determinant of student persistence. Help clients imagine a new future, with questions like this: What would it be like to have completed your degree? Would it change the way you feel about yourself? Would you feel more confident in your work? Would it help you achieve your career aspirations? How would it affect your relationships with others?

Identify the Barriers

What is stopping your client from returning to (or persisting in) college? Anticipate these kinds of concerns: (1) financing the costs, (2) fear of failure, (3) lack of support from spouse or family, (4) guilt (about working less or taking time from other obligations), and (5) interference with work. Help clients generate ideas for lowering or working around these barriers. For example, the financial aid office at the local community college can help your client develop a reasonable cost estimate and connect them to sources of scholarships, loans, and on-campus employment opportunities. Some of these are targeted to older learners, students who are mothers, or those seeking midlife career changes. In another example, feelings of guilt are often ameliorated when clients weigh the long-term financial and psychological benefits associated with degree completion, for themselves and for their families.

Clients may need encouragement. See *Appendix A* for success stories told by midlife students who overcame barriers and successfully completed their education. Support groups are an important resource for students who lack confidence. Most colleges have one for older students.

Explore Myths and Realities

Here are three of the more common myths and realities:

Myth: I don't have the skills to succeed in college.

Reality: Returning students often underestimate their ability to perform in the college classroom. In fact, older students are often more hardworking, persistent, and organized than their younger counterparts. Some need to take refresher courses or seek tutoring in such subjects as math, computer skills, or composition but many outperform traditional students.

Myth: The younger students won't like me.

Reality: In general, younger students respond positively to returning students, particularly those who show an interest in, and respect for, their younger peers. Of course, many younger students are struggling with their own college insecurities and adjustments. Most are just not paying that much attention to the older student sitting next to them in class.

Returning students tend to ask more questions in class and, due to their more extensive experience, they often share more information when instructors invite participation. On occasion, younger students resent this behavior because it seems like an effort to curry favor with the professor. To avoid dominating classroom discussion, a relative few returning students benefit from increased self-monitoring and self-regulation.

Myth: The professors don't like older students.

Reality: Wrong. Almost all professors enjoy older students because of their serious approach to education, their willingness to ask questions, and the real-life experience they bring to classroom discussions. In rare cases, a younger professor will complain that an older student treats them with disrespect, apparently in the belief that "real world" experience is more important than the instructor's academic credentials. This is not a winning strategy.

Cultivate Supporters and Mentors

Returning students need relationships that support their sense of efficacy. These can involve friends, family, counselors, and teachers. Encourage your clients to participate in the formal mentoring program (offered on most campuses) or to seek an informal mentor among the faculty. Clients who lack support from their spouses will need special assistance. In counseling, he or she can develop persuasive arguments to help the spouse understand why a return to school is important for the client and the marriage. Increased income, role modeling for children or grandchildren, and the desire to be a more interesting and well-rounded person are three persuasive rationales for returning to college later in life (also see Scala, 1996). Reluctant partners can often see that these benefits outweigh short-term inconveniences. However, spouses who feel threatened may need reassurance. They may respond well to being involved in planning the new educational effort. Some will find it assuring to attend school events or meet new school friends.

Manage the Impact: Renegotiate Routines and Roles

Some clients will try to limit the impact of their schooling on the marriage by adding new responsibilities to existing ones. They will simply force more tasks into less time, reduce their sleep, and hide feelings of fatigue and stress. Although increases in efficiency may be possible, this approach can result in stress, resentment, and, ultimately, failure. You can help by recognizing the symptoms of overwork and encouraging the client to explore other approaches—such as renegotiating work loads with the spouse. As suggested in chapter 4, changes in familiar domestic routines may be inevitable when partners commit to new activities. The pair may need to renegotiate housecleaning, meal preparation, social schedules, transportation, income production, and other aspects of married life. Flexibility in the marriage is a key to student success.

Take Advantage of Resources

Some midlife students are reluctant to use student support services. They sometimes assume that services were intended for younger students or feel that older students should be able to "do it alone." One of the authors directs a scholarship program targeted to "reentry students" (ages 25 to 50 years), who intend to return to the workforce after completing their degree. His largest challenge is convincing eligible students to apply. Many assume incorrectly that they do not "deserve" the scholarship or that the money will be awarded to younger students. Encourage clients to take full advantage of the advising, counseling, tutoring, and personal enrichment opportunities offered at their educational institution. These services enhance the success of all students, including middle-aged ones, and make for a richer educational experience.

CONCLUDING THOUGHTS

Losing a job and returning to school are quite different experiences. But as we have seen, clients in the midst of these transitions have some stressors in common. They have common needs as well, including enhanced self-efficacy, support of the spouse, and connecting with services and resources. In particular, spouses may underestimate the impact of job loss and retooling on their marriage relationship. Helping partners learn to help one another can turn marital stress into marital strength. We have included some exercises that should prove useful. In addition, you can steer clients to the resources provided in *Appendix A*. For example, their resolve may be bolstered when they see how income increases with college education or by reading the stories of successful returning students. Persistence is important when seeking a job or completing an education. Both processes can be lengthy and, at times, discouraging. Regular counseling sessions will help clients negotiate the personal and relational barriers that undermine success. Due to changing circumstances or personal choice, your clients have steered their lives in new directions. You can help keep them on track.

QUESTIONS FOR CLIENTS

1 How has the loss of your job affected your identity? How has your job loss affected your relationship with your partner?
2 Consider the eight ways of coping presented in Table 5.1. Which are you using? Which would you like to develop?
3 What is most stressful about your job loss? About looking for a new job/career? About returning to school? Have you discussed these feelings with your partner?
4 What types of support do you need from your spouse? What support does your spouse need from you? Describe concrete behaviors such as resume writing, helping with household chores, listening to ideas, discussing plans for the future.
5 How will your plans need to change in response to your new circumstances? Will roles need to be assessed and adjusted? Which roles need updating?
6 Reflect on previous transitions in your relationship. What did you learn that would be useful now?
7 What sources of expertise and assistance would help you secure employment or return to school? Consider your social and professional networks, online resources, career counselors, financial aid specialists, and university advisors.
8 What knowledge or skills do you think you need to complete this transition smoothly? How could you acquire them?
9 List the most positive outcomes you can imagine. Discuss these with your spouse and devise a plan.

EXERCISES

Exercise 5.1 Identifying Job Loss Distress

The goal of this exercise is to help you identify how job loss is causing distress for you and your marriage.

As a couple, discuss the following questions:

1   What percentage of your "self" was wrapped up in the job you just lost?

    0%————25%————50%————75%————100%

2   Has the job loss affected how you feel about yourself? If so, how?

3   How do you feel about your ability to get a new, meaningful job? (Circle all that apply.)

    Excited, worried, frustrated, motivated, bitter, expectant, overwhelmed, lost, active

4   Regarding the job loss, to what extent do you feel worried about finances?

    Very little worry (I seldom think about it.)

    Concerned (I've worked through our budget and watch it closely.)

    Very worried (I can't get it off of my mind. I'm not sleeping well.)

5   In what ways will the job loss affect you and your family financially?

    Major bills (e.g., mortgage, car payments)
       Short term:
       Long term:

    Lifestyle issues (e.g., going out to eat, playing golf, traveling)
       Short term:
       Long term:

    Providing for family members (e.g., family vacations, financial help)
       Short term:
       Long term:

6   Are there important relationships at work that you will miss? Below, list the names of people you will miss, whether you'd like to stay in contact with them, and ways you can stay in contact with them.

    Who will be missed?

    Want to stay in contact with:

    Ways to stay in contact.

Exercise 5.2 Identifying Returning to School Distress

The goal of this exercise is to help you identify how returning to school is causing distress for you and your marriage.

1   To what extent do you feel "competent" in your academic abilities?

not very competent————————————very competent

■ What steps can you take to develop your academic skills?

2   To what extent are you anxious about "fitting in?"

not anxious————————————————-very anxious

■ What student services resources, clubs, and activities does your campus have for returning students?

3   What are your academic and social expectations for your first semester?

Academic:

Social:

■ Talk with your spouse, a friend, or admissions counselor as to whether these expectations are realistic.

Exercise 5.3 Anatomy of Risk Taking

The goal of this exercise is to determine how you and your spouse handle risk.

On a scale of 1 (low) to 10 (high), rate your comfort with risk taking.

Husband:

Wife:

Now, take time to do an assessment on how you handle risk.

1   Describe a time in the past where you had to take a risk as a couple.

2   What type of risk was involved (e.g., financial risk, moving, high uncertainty...)?

3   List the approach or approaches that kept the risk manageable (this doesn't necessarily mean everything went just they way you wanted it to, but how you kept it from becoming overwhelming).

4   From the list generated at *Step 3*, identify the approaches that "work" for you and that you'd like to keep using. Next, identify

what didn't work and why. Are there news ways of handling what didn't work last time?

- Worked for us, or one of us:
- Didn't work and why:
- New strategies:

5   Finally, describe how you are going to apply your list of "worked" and "new" strategies to your current situation.

Exercise 5.4 Using Your Internal Resources

The goal of this exercise is to identify each person's internal resources and use each other's strengths.

As individuals, rate each of the following on a scale of 1 (strongly disagree) to 10 (strongly agree).

1   *Self-efficacy*—I believe I can complete what I start.
     Husband:
     Wife:
2   *Secure attachments*—I believe my spouse will do whatever he or she can to support me.
     Husband:
     Wife:
3   *Skills and competencies*—I believe I have the skills to be suc-cessful at school or do well at a new job.
     Husband:
     Wife:
4   Now that you've rated each category, discuss your internal strengths as a couple. How can you work together to achieve each individual's goals during this time?

Exercise 5.5 Negotiating Changing Roles

The goal of this exercise is to help you identify how your roles may be affected by a change of career or return to school.

1   Make a list of the various ways that beginning a new career or returning to school might change the roles that each spouse plays at home. For example, it might change one spouse's ability to stop at the store, do laundry, manage the cars or mow the lawn.
2   Next, discuss each of these changes and how acceptable they are to each of you. (Note: this is not a time for blame, accusations or

defensiveness. The goal is simply to identify tasks that need to be negotiated.)
3   Finally, work it out.
    a   First, talk about each issue that you've identified in the previous step.
    b   Second, create a short-term plan of how each of you can collaborate and compromise to adapt to this lifestyle shift.
    c   Third, plan a follow-up meeting to discuss whether each partner is satisfied with his or her new or adapted roles. (The follow-up meeting should be no later than 2 weeks after the initial decision has been made.)
    d   Fourth, discuss what you've learned by shifting roles.

Exercise 5.6 Learning to be Supportive During Career Change

The goal of this exercise is to identify how to be supportive of your partner during career change.

1   Privately write down how you would best like to be supported during this time of change. (Both partners should do this. While the individual who lost his or her job or is returning to school may have the most obvious need for support, his or her spouse may actually need help as well.)
2   Next, privately, write down how you think your spouse would best like to be supported.
3   Now, share your lists. Identify points of understanding and areas of misperception.
4   Finally, get *behaviorally specific*. In other words, if your spouse lists "show appreciation" as a way to support him or her, ask how she or he best likes to be appreciated—flowers, a note in the lunch bag, a clean kitchen? (A final note here: Don't assume old expectations still apply. Flowers might have been great at one point; a clean kitchen might be much more meaningful now.)

REFERENCES

American Council on Education. (2007). *Framing new terrain: Older adults and higher education.* Retrieved November 6, 2008, from http://www.acenet.edu/Content/NavigationMenu/ProgramsServices/CLLL/Reinvesting/Reinvestingfinal.pdf
Andom, M. (2007, October 26). Older students' struggles. *Chronicle of Higher Education,* 39–39.

Bowlby, J. (1988). *A secure base: Parent-child attachment and healthy human development.* New York: Basic Books.

Clinton, H. (2008). *Clinton, Graham to Back Bill to Aid "Non-Traditional" Students.* Retrieved November 14 2008, from http://clinton.senate.gov/~clinton/news/2004/2004211531.html

Cummings, J. (2007, January 21). Laid-off middle-aged workers face job-finding ordeal. *Dayton Daily News,* p. A12.

Folkman, S., Lazarus, R. S., Dunkel-Schetter, C., DeLongis, A., & Gruen, R. (1986). The dynamics of a stressful encounter: Cognitive appraisal, coping, and encounter outcomes. *Journal of Personality and Social Psychology, 50,* 992–1003.

Gearon, C. L. (2008). Back-to-school days for adults. *U.S. News and World Reports, 144,* 46–48.

Hobdy, J., Hayslip, B., Kaminski, P., Crowley, B., Riggs, S., & York, C. (2007). The role of attachment style in coping with job loss and the empty nest in adulthood. *International Journal of Aging and Human Development, 65,* 335–371.

Leana, C. R., & Feldman, D. C. (1992). *Coping with job loss. How individuals, organizations, and communities respond to layoffs.* Boston: Lexington Books.

Malen, E. A., & Stroh, L. K. (1998). The influence of gender on job loss coping behavior among unemployed managers. *Journal of Employment Counseling, 35,* 26–39.

Philibert, N., Allen, J., & Elleven, R. (2008). Nontraditional students in community colleges and the model of college outcomes for adults. *Community College Journal of Research and Practice, 32,* 582–586.

Quimby, J., & O'Brien, K. (2006). Predictors of well-being among nontraditional female students with children. *Journal of Counseling and Development, 84,* 451–460.

Sander, L. (2008, January 18). Blue collar workers take work ethic to college. *The Chronicle of Higher Education,* 1A, 22A.

Scala, M. A. (1996). Going back to school: Participation motives and experiences of older adults in an undergraduate classroom. *Educational Gerontology, 22,* 247– 274.

Schlisserman, C. (2008). *U.S. initial jobless claims fell to 357,000 last week.* Retrieved November 6, 2008, from http://www.bloomberg.com/apps/news?pid=20601087&sid=aS2qus.tsaq0&refer= home

Siebert, A. (2000). *Proceedings of NCAL '00: Teaching adult students the way they learn: The instructor's role in retaining adult learners and increasing their chances of success in college.* Retrieved November 6, 2008, from http://www.adultstudent.com/

Taniguchi, H., & Kaufman, G. (2007). Belated entry: Gender differences and similarities in the pattern of nontraditional and traditional college enrollment. *Social Science Research, 36*(2), 550–568.

Third Age News Service. (2008). Laid-off middle-aged workers face job-finding ordeal. Retrieved November 14, 2008, from http://www.thirdage.com/age-discrimination/laid-off-middle-aged-workers-face-job-finding-ordeal

United States Department of Labor, Bureau of Labor Statistics (2008). *Employment situation.* Retrieved November 21, 2008, from http://www.bls.gov/news.release/empsit.toc.htm

United States Department of State. *Nontraditional Students Enrich U.S. College Campuses* [data file]. Retrieved November 21, 2008, from http://www.america.gov/st/educ-english/2008/April/200804281212291CJsamohT0.3335382.html

Managing Boundaries: Boomerang Kids, Adult Children, and Grandparenting

6

KATHLEEN M. WALDRON AND VINCENT R. WALDRON

Rob and Betsy: The Boomerang Kid

Rob and Betsy envisioned their post-childrearing years as a time to enrich their marriage through candlelight dinners, slow dancing in their living room, and spontaneous romantic moments anywhere in their house. They hadn't counted on their younger son moving back home after graduating from college . . . and showing no signs of moving out two years later. They are unsure what to do to hasten his "exit process" and argue—mainly with each other—over how supportive, patient, and understanding they should be.

Pete and Jean: The Overtaxed Parents

Pete and Jean, who run their own real estate brokerage, had the same visions as Rob and Betsy, but have found they spend more time and energy on their adult children than they ever imagined. Their oldest son's wife was in a car accident 2 years ago and has had ongoing health problems. To help out, Pete and Jean babysit for their 3-year-old twin granddaughters 1 or 2 days a week. Their second child, a daughter, runs her own business, and they help her one day a week, as well. Finally, their younger son has recently gone through an emotionally devastating relationship break-up as well as the loss of his job to outsourcing. They are trying to "be there" emotionally for him, as well as aid him financially. Mostly they find they are exhausted and frequently resentful of these unanticipated demands.

Gail and Dan: The Exploited Grandparents

Gail, age 52, has gone back to college. She is excited to focus on her dreams and goals after raising three children. Unfortunately, Gail's oldest daughter Kim has had problems with drugs and is an ineffective single parent to children ages 9 and 7. Gail has taken on the responsibilities of calling the children every morning to waken them for school, driving 20 minutes to their house to make them breakfast, and picking them up from after-school care to make sure they have their homework done before returning them to their mother around 6:30. Most weekends the children are with Gail and her husband Dan. Gail and Dan frequently argue over how much help they should provide their daughter and whether taking the children on the weekends simply results in less responsible behavior on Kim's part.

The challenges faced by these three couples are commonly encountered at midlife, but nearly always unanticipated. Each of the three situations addressed in this chapter involves the management of family boundaries. Most couples want their "boomerang" children to achieve independence as soon as possible. But where is the boundary between temporary assistance and long-term dependence? As Rod and Betsy found, a boomerang kid can alter a couple's long-held midlife plans and stretch the boundaries of privacy. Even children who live away from home need considerable assistance at times. But centerstage couples like Pete and Jean walk an emotional tightrope. When does helping become enabling or meddling? For this couple, the commitments to helping the kids were undermining commitments to their own marriage. Finally, the once bright line between parenting and grandparenting is dimming. At a time when lower- and middle-class parents are struggling to keep their heads above water in a turbulent economy, more centerstage couples are asked to provide hands-on help with grandchildren. As a result, Gail and Dan felt almost under siege as grandparenting responsibilities crept into every corner of their lives.

Negotiating relational boundaries can be a perplexing task for even the most well-adjusted centerstage couple. The consequences of their decisions will have long-term impact on their own relationship and those they share with other family members (Greenfield & Marks, 2007). Some will find themselves to be stressed, angry, emotionally distant, resentful, frustrated, and in need of counseling assistance to get their lives back on track.

BOOMERANG KIDS

Boomerang kids are adult children who have moved out of their parents' house—usually for college, marriage, or employment—and then, some time later and usually unexpectedly, move back home. The primary reason kids "boomerang" is financial—they have not located a job after college, they lost a job, or they have recently divorced and cannot afford to pay their mortgage or rent. They may be trying to save money for a down payment on a house or condominium; living with their parents for 6 months or a year, with reduced living expenses, allows them to do that. Adult children may also return for other reasons. Some need help with childcare due to a divorce or unexpected pregnancy. Others seek psychological support during a time of emotional turmoil (also common after a divorce), or physical assistance due to a serious health issue.

BOX 6.1 WHY KIDS BOOMERANG

- Job and income losses
- Recovery from divorce
- Help with childcare or pregnancy
- Saving money for college or to purchase a house
- Recovery from illness
- Emotional support
- Physical assistance

In the 1950s through 1970s, it was typical for children to move out of their parents' home between the ages of 18 and 22 years, either to go to college and then directly into the workforce, or to marry, or to join the military. The median age of marriage was much younger then (20 to 21 years for women and a year or two older for men, versus around 25 and 27 today) (US Census, 2004), and well-paying jobs were plentiful for those with a high school education. Adult children were expected to be independent of their parents by their early 20s.

Since the 1980s, however, it has become more common for adult children in North America to live at home, for a variety of reasons. In 2001, 41.1% of persons aged 20 to 29 were living with their parents, compared to 27.5% in 1981 (Beaujot, 2004.) As we mentioned above, some of the reasons are economic, as adult children cannot find jobs or are laid off from their jobs. The tendency to marry later in life is another contributing factor, as marriage typically increases resources available for rent or mortgage payments. Recent generations of midlife couples have chosen smaller families and enjoyed a higher standard of living and these trends feed the surge of boomerang children. With only two children in a family, it is easier for one, or both, to return home, than if there are five or six (younger) children still living at home. In the United States, many young adults are now accustomed to a comfortable lifestyle that is unsustainable when living on their own. For all of these reasons, returning home can be an attractive option, especially if mom or dad is preparing dinner and washing the dishes. Many times, the boomerang experience works out just fine, but in other cases, there are problems, sometimes serious ones, that require professional counseling.

HELPING ADULT CHILDREN

For generations, parents in the United States have helped adult children get started in their careers and launch their households, as well as assisted in times of crisis. These tendencies continue today, but with some twists. Societal trends (see Box 6.2) are changing the family, and some of the differences result in a need for more parental assistance over a longer period of time. Consider divorce and unwed parenthood—far more children today are raised by never-married single parents than was true 30 or 50 years ago. Due to higher divorce rates, compared with the 1960s and earlier, many single parents require financial and childcare assistance from their own parents.

The economy also affects the need for assistance. Housing prices climbed steeply for several decades, and most young adults could not

---

BOX 6.2 SOCIETAL TRENDS BEHIND THE INCREASE IN BOOMERANG CHILDREN

- Higher divorce rate
- More single parents
- Increased housing and college costs
- Economic downturns

---

afford to buy a house or condominium without at least some help from their parents. More recently, the inability to obtain credit may prevent young adults from purchasing a home. The same is true of college tuition; it is increasingly common for college graduates to be heavily in debt for student loans. The economic downturns in 2001 and 2007 have also meant many young adults have had trouble finding, or holding on to, adequate employment (New York Life, 2008). Parents may find they are helping their late-20-somethings with car payments, utility bills, and other monthly obligations.

Parents help adult children in other ways. They offer advice on a myriad of matters ranging from which brand of washing machine to buy, to how long to let a baby cry, to whether it's better to fix the transmission or buy a new car. They have decades of experience in home ownership, home maintenance, car ownership and maintenance, child-rearing, career decisions, relationship dynamics, financial management, and many other areas. Teenage children often dismiss their parents as out of touch, but most realize by their early 20s that mom and dad really do know "a lot about a lot" and turn to them for advice.

Although it is normal for parents to act as helpers, mentors, and cheerleaders for their adult children, sometimes the needs of the adult child can exceed what the parents are capable of providing. Some parents find that they are tapping out their own savings. Some come to counseling offices because they are emotionally exhausted; physically depleted; or feeling frustrated, resentful, or guilty. In these cases, midlife parents often find themselves enabling an adult child to be overly dependent or find they have helped create a codependent relationship. Many are looking for ways to simultaneously withdraw assistance and preserve healthy relationships with their adult offspring.

GRANDPARENTING

Although many couples view the prospect of becoming a grandparent with pleasure, none get to choose when they will assume the role. For some midlife couples, it is far too soon—sometimes a decade earlier than anticipated. For the most part, middle and upper-middle class parents become grandparents later in life than lower-income parents. The adult children of higher-income, better-educated parents tend to postpone childbearing until they have completed their education and become established in a career. Members of this group are often well into their

30s (with parents in their late 50s and 60s) before they have children. In contrast, adult children of lower-income, less-educated parents tend to have children in their early- to mid-20s, when their parents are typically in their 40s.

Whether they perceive the arrival of grandparenting to be "on-time" or "off-time" is an issue that affects a couple's response to the role. Joel and Sharon illustrated that point for us. They are members of the Church of Latter-Day Saints, who tend to marry and start their families at a relatively young age. Joel and Sharon both completed college and they enjoy an upper-middle class income. They became grandparents when they were 44 and 46 years old—exactly when they expected to, and right in sync with most of their church peers. They were "on-time" with their grandparenting role. In contrast, Erica and Alan are Ivy League graduates, who married immediately after college and had their first child a year later. Not one of their college friends married before the age of 28. Most were older than 30 and delayed having children for several years after that. Erica and Alan became grandparents at age 47, when their daughter was 24, and their college friends were still raising young teenagers. Erica and Alan feel "off-time" compared with their college friends.

Varieties in Grandparenting Experience

The experience of grandparenting is anything but uniform. Some couples enjoy the "traditional" grandparenting experience, with reasonably stable adult children who live fairly close by, but remain relatively independent. Traditional grandparents see their grandchildren regularly, provide some baby-sitting help, and experience their family relationships as generally positive, rewarding, and undemanding.

BOX 6.3 TYPES OF GRANDPARENT EXPERIENCES

- Traditional: Occasional visits and moderate involvement
- Caregiving: Increased responsibility for childcare
- Long-Distance: Limited contact with grandchildren
- Stressful: Unpredictable involvement due to unstable parents
- Custodial: Full responsibility for grandchildren

Caregiving grandparents provide regular, ongoing care to the grand-children, usually to help the parents avoid the expense of daycare or out of fear of having strangers care for the children. They are a great help to young families, but caregiving grandparents may find themselves at the center of confusing and stressful family dynamics. Two fairly common examples are: (1) When the grandparents are babysitting, they are expected to be "in charge"—but their rules and habits may conflict with those of Mom and Dad. Children may be confused, not knowing whom to turn to for permission or which rules to follow. (2) Parents are sometimes distressed to learn that a child prefers the comfort provided by a care-giving grandparent to their own parent. In most cases, these issues are fairly easily resolved, but some families benefit from the insight of a coun-seling professional. In some cases, it becomes obvious that professional childcare is a better option.

Long-distance grandparents are those who live far from their grand-children and see them only once or twice a year, or even less. Economic and demographic trends have made this a common mode of grandpar-enting. In the past, it was much more common for extended family members—grandparents, aunts, uncles, and cousins—to live within the same county, the same town, or even the same city block. Now, families are more likely to be spread among four or five noncontiguous states, or even different countries. It can be hard to maintain close relationships with grandchildren in one distant location, and it is truly challenging when multiple grandchildren live in different far-away places. Some midlife couples will be depressed or frustrated by the long distance role, others simply accept it or even prefer it.

Although most traditional and long-distance grandparenting relation-ships are positive or at least neutral, other grandparenting relationships are *stressful*. Stressful grandparenting means the grandparents are wor-ried that their grandchildren's basic needs are not being met or that there are serious strains in the relationship between the grandparents and the grandchildren's parent(s). Whether by choice or circumstance, some midlife couples take on many of the parenting roles, involving them-selves deeply in the lives of grandchildren whose parents are unstable. Gail and Dan, introduced in an opening vignette, illustrate some of the stresses these grandparents may face.

In severe cases, a crisis makes it necessary for the grandparents to take custody of their grandchildren. *Legal custody* involves going to court and drawing up papers that legalize the new relationship status. More com-mon is *physical custody*, where the grandchildren live predominantly with the couple, but the grandparents have no legal rights or responsibilities (Grandparents with legal custody typically also have physical custody). Legal custody is "cleaner" in the sense that grandparents can authorize medical treatment, sign field trip permission forms, enroll the grandchildren in school, and so forth. Unfortunately, if the parents temporarily abandon their children or refuse to sign over legal custody, the grandparents are often caught in a legal limbo—they have the children, but they cannot legally act on their behalf. Clients caught in these situations often need counseling, community support, and professional advice.

BOX 6.4 PHYSICAL VERSUS LEGAL CUSTODY

- Grandparents with *physical* custody have the grandchild living in their home and act as parents would. They have no legal authority over the grandchild and cannot sign legal papers on behalf of the child. The grandchild can be removed from their home by the parent at any time.
- Grandparents with *legal* custody have the grandchild living in their home, but they also have legal authority over the child. A court must grant legal custody. Parents cannot remove the child from the grandparents' home. However, a court could decide that grandparents are providing an inadequate home environment and remove the grandchild to the foster care system. For this reason, some grandparents, especially those with health problems, do not want legal custody of their grandchild, for fear he or she could be legally removed from their care.

If grandparents do have custody—whether legal or physical—they typically perform the full range of parenting duties. They feed, clothe, and shelter the children; get them to school; help with homework; sign them up for sports teams and music lessons; drive to dentist appointments and karate class; enforce discipline; plan birthday parties; and tuck them into bed at night. There are literally raising their grandchildren—which can be exhausting.

Custodial grandparents face a particularly difficult task. In nearly all cases, they are simultaneously stressed by serious and ongoing problems in their adult child's life. The most common circumstances under which grandparents take custody of their grandchildren are drug abuse by the parent(s), imprisonment of the parent(s), and abuse by the parent(s) of the grandchild(ren).

Custodial grandparents face numerous issues that are beyond the scope of this book. They typically include:

- Emotional problems of the grandchildren (for example, abandonment issues, nightmares, aggressive behavior, and depression)
- Financial issues (grandparents often quit or cut back on work to care for the grandchildren; they may not have health insurance or government assistance to help cover the increased financial obligations)
- Conflicts with their own adult child (the adult child may be angry at the grandparents' "interference," or the grandparents may be angry at the adult child for their irresponsible behavior).
- Physical and emotional exhaustion from dealing with these issues, as well as raising young children at an age when a midlife couple may find that their parenting stamina has diminished.

SOURCES OF DISTRESS

In this section, we identify the specific problems your midlife clients may bring to therapy to manage their relationships with adult children and grandchildren.

Problems with Boomerang Kids

Many parents and children manage the boomerang period without assistance. Others are perplexed, not sure what to expect of this new relationship. Will the boomerang kid be treated as a tenant, with the parents playing the role of disinterested landlords? Or, will this young adult resume the lifestyle he or she enjoyed as a teenager, with doting parents providing active support and oversight? It is when differences in these expectations emerge—whether between the returning child and parents, or between the parents themselves—that problems arise.

Some common areas for disagreement include:

- length of stay
- financial contributions by the *boomerang kid*
- household chores
- privacy expectations
- household "rules"

Length of Stay

The boomerang kid may move back in "temporarily" after graduating from college (as Rob and Betsy's son did), intending to stay only until he or she finds a job and saves a little money. But, the job search may drag out. Perhaps jobs are scarce at the moment. Maybe the child is a little too picky. For whatever reason, what the parents had typically envisioned as a 3- or perhaps 6-month assistance period has turned into a year, 2 years, or 5 years. They wonder if their son or daughter will *ever* leave.

In some cases, though, one parent is perfectly happy having the boomerang kid living at home. That parent may enjoy the companionship, or the continuation of the active parenting role, or the opportunity to make up for time "lost" when the child was younger. (Men are more likely to fall into the last category.) Then, there may be arguments and resentment between the parents, as one strives to maintain the status quo and the other is itching to move on to the true "empty nest" stage of life.

Financial Contributions

Because most boomerang kids are struggling financially, parents feel that providing free room and board is the least they can do to help their adult child get on his or her feet. But, when they see their child spending money on ski trips, enhanced car stereo systems, or $80 shoes, they begin to question the wisdom of this "assistance." In some cases, one parent may see the child's expenses as justified or "deserving," and the other feels their son or daughter is being irresponsible (a prime source of potential argument and resentment between the parents). The parties may have conflicting expectations about financial contributions the child will make to support household operations and the extent to which he or she should expect to use the parents' property (such as a car or computer).

Household Chores

Household chores can be a source of conflict. The boomerang kid may assume the parents will continue to do his or her laundry, make dinner, and generally treat him or her as a dependent. The parents feel otherwise. Or, they may enjoy feeling "needed" again and implicitly encourage the kid's dependence. Some children resent overly involved parents who act as if they don't think he or she is "capable" of maintaining a car, paying bills, or managing meals. Either way, resentment and arguments can ensue.

Privacy Violations

Both parents and boomerang kids are likely to express questions and concerns about privacy. Are parts of the house "off-limits" to parent or child? Do parents expect to be informed about the status of their adult child's romantic relationships, financial affairs, or job seeking efforts? Will the parents express their concerns about the child's relationships, eating habits, or alcohol use? Or will they agree that these concerns are "none of our business?"

Household Rules

Finally, there may be disagreements regarding general household codes of conduct. These could involve curfews, pets, visits by romantic partners, smoking, use of "public areas" (living room, kitchen, front porch), and cleanliness standards, among many other issues.

Stressful Relationships with Adult Children

Most parents continue to help their children as they transition into adulthood. Many provide financial assistance, including helping to buy a car or house. Sometimes, though, helping adult children causes problems for the parents, the adult child, or the relationships between the two parties. Pete and Jean (introduced at the beginning of this chapter) are well-meaning parents who became overwhelmed by a growing list of demands. When they volunteered to baby-sit for the twins, this midlife couple expected to help for only a few months. They could not anticipate the seriousness of their daughter-in-law's health problems or the economic downturn, which slowed their daughter's business and made it impossible for her to hire help. Pete and Jean want her to succeed, but it's difficult to assist her with bookkeeping, record-keeping, and other tasks while also providing childcare and tending to their own business. Adding to these burdens are worries about their younger son, who shows signs of depression. They want to help him through this rough period, but they are starting to feel overwhelmed.

Clients often need assistance in prioritizing needs and learning how and why to say "no." In therapy, overtaxed couples can explore creative ways to provide reasonable levels of help and preserve their own relational resources (see *Working With Clients* below).

Grandparenting Complexities

Many parents are delighted to find out they get to add "grand" to one of their roles. They eagerly look forward to spoiling their grandchildren, passing on family traditions, and re-living childhood with a new generation. For others, though, it is a shock, or grandparenting brings much heartbreak and stress. Even when grandparenting is welcomed, there can be issues and conflicts.

We will focus on three types of grandparenting experiences that are most often addressed in counseling: stressful, long-distance, and traditional.

Stressful Grandparenting

Some midlife couples are continually stressed because their grandchildren live in unpredictable and unstable homes. The grandparents must intervene repeatedly with financial, emotional, and physical assistance. Kent and Susan face this situation because their daughter, a single parent, suffers from mental illness. Her employment has been sporadic and low-paying. Kent and Susan pay her rent, cell phone bill, and car insurance. They provide childcare at least two nights a week and many weekends. They try mightily to be a stabilizing influence to their two grandsons. Like Gail and Dan, this couple feels some resentment, especially when their daughter refuses to see a counselor and fails to take her medications on a consistent basis.

Grandparents in these situations often disagree with each other over the types of assistance they should provide, and for how long. Are they enabling their adult child to abdicate their own parenting responsibilities? Should they take a "tough love" approach? Should they seek custody of the grandchildren? Unfortunately, grandchildren are sometimes pawns used by the adult child to gain financial or other assistance—"If you don't help me, your grandchildren will end up on the street." There is seldom a "right" response, and grandparents may bounce back and forth between offering assistance and standing back.

BOX 6.5 EMOTIONAL CONSEQUENCES OF STRESSFUL GRANDPARENTING

- Resentment at excessive responsibility
- Anger at adult children and spouse
- Ambivalence about whether to help or not
- Guilt from not helping "enough"
- Anxiety/fear for the safety and health of the grandchildren

---

Long-Distance Grandparenting

Long-distance grandparents face the challenge of building and maintaining a relationship with grandchildren who live far away. All other things being equal, it is far easier to be an active and engaged grandparent when the grandchildren are only a half hour drive, or 5-minute walk, away.

BOX 6.6 DIFFERENCES IN CLOSENESS

Four of our grandchildren live within 15 minutes of us, and we see them all several times a month. We never miss the 7-year-old's t-ball games, we have a slumber party once a month for all of them—we're just very involved in their lives. But our other two grandchildren live over 1,000 miles away. They've been coming here in the summer for a week to visit, and we go out there just after Christmas, but it isn't the same. They're only 6 and 4, and they just don't know us. It takes at least 2 days to really warm up to us, and by the time we're all feeling comfortable, it's time to leave.

As this quotation suggests, young grandchildren who see their grandparents only once or twice a year may be frightened of these "strangers" who suddenly want to hug and kiss them. Older grandchildren may be uncomfortable or reticent, as well. The grandparents may feel sad that they are not involved with their grandchildren's lives and resentful of their adult children (or their partners) for moving far away. It behooves grandparents to take the time (and spend the money) to be an active part of their grandchildren's lives through visits, phone calls, e-mails, and the exchange of pictures and gifts.

Traditional Grandparenting

Traditional grandparents live relatively near their grandchildren (close enough to see them at least monthly) and have regular, ongoing contact with them. Typically, traditional grandparents report positive relationships with their grandchildren (and the grandchildren's parents), but problems do arise. Grandparents may, for instance, disagree with the parents' parenting philosophy. Amy and Landon believed in using "time-out" and reward charts as discipline techniques, and they were appalled to discover Landon's mother was spanking their 2-year-old when she baby-sat 1 day a week. They quickly found another sitter, and family relations were strained for months. Nicole and Clark were concerned about family allergies and determined to avoid exposure of their children to dairy products and sugar until they were at least 2 years old. This was clearly conveyed to both sets of grandparents. They were none too pleased when they arrived home after a movie date to find Nicole's parents feeding their 10-month-old ice cream! Julie and Ian were angry when Ian's parents neglected to strap their 3-year-old into his car seat. (Ian's dad argued that "it was too hard to figure out. And, besides, we were just going to the corner store.")

In all of these cases, there are issues of trust and respect at play— the parents (the adult children) expect the grandparents will honor and respect their wishes for their children. The grandparents may feel that their years of experience in child-raising are disregarded and trivialized. You can help your clients identify their contributions to these conflicts and make the adjustments needed to preserve trusting relationships.

ANALYTICAL TOOLS

These conceptual approaches have been helpful to us in understanding the challenges midlife couples face in managing relationships with adult children and grandchildren.

Applying the Dialectical Framework

Two dialectical tensions stand out in conversations with midlife couples.

Helping versus Independence

Parents voice conflicted feelings when offering extended assistance to adult offspring who are struggling. Given years of parental investment and strong emotional bonds with their children, the urge to help is strong. Parents worry out loud that their kids will fail, that they are not yet "ready" for independence, that things are "tougher now," that adult children just need time to get back on their feet. At the same time, one or both partners raise concerns about the effects of "coddling," the need to grow up, and the benefits of failing and "pulling yourself up by the bootstraps." Counselors can help parents find ways to integrate these ambivalent impulses by, for example, setting limits for boomerang children and defining age appropriate kinds of assistance. In some cases, clients need help in understanding the value of "controlled" failure in a person's life and the deleterious effects of overdependence. When an adult child (or his/her offspring) appears to be at serious risk, a client may need help in convincing a reluctant spouse that certain kinds of parental intervention are necessary and appropriate.

Couple Autonomy versus Family Connectedness

Midlife couples are sometimes ambivalent about the degree to which their own relationship, or family relationships, should take priority at midlife. The potential return of a boomerang child is one impetus for these conflicting feelings, as it forces the couple to sacrifice some of their newly experienced privacy and autonomy. Often, the couple is simultaneously glad to help and rueful over the need to once again share their home. As we mentioned earlier, spouses may express these feelings with different degrees of intensity, or they may simply disagree about such things as time limits, household rules, and the kinds of help to provide. Clients often need guidance to express these opposite perspectives, affirm their legitimacy, and devise strategies for meeting their commitments as partners and parents. One strategy is to sequence these opposing desires through an agreement, which allows the child to return for a limited amount of time, after which the parents will reclaim their privacy. A sibling or relative could be enlisted to provide further support after the designated period expires. Couples may find ways to meet both relational goals by, for example, taking more trips together during the boomerang period, assuming they trust their adult child to look after the home during the absence.

Applying the Resilience Framework

The resilience framework encourages midlife couples to build on strengths, draw on existing resources, and devise flexible responses to life challenges. We present several ideas culled from interviews with resilient couples.

Be Aware of and Use Existing Community Resources

Most communities have a plethora of resources available for people experiencing stress. Resilient people use them before stress levels exceed their levels of tolerance. Stressed grandparents often can find respite services in their community. Parents of drug addicted children find support from Al-Anon and similar groups. When adult children lose their health insurance, parents should encourage them to take advantage of state-subsidized programs until they get back on their feet. These moves relieve some of the burden from midlife parents (and some of the accompanying exhaustion) and also encourage adult children to handle problems on their own. Although some parents will feel guilty about not providing direct aid, they may be comforted at the thought of preserving their own resources and by the knowledge that community professionals are trained to provide appropriate support.

Draw on Family Resources

Some midlife couples are reluctant to ask for help from community resources, relatives, or other adult children, preferring to keep problems close to the vest. However, in therapy, they can explore the reasons for their reluctance (e.g., shame?) and possible strategies for requesting assistance. Custodial grandparents can benefit from the assistance of stable adult children who often view such assistance as a privilege rather than a burden. Siblings can sometimes be helpful. Rob and Betsy discussed their boomerang child with Betsy's brother. He offered to make his guesthouse available to their son (in exchange for a modest rent) if their boomerang situation didn't resolve itself in 3 months. That "safety valve" gave the couple and their son a feeling of security and relief.

Use Past Experience to One's Advantage

Experienced parents know that all children experience turbulent times and that even the darkest parental moments tend to eventually clear. Midlife couples have experience in negotiating rules, managing conflicts, and "waiting out storms." That experience can be applied to conflicts with

adult offspring, with some modifications. Therapists can remind co
of their past successes and encourage them to follow their parenting
stincts. The knowledge that most parents eventually find the right bala
between firmness and support can be comforting. So is the knowledg
that the couple has adapted to changing circumstances in the past and
can do so again. The enduring value of the marital relationship is affirmed
when midlife couples work collaboratively to negotiate the boundaries of
their family relationships.

Applying the Roles Framework

Role stress, the distress that accompanies conflicting role demands, is a
common theme in client experiences. This is particularly true of grandparents with legal or physical custody of their grandchildren. Parenting
is a very demanding role under the best of circumstances. When grandparents add it to existing roles such as employee, spouse, and volunteer,
the burden can be crushing. Role stress is relieved when some of the
roles are shared or dropped. Role occupants may need help in accepting
it is "ok" to ask for help in addition to providing it. Learning to accept
adequate rather than superior performance in one or more roles may
bring emotional relief for some clients. Support groups provide a safe
place for role-stressed midlife couples to vent emotions, seek advice, and
connect with supportive people and services.

WORKING WITH CLIENTS

Responding as a Couple

Each of the three areas discussed in this chapter may put inordinate
stress on the marriage. It is important when dealing with boomerang
kids, adult children, and grandchildren, that the couple utilize many of the
communication skills discussed thus far in the book. Setting aside regular
time to discuss the effectiveness and appropriateness of boundaries with
children is essential. Married partners want to be clear on their "couple
goals" as they manage issues regarding their adult children. Not only does
this provide time to nurture the marriage, but it also minimizes couple
conflict as they deal with two of the most difficult issues in any marriage:
Finances and children.

Negotiating Expectations With Boomerang Kids

Most problems with boomerang kids result from a failure to plan for the boomerang experience. The adult child suddenly needs a place to stay, and the parents say "of course you can come home," without much discussion or thought. Taking time to think about the ramifications, discussing them with each other (parents and adult child), and signing a contract can ease most problems that might occur.

BOX 6.7 WHAT YOU MIGHT HEAR FROM CLIENTS: WHEN WILL MY BOOMERANG KID LEAVE?

We were actually very happy to have Stephanie move back in with us after college. She went to college out of state, and we viewed it as a chance to re-connect with her. She didn't have a job, but we knew she was well-qualified, and we thought she'd find one in a couple of months, stay with us another 3 or 4 months to save some money, and then move out. We figured 6 or 7 months tops! But her idea of 'looking for a job' was mostly surfing the internet a few times a week. After 6 months, she had had only two interviews, neither of which resulted in a job offer, and we were starting to wonder what we had gotten ourselves into.

Some parents of boomerang kids choose to view their relationship as more landlord-tenant than parent-child. They draw up a contract and both parents (landlords) and child (tenant) sign the agreement. Other parents may feel that is too formal or "cold." Whether an actual contract is signed or not, the parties need to discuss potentially volatile issues and come to agreement. Most clients will agree to do so rather than jeopardize the future of their relationship with their child because of petty irritations that could have been prevented. In Stephanie's parents' case, the irritations were already multiplying when they decided to sit down and discuss "the situation." The family ended up composing an informal contract, which eased the tension and spurred Stephanie to a more diligent job search. Six months later, she had landed a job and saved enough money for the deposit on an apartment and several pieces of decent furniture. Stephanie moved out on good terms with her parents.

BOX 6.8 DEVELOPING A CONTRACT WITH BOOMERANG KIDS: KEY QUESTIONS

1 How long will the adult child live in the parents' home?
2 Will the adult child contribute room and/or board to the parents?
3 Will there be other expenses the adult child is responsible for?
4 What other responsibilities will the adult child have around the house?
5 What responsibilities will the parents have for the adult child?
6 What rules and expectations need to be clarified?
7 What other issues particular to your situation need to be addressed?
8 Do any of these apply to the parents as well?

Before committing to having an adult child move back in, parents should discuss the following issues, with each other and with their adult child:

How Long Will the Adult Child Live in the Parents' Home?

Is the return based on a particular situation, such as a temporary hiatus between college and graduate school, or the start of a new job? Or, is the return more open-ended, with no clear "leave" date in sight? Adult children who have lost a job, been divorced, or filed for bankruptcy, may need a year or longer to get back on their feet. Clients need to assess their own comfort with an indefinite timeline. Additionally, it is essential to help them assess what they will do if the time exceeds expectations by a significant amount.

If parents limit the adult child's stay, will the limit be based on time, such as a certain number of months, or situation, such as the child finding a job or saving a certain amount of money? If the latter, what will be done if the situation takes substantially longer than expected to be resolved? If an actual contract is drawn up, it might be a good idea to note this issue will be revisited if the child is still living at home after a certain date.

Will the Adult Child Contribute Room and/or Board (Grocery Expenses) to the Parents?

Parents can differ here, as noted above. For a child who has just graduated from college or who is facing serious financial difficulties, it may be reasonable to offer free room and board for a certain period of time. If the parents do decide rent should be charged, what is a reasonable amount? Will there be a sliding scale—for example, a gradual increase as finances become more fixed? Will it be based on a percentage of the adult child's income?

In some cases, parents charge room and board, but then return a portion of the money to the child when the child leaves, especially if the child is saving toward buying a house or furnishing an apartment.

Will There be Other Expenses the Adult Child is Responsible For?

Who will pay for cable TV or internet to be connected in the adult child's bedroom? What if the toilet in his or her bathroom needs plumbing work? Will the adult child contribute to the electric, gas, or phone bills?

What Other Responsibilities Will the Adult Child Have Around the House?

May the adult child use the laundry facilities? If the bathroom is shared with other members of the household, who cleans it and when? Will the adult child clean her room or bathroom? How neatly is he expected to maintain his bedroom? Are there other chores, inside or out, that she or he will be responsible for? What specifically are they, and how will they be performed? For instance, should dirty dishes be stacked by the sink; placed in the dishwasher; or washed, dried, and put away? Be as specific as possible, to avoid frustration and resentment later on.

What Responsibilities Will the Parents Have For the Adult Child?

Will the parent do the cooking? Will the parent "pick up after" the adult child? Will they keep track of phone messages? Are they responsible to do all grocery shopping? Do they need to keep him or her on their car or medical insurance?

What Rules and Expectations Need to be Clarified?

Does the adult child have full use of the house? Can he or she entertain guests in the public areas of the home? Will private areas be respected? Does the adult child need to let the parents know where he or she is going and what time he or she expects to return? Can the adult child entertain romantic partners in the home? In the adult child's bedroom? Can the adult child have overnight visitors?

Does the adult child have her or his own vehicle, or will she or he be using the parents' vehicle(s)? (Who pays for gas? Insurance? Runs errands? What if there is a conflict over vehicle use?)

Is the adult child expected to abide by other household customs, such as arriving for dinner at a specified time, making one's bed, attending a worship service, respecting privacy, respecting "quiet hours?"

What Other Issues Particular to Your Situation Need to be Addressed?

Does the adult child have children? A pet? Smoke? Does the parent have physical limitations that may require extra accommodations by the adult child? Circumstances such as these must be addressed.

Do Any of These Apply to the Parents As Well?

As a way of demonstrating mutual respect, parents may place themselves under some of the same rules as their adult child. Should the parents let the adult child know where the parents are going, and when they expect to be home? Are there other expectations the adult child has of the parent, such as respecting his/her privacy, interacting with his/her friends, or using possessions?

The most important step to a pleasant boomerang kid experience is starting off with frank communication. "Checkpoints" should be built into the agreement. The parties should assess their arrangement periodically and make adjustments. All parties should be encouraged to raise concerns before they become serious sources of irritation. Naturally, most families will experience some discord from time to time. Parents should expect this and avoid overreactions.

Transitioning Relationships With Adult Children

Nearly all adult children turn to their parents from time to time for advice or assistance. Nearly all parents are happy to provide it. But, as with Jean and Pete, at some point the needs of the child (or children) may become overwhelming. Recall that this couple was approaching exhaustion and experiencing marital discord over their commitments to the adult children. They realized they may have "bitten off more than they could chew," and must begin to set some *boundaries* around what they are willing—and able—to do.

Rethinking Financial Boundaries

Jean and Pete considered whether financial assistance needed to be cut back or used to substitute for other kinds of help. First, they could offer to pay for their twin granddaughters to attend a quality preschool 3 half-days a week. This would give their daughter-in-law as much of a break from the children as she has when Jean and Pete babysit 1 or 2 days a week. In addition, the girls would benefit from the structure and social opportunities offered at preschool.

Second, they considered hiring a part-time bookkeeper for their daughter for 1 year. That would allow her enough time to reorganize her business and decide if it is worth continuing.

Third, they could offer to pay for counseling for their son, who lost his mental health benefits when he lost his job. While they will continue to "be there" for him and to provide some financial assistance, he will also have professional advice to rely on.

Upon reflection, Jean and Pete decided on the first and third options. They continued to help their daughter for another 6 months with her business, as that was the least time-consuming and least-stressful demand. They planned to reassess their stress level and her economic prospects after the 6 months.

Parents also may provide financial assistance as a loan, with the expectation that the adult child will pay them back. Parents can formalize this loan, with a signed contract, defined interest rates, and calculations of payments and due dates. Most parents, however, prefer a more informal route, unless the child has repeatedly needed financial assistance or shown poor judgment. If they are making a large loan, parents may want to consider modifying their wills to reflect that. They may leave that child less money (equivalent to the unpaid balance of the loan) than other children. This can prevent family discord regarding perceived inequities in inheritance.

BOX 6.9 DOING VERSUS PROVIDING

Parents can help their kids by "doing" and by "providing." When parents "do," they take on the responsibility themselves—as when Jean and Pete babysit for their granddaughters. When parents "provide," they find other resources to fill the need. They may hire professional help, suggest a support group, or recommend a book or Internet Web site. They are still helping their children, but at less emotional—and physical—cost to themselves.

Finding a Balance: Substituting and Recalibrating Support

Not everyone has the financial resources of Jean and Pete, but parents can lessen stress by substituting less demanding kinds of assistance for the ones they provide currently. Some examples include asking extended family members to take over some kinds of support, connecting the adult child to community resources such as subsidized preschools or daycare centers, or having a stressed child move back home to eliminate helping pay his or her housing expenses.

Even when parents limit financial help, they can continue to offer appropriate levels of advice and counsel. But a child who needs nearly constant advice, or who is emotionally fragile, can be extremely draining on a parent. At some point, parents need to ask whether they are enabling the adult child to remain dependent. Recalibrating the level and type of assistance will relieve pressure on the parents and encourage the child to mature. Parents might decide to buy the adult child a book on home repair, for instance, rather than running over every time something stops working. They may simply need to encourage more reliance on professional sources of assistance, such as car mechanics, therapists, or a financial manager.

Communicating Expectations

Some parents react to any sign of distress in their adult child's life with an anguished "Oh, dear, what can I do to help?" Parents need to signal that their children are adults, who are expected to handle their own problems. Conversations about the child's problems should begin with phrases like "What do *you* see as the most important issues?" and "What office do *you* think you should contact first?" Parents can continue to be supportive, but they can also make it clear that the responsibility for action rests with the adult child. The ball, in other words, needs to be in the child's court.

Using Community Resources

Counselors can help parents by directing them to the resources that can help their children (and encouraging them to make the referral). Most communities provide a resources guide for everything from alcoholism to bankruptcy, child- and elder-care to small business assistance. Parents cannot fully replace these community resources and they need not try to.

Addressing Grandparent Challenges

Help provided to clients must be adjusted to the kinds of grandparenting situations they face. Here we consider the three more common ones:

Working With Stressed Grandparents

In the typical "stressful" grandparenting situation, the parents of the grandchild are not competent to raise a child in a nurturing, supportive way. The parents may be distressed, addicted to drugs, immature, emotionally unstable, or experiencing domestic abuse. Grandparents in these kinds of circumstances are generally trying to give their grandchildren as much of a "normal" life as possible, while not angering the grandchildren's parents. It can be a very delicate balance—do too much or seem to criticize the parents, and the parents forbid access to the grandchildren; do too little, and risk emotional, physical, or other harm to the grandchildren.

In most, but certainly not all of these cases, the grandchildren are being raised by a single parent, typically the daughter of the grandparents. Gail and Dan, from the initial vignette, are representative of "stressed" grandparents.

BOX 6.10 HOW DO I USE IT? WORKING WITH STRESSED GRANDPARENTS

1 List the grandparents' concerns.
2 Brainstorm several ways to address each concern.
3 Consider which potential solutions are realistic and feasible.
4 Reflect on the likely reaction of the grandchildren's parent(s) to the potential solutions.
5 Select one or more solutions that seem most likely to work.
6 Implement the solution(s).

Limit the tendency to make many changes at one time. One change, consistently implemented, is better than four or five changes, even if all seem important.

7 After several weeks, reflect on how the solution is working and make needed adjustments.

In working with stressed grandparents, one of the first issues to address is the areas in which the grandchildren's lives are being compromised. Are they not being fed adequately? Are they not going to school? Are they being emotionally or physically abused? Try to pinpoint the specific areas of concern in concrete terms.

BOX 6.11 WHAT YOU MIGHT HEAR FROM CLIENTS

Example 1: "Our granddaughter Serena is only 10, but her mother has mental health and other issues. Serena is basically functioning as the adult in the household. She tends to her mother's needs, she does their laundry, and cooks their meals, she misses school A LOT—last month she missed 4 days and was tardy 5 other days. I can see the strain in her eyes. She's not being allowed to be a kid, and her schoolwork is suffering."

Example 2: "Our grandsons are ridiculed by . . . well, he's our daughter's boyfriend of about 3 years, but he's not their step-father because they aren't married, which is probably a good thing. But he calls them terrible names, humiliates them, shames them—it is awful, and they have become fearful, withdrawn, scared children. They're only 7 and 5. We're afraid the damage he has done is permanent, and we have no idea what to do. We have no rights and our daughter tells us to quit sticking our nose in her business."

Once a list of concerns has been drawn up, brainstorm what—realistically—can be done to address each of them. In cases of abuse, government intervention is obviously called for, but clients will need to see that it can make the situation better, not worse. Gail and Dan listed nutrition, lack of schedule, school problems (not going, not doing homework), and too much TV/video gaming as their four main areas of concern. They brainstormed ways to address each concern. Here are the solutions that Gail and Dan decided to try:

1   They rearranged their schedules to make sure the children are at school on time every morning. Gail takes the children to school, which means she cannot take a college class before 9:00 A.M.

2   Gail makes sure the children eat a healthy, but simple, breakfast before driving them to school. The breakfasts are typically cold cereal (sugar-free) or toast, with juice and milk.

3   They arranged for the children to attend the after-school program instead of going home to a TV-intensive afternoon of unhealthy snacks. (They pay for the after-school program.)

4   Dan picks the children up from the program around 4:30 P.M. This means Dan must arrive at work by 7:00 A.M., so he can leave by 4:00 P.M.

5   Gail and Dan then supervise the children's homework while simultaneously cooking a healthy but simple dinner.

In doing these five things, Gail and Dan addressed all four of their areas of concern: nutrition, schedule, school, and TV/video games. Their daughter Kim offered no resistance to any of their suggestions, as her main priorities are to sleep and avoid the stress of parenting. The cost to their own lives was manageable, especially because their weekends were their own. However, Gail began to worry about the grandchildren's weekend experiences when their mother began having "boyfriends" spend the night. She lobbied to have the grandchildren spend Friday and Saturday nights with her and Dan, which Kim was very agreeable to, but which Dan soon resented. Weekends were his time to work in his wood shop, go fishing, and otherwise unwind from his stressful week. Including the grandchildren just made his "hobby" time into "work."

Gail and Dan need to continue to reassess their commitments to their grandchildren and what, realistically, they can do for them. They also need to consider how much they are enabling Kim to live irresponsibly. Kim is the parent, but so far, she is relieved of almost all parenting responsibility. They are seeking guidance from a grandparent support group at their church as well as a professional counselor through Gail's college.

Working With Long-Distance Grandparents

Most grandparents long to be close to their grandchildren—physically close, where they can hug them and read to them and teach them how to do things the grandparents love to do, but if you live far from your grandchildren, those simple and expected pleasures are not available to you. Long-distance grandparents must come up with ways to stay close to their grandchildren, despite the distance. Here is some advice that might be useful to clients.

Stay Relevant. At least once a month, send something in the mail. It does not have to be expensive. Pick up some long, dangly necklaces and a floppy hat at a garage sale or thrift store for your granddaughter who loves to play dress-up. Send books, markers, stickers, small cars, an age-appropriate DVD (that you have watched and can talk about), postcards from your hometown—anything your grandchild will find interesting and be able to associate with *you*.

BOX 6.12 STAYING IN TOUCH WITH YOUNGER GRANDCHILDREN

When our granddaughters were small, we sent them packages every 2 or 3 weeks. Because they live in Florida, where there isn't any fall, we ironed red, orange, and yellow maple leaves between sheets of waxed paper and mailed them to them. They loved the bright colors and took them to preschool for show-and-tell. They also hung them in the windows of their bedrooms, so the light would stream through them. I like to draw, and every so often, I'd send them a picture-story of what Grandpa and I were doing in our daily lives—whether planting our garden, building a snowman, or canoeing on one of the rivers near here. Our daughter-in-law saved all of my stories in a special binder notebook that the girls could pull out and look at any time they wanted.

Make Personal Contact. Call them on the phone at least once a month. Once children are 2 or 3 (depending on their verbal skills), they can carry on short conversations.

Let Them Hear Your Voice. Make audiotapes of you reading a picture book, and mail both the tape and the book to the grandchildren. They can listen to you read, as they turn the pages, and become comfortable with your voice. Read as if you were sitting next to your grandchild. Include comments on the pictures, questions to them ("Oh, my! I hope that monster doesn't find her! What do you think will happen, Sophia?"), and reminders to turn the page. Making the story personal will be comforting to the grandchild as he or she relistens to it over the coming months and years.

Older grandchildren will also enjoy receiving packages in the mail. Include items that are personal to them—baseball cards for the baseball fanatic, interesting rocks for the budding geologist, or the 17th book in the series the avid reader has discovered.

BOX 6.13 TALKING WITH OLDER GRANDCHILDREN

To connect with older children, "stay up" with their changing lives—do you know their friends' names? Their teachers? Their activities? Their favorite movies and TV shows? (Do you watch their favorite movies and TV shows, so you can talk about them?) In a typical phone conversation, you should be able to ask questions and make comments such as these:

- "How'd the soccer game go? Did you get to play goalie finally?" (The grandparent knows there was a soccer game, and that the grandchild is itching to play goalie.)
- "How'd that math test go? Was it as easy as you thought it would be?" (The grandparent knows there was a math test, and that the grandchild felt confident he or she would do well on it.)
- "How was Jaden's birthday party?" (The grandparent knows the grandchild's friends.)
- "What did you think about [favorite TV show]? I couldn't believe [X] happened!"

Staying up on their lives will help you have a close relationship with your grandchildren through the teen, college, and young-adult years.

Using New Technology. With older grandchildren, you can have longer telephone conversations and you can chat via IM (instant messaging) or various video-chatting programs that are free. One key variable here is for the grandparents to be flexible by adapting to the communication tools that teens themselves use (MySpace, Facebook, text messaging; you can even play chess online), in addition to more familiar ones (handwritten letters).

Working With Traditional Grandparents

Traditional grandparents generally have the easiest task. They live near their adult children and grandchildren, and they are not unduly worried about their grandchildren's safety or well-being. They can "spoil" the grandchildren and then "hand them back" to the parents. But traditional grandparents may need assistance with these tasks.

Managing Differences in Philosophy. There are many ways to raise children, and people can have honest differences of opinion. Some may think fussy young children should just "cry it out," and others believe in offering comfort and reassurance. Some have strict rules and regulations and others are more laid back. The point grandparents must keep in mind is that: They are not the parents.

If parents feel strongly that their children need rules or must be reassured, grandparents should respect the parents and comply as best they can. Remember: The parents can decide to limit the grandparents' time with the grandchildren, so maintaining a positive, respectful relationship with the parents is important.

Grandparents can ask the parents "How do you want me to handle it when the grandchild cries or refuses to obey?" and then listen carefully to the parents' reply. Grandparents can also simply watch the parents with the grandchildren, and over time, pick up the parents' parenting philosophy from their interactions.

Understanding the Difference Between Spoiling and Indulging. This is a common complaint by many parents: The grandparents go overboard in indulging their beloved grandchildren, handing out-of-control children back to the parents when the grandparent visit is over. As one parent noted:

I love having Mom and Dad take the kids for the weekend, but when they come back they are off their schedule, they've eaten cookies and ice cream for breakfast, and they want to sleep in our bed! I'm about to tell them they can only visit the kids at our house, for an hour!"

Grandparents do need to keep in mind that the grandchildren's lives continue after they leave the grandparents' house. They want the grandchildren to return, which means making sure the aftermath of the visit is positive for the parents. They also want to make sure the grandchildren have a special time while they are visiting. Meeting both goals is not that hard to accomplish. There is a difference between "spoiling" (which means "to ruin," as in spoiled fruit) and "indulging."

BOX 6.14 SPOILING VERSUS INDULGING

Spoiling	Indulging
* having no bedtime	* letting grandchildren stay up half an hour later than usual
* watching five videos	* watching one video
* eating two bowls of ice cream for dinner	* having a scoop of ice cream for dessert
* buying seven trucks on a shopping spree	* buying one truck on a shopping trip

---

Spoiling generally involves an excessive number of "treats," combined with few rules or consequences. Encourage grandparents to *indulge in moderation*. One or two "treats" a day makes for a special time at Grandma and Grandpa's house; the grandchildren do not need endless catering and coddling. And bear in mind that it is a treat for most young children to partake in the daily life of their grandparents, which may vary considerably from their life at home.

Planning Time With Grandchildren. One of the best things grandparents can give their grandchildren is time. Endless games of "Go Fish" or "Trouble" may make for better memories, and more laughter, than an elaborate outing to an amusement park. Plan for unhurried time together, whether making dinner, weeding a garden, or folding laundry. Grandparents who listen to their grandchildren and tell interesting stories, create tight emotional bonds that will last well into the grandchild's adulthood. Parents appreciate the investment of time and creativity.

Our children love visiting Nana and Papa because they get to do all of these amazing things—like fill the half-dozen bird feeders in their backyard, and add potato peelings to the compost pile, and run through the sprinklers. For kids who live in a city apartment, these are exotic adventures!"

Consulting With the Parents. It's a good idea for grandparents to run any plans by the parents, just in case it conflicts with plans the parents have already made. Grandparents have been known to buy a gift for a visiting grandchild, only to discover that the parents had already purchased that very item for the child's birthday a few weeks later. Grandparents should also avoid doing anything "drastic." One mother wanted to clip her 2-year-old daughter's bangs back with barrettes and was growing the bangs out. The grandmother, baby-sitting on a weekend afternoon, was unaware of that. She decided the child's bangs were too long and proceeded to trim them well above the eyebrows. Her daughter, the child's mother, found this presumptuous and was angry with the grandmother for overstepping her role.

Grandparents should avoid *making promises* that can only be fulfilled by the parents, whether it is something minor ("I'm sure Mommy and Daddy will let you have cookies later on") or major ("I bet you'll have a little brother or sister some day!").

Respecting the Parents' Wishes. This is a problem cited frequently by many parents. Grandparents can ask parents to detail exactly how they want certain situations handled. They can also apologize if they are unable to adhere to the parents' wishes and ask for assistance (such as with the difficult-to-use car seat) or alternative ways to handle a situation (e.g., discipline measures that do not include physical punishment). People, in general, cooperate more and perform better when they understand the reason behind a certain course of action. Grandparents might ask the parents, in a curious, "I'd really like to know more about this" manner, why the parents prefer X to Y.

CONCLUDING THOUGHTS

The theme of this chapter has been managing boundaries. As we have seen, midlife couples can become stressed and exhausted if they fail to negotiate healthy relationships with their adult children. A time of life that could be creative and energizing becomes personally and relationally taxing. However, many of the problems encountered by midlife parents can be addressed through modest changes in expectations and communication. In counseling sessions, you can help couples recognize the signs of poor boundary management. You can also help them regain solidarity and improve the communication practices they use with each other and their adult children. By keeping their own relationship needs on center-stage, midlife couples will, in the long run, be better able to maintain healthy relationships with their children and grandchildren.

QUESTIONS FOR CLIENTS

Boomerang Kids

1   What are the benefits and challenges of having your child move back home?
2   On what key issues do you, as a couple, differ regarding your son's or daughter's return?
3   How will your marriage be affected by the return of your adult child?
4   Do you trust your child to be back in the home? (Might she/he use money or cars without asking?)
5   Can you agree on the terms of a contract for your child's return?

Helping Adult Children

1   To what extent do you feel like you are "helping" your child rather than "enabling" him or her?
2   Do you consider your child's problems to be short– or long-term? How long will your commitment last?
3   To what extent is your child taking steps to help him or herself?
4   To what extent do you, as a couple, agree regarding the help you offer your child?
5   Do you have both the emotional and financial resources to help your child at this time?
6   What other people, services, or resources could be helpful to your child?
7   What limits have you imposed on your assistance?

Grandparenting

1   Are you able to balance your roles as grandparents and partners in marriage? What stresses and rewards are flowing from your grandparenting role?

2 To what extent do you believe your grandchildren are safe physically and psychologically? Who can help you decide?

3 Do you have the time, emotional stamina, and finances to help your grandchildren in the way you think is best? Where can you get help in your community?

4 How is your relationship with your adult child affecting your relationship with your grandchildren? Could other caretakers supplement the support you provide and reduce the strain.

5 What boundaries and limits have you stipulated? Are you able to stick with them? Have you fully discussed them with your adult children?

6 Can you think of creative ways to involve the grandchildren in activities you enjoy as a couple?

7 What steps can you take to stay relevant in the lives of your long–distance grandchildren?

8 Are you communicating sufficiently with your adult children about your role as a grandparent, and their expectations for your grandchildren?

EXERCISES

Exercise 6.1 Making a Boomerang Plan

The goal of this exercise is to create a plan with your "boomerang kid" that makes expectations explicit.

Sit down as a couple and review the following issues. Try to come to consensus about each topic. Afterward, meet with your returning child to make a plan. The goal of the first meeting is to build solidarity, *not* to gang up on your child. Approach both meetings in the spirit of dialogue.

Issues to be discussed:

■ Length of stay (specific amount of time or related to time after getting financially stable)
■ Financial contributions (room, board, utilities...)
■ Household chores (laundry, yard work, cleaning...)
■ Privacy guidelines (entering bedrooms, checking mail, asking questions about jobs)
■ Household rules (curfew, guests in rooms, use of public space)

Exercise 6.2: Using the Past to Manage Boundaries

The goal of this exercise to draw on the past to manage current struggles with children.

1 As a couple, identify two past experiences where you had to handle difficult issues with the child you are currently struggling with. (Or if this child was previously the "golden child," draw on experience with your other children.)

2 Think carefully about what made each of these situations successful or unsuccessful. (What was unique about the situation? About the child? About both of you as parents?)

3 Apply the elements you've identified to the current situation.

Exercise 6.3 Couple Boundary Meetings

The goal of this exercise is to help you have regular couple times to discuss parent-child boundaries.

1 Identify a regular time and place to talk about your relationship with your children.

2 Set a time limit on the discussion (if you have too much to discuss, put aside certain items until the next meeting or set another meeting to continue the discussion).

3 Discuss your honest feelings related to your relationship(s) with your adult children.

4 Identify what is "working" or not "working."

5 Brainstorm possible solutions.

6 Select a solution that will "work" for both of you and, you hope, your child.

7 Be prepared to discuss, at your next couple meeting, whether the decision is working or not. Make necessary adjustments.

Exercise 6.4 Grandparent Couple Time

The goal of this exercise is to help you use "grandparent time" to double as "couple time."

1 Identify three activities you enjoy doing as a couple that children can be involved in. (This can be as simple as cooking breakfast or hiking.)

2   Brainstorm how grandchildren can be included in the activity. (Give children age-appropriate tasks, such as setting the table or flipping the pancakes; pick a hike that is less strenuous than your normal hikes, but that you and your spouse both enjoy for its scenery.)

3   Spend couple time getting ready for the children's arrival. (Doing special things to the guest room, buying a new game, or baking together are ways to spend time as a couple while readying yourselves for the grandkids.)

REFERENCES

Beaujot, R. (2004). *Delayed life transitions: Trends and implications*. Retrieved November 12, 2008, from http://www.vifamily.ca/library/cft/delayed_life.html

Greenfield, E. A., & Marks, N. F. (2007). Linked lives: Adult children's problems and their parents' psychological and relational well-being. *Journal of Marriage and the Family*, 442–454. Retrieved November 12, 2008, from http://www.pubmedcentral.nih.gov/articlerender.fcgi?artid=1950122

New York Life. (2008). *Adult children moving back home: Don't let "boomerang kids" derail your goals*. Retrieved November 12, 2008, from http://www.newyorklife.com/cda/0,3254,13762,00.html

U.S. Bureau of Census. (2004). [Table explaining estimated median age at first marriage from 1890 to present]. *Estimated Median Age at First Marriage, by Sex: 1890 to Present*. Retrieved November 12, 2008, from http://www.census.gov/population/socdemo/hh-fam/tabMS-2.pdf

7

Relocation at Midlife: Marking a New Era

DAYNA KLOEBER AND VINCENT R. WALDRON

For years, the comfortable house owned by John and Elizabeth had served as a gathering place for local teenagers. After countless sports practices and Science Olympiad competitions, their twins, Leah and Bradley, had invited their various teams home for a few relaxed hours of snack eating and spirited post-game analysis. Their dining room table was frequently commandeered for use as a study table, as the kids and their classmates prepared for exams and worked on team projects. When the twins finally left home for college, John and Elizabeth both felt twinges of loneliness and loss. Elizabeth described it in physical terms—a deep ache. John felt disoriented as the familiar hustle and bustle gave way to quiet. The veteran parents missed not only their own children but also the laughter and energy that came with so many young visitors. It was always part of the plan to relocate when the kids moved out. Finding and renovating an older home would give them a project to share as they launched this new era of married life, but the pair suddenly felt some trepidation. Why leave the old neighborhood when so many friends lived close by? What if the new neighborhood was less friendly? Why incur the expense of moving when their current mortgage was mostly paid off? John and Elizabeth needed more time. The couple crafted a new plan. With tuition costs rising and more time on their hands, John and Elizabeth decided to purchase a modest investment property. They would spend their weekends planning, shopping, and remodeling the small house, and then (they hoped) sell it for a profit. As it turned out, the project was a qualified success. John and Elizabeth did most of the work themselves, and the physical demands felt good to this energetic couple. By keeping busy on weekends, the pair kept feelings of loneliness at bay. They enjoyed a sense of teamwork and camaraderie and found great satisfaction in the "before and after" photos that documented their collective handiwork. The modest profit motivated them to launch additional projects until, eventually, John and Elizabeth tackled a major remodel—a new home for themselves.

UNDERSTANDING THE RELOCATION EXPERIENCE

Like John and Elizabeth, many centerstage couples intend to relocate after their children leave home. And many do end up moving. The National Association for Realtors (2007) reported that 31% percent of homes were purchased by people aged 45 to 64. However, as our opening narrative suggests, the decision to relocate at midlife is complicated by a number of social, emotional, and financial factors. Of course, relocation can be taxing at any life stage. It is considered by social workers and health professionals to be one of the most taxing events in a person's life, potentially as stressful as the death of a parent or a divorce, but centerstage couples make this transition at a time when marital satisfaction may be at a low ebb (Gecas & Seff, 1990; Gottman & Levenson, 2000; Stienberg, 2001). As the children leave home and parental responsibilities subside, some couples struggle to redefine their relational identity (Wallerstein & Blakeslee, 1995). Like Elizabeth and John, many couples plan to relocate or remodel to address an identity gap that opened when the children left home. All of this suggests that the relocation decision may be one of the issues that midlife clients raise in therapy.

Marriage researchers report that long relationships are often strengthened after periods of redefinition and adaptation (Wallerstein & Blakeslee, 1995). The quest for a new home may be part of this larger transformation—one that is both emotionally taxing and potentially revitalizing. Accordingly, the first purpose of this chapter is to examine variations in the relocation experiences of centerstage couples. What kinds of moves do couples make, and what are their motives for relocating? Next, this chapter outlines stages of the relocation process. The factors that promote resilience and stress at each stage are our special concern. Third, we use the analytical tools developed throughout this book to interpret client reports about this important transition. Fourth, in *Working With Clients*, we provide practical suggestions for helping clients work through the relational issues that often accompany relocation. As in other chapters, we end with questions for clients, exercises, and resources to facilitate the integration of this chapter's principles.

The following identifies stresses and opportunities associated with different types of relocation and raises questions that will help clients prepare for this major life transition.

Types of Relocation

Table 7.1 provides a relocation typology. We also note some concerns raised by clients when they consider the implications of relocation.

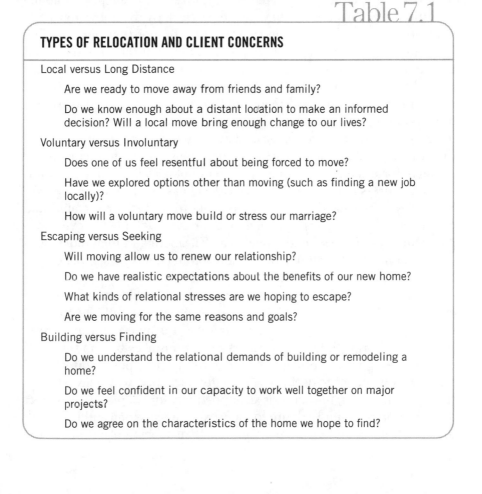

Table 7.1

TYPES OF RELOCATION AND CLIENT CONCERNS

Local versus Long Distance

    Are we ready to move away from friends and family?

    Do we know enough about a distant location to make an informed decision? Will a local move bring enough change to our lives?

Voluntary versus Involuntary

    Does one of us feel resentful about being forced to move?

    Have we explored options other than moving (such as finding a new job locally)?

    How will a voluntary move build or stress our marriage?

Escaping versus Seeking

    Will moving allow us to renew our relationship?

    Do we have realistic expectations about the benefits of our new home?

    What kinds of relational stresses are we hoping to escape?

    Are we moving for the same reasons and goals?

Building versus Finding

    Do we understand the relational demands of building or remodeling a home?

    Do we feel confident in our capacity to work well together on major projects?

    Do we agree on the characteristics of the home we hope to find?

Although any number of categorizing schemes have been proposed, we consider four questions when assessing the potential relational impact of relocation. First, is the move local or long distance? Long-distance moves are more likely to disrupt the social network of the couple. They should expect a longer period of adaptation as they locate services and sources of support in a new community. Social and cultural practices may be quite different, particularly when clients move to new regions or from urban to rural settings. Local moves have the advantage of introducing novelty into the lives of veteran couples, while maintaining close geographical ties to familiar family, friends, and service providers. However, local moves may fail to bring the excitement and novelty that some couples seek at midlife.

Second, is the motivation to relocate voluntary or involuntary? Involuntary moves are often mandated by employers or changing economic conditions (see chapter 5). They can be particularly disruptive to a partner who values predictability and control. One or more partners may feel resentment when relocation is imposed by circumstances rather than choice. Forced moves are complicated by unwanted losses in social support, difficulty making new friends, aversion to an unfamiliar climate, and full-blown culture shock (Klopf, 2001). Couples may need assistance in considering alternatives to relocation or in developing resilience in the face of relocation challenges. They may need help imagining how they will maintain important social connections with children or friends through, for example, communication technologies like online communities, picture-sharing, and Internet video links (Waldron et al., 2005). Strategies for making the moving process more gradual, predictable, and psychologically safe may be needed. In the case of voluntary moves, couples sometimes have second thoughts as Elizabeth and John did. Counselors can help them rethink their plans and recognize discrepancies in the desires of individual partners.

Third, is the move designed to escape present problems or seek new experiences? Moving is sometimes perceived as the antidote to long-standing marital problems. It may also allow a couple to escape stressful relationships with family members or put mistakes behind them. Of course, fleeing from a problem may not resolve it. Couples often need third-party guidance to decide if a "change in scenery" will really be helpful. Often, however, relocation is an opportunity for couples to reconnect and collaborate around a desire for new experiences. John and Elizabeth took the time to build consensus around their moving plans and in the process developed the experience and teamwork needed to remodel a home that suited their next phase of life.

Fourth, has the couple considered building versus finding? We include the building versus finding category because couples may need to consider building (remodeling) rather than finding a new home. Of course, remodeling projects are not for the faint of heart, as they require expertise, patience, and seemingly unending investments of cash. Couples contemplating a remodel should first take an inventory of their tolerance for frustration and pledge not to let the stresses of building a home undermine the foundations of the marriage.

Why Couples Move: Expectations and Motives

We suggested that relocation comes in a variety of types, each with its own difficulties and opportunities, but a fuller understanding of why moving can be problematic for centerstage couples requires a closer look at their expectations and motives. Box 7.1 provides a list of commonly reported motives. We discuss several in more detail.

BOX 7.1 MOTIVES FOR MOVING

- Accepting career opportunity
- Exploiting economic advantage
- Escaping financial distress
- Seeking improved climate
- Changing/enriching lifestyle
- Moving closer to family/away from family
- Preparing for retirement
- Collaborating on a project
- Reinventing relational identity
- Leaving problems behind

Closer to Family/Away From Family

A desire to be closer to family spurs some centerstage couples to relocate. Some fail to adjust when adult children leave home. They move to be closer to the kids (or grandkids). Midlife offers an opportunity for some couples to "return to their roots." They return home to renew kinship ties. In other cases, moving back home makes it possible for one or more offspring to care for parents and older relatives. Of course, difficult family relations motivate some couples to move away. With the children gone, ties to difficult parents and relatives can be more easily loosened, if not actually broken.

Collaborating on a New Project

In interviews, married couples frequently described the middle years of marriage as a transitional time of getting reacquainted and developing new and mutual interests. One insightful student shared after interviewing her parents, "My parents really had to work on focusing everything back to each other. Activities such as dinner, church, and vacation left them feeling void of something." We read countless similar accounts of parents feeling sad, angry, useless, and lonely. Many described periods of feeling estranged from their partner as a result of these feelings. "I looked at him and felt like I didn't know him and wasn't sure if I liked him," said one 51-year-old wife regarding her husband. During this period, resilient couples often made a purposeful effort to reconnect, often through shared projects or new goals. For some, (recall Elizabeth and John) the process of finding a new home served this purpose.

Reinventing Relational Identity

In relational narratives, parenting is often mentioned as one of the key transformational experiences in long-term marriage (Kelley & Waldron, in press). It profoundly changes relational identity in a way that may not be experienced again until the kids leave home. Relocation can be a symbolic way of marking this second identity change. For our opening couple, John and Elizabeth, the work of purchasing and remodeling an investment property was emblematic of the years of cooperative effort they invested in their children. It also signaled a transitional phase in their relationship, one that marked a new independence and new goals. For them, the purchase of a new home marked the arrival of a new era in their lives, one in which their marriage reclaimed centerstage.

Stages of Relocation

As a marital process, relocation begins long before the boxes are packed. In fact, many couples anticipate and plan, and sometimes argue, for many years before they finally move to a new home. Relocation is a multistage process. The relational tasks performed at each stage have the capacity to strengthen a marriage, but each stage also brings opportunity for stress and discord.

BOX 7.2 STAGES OF RELOCATION

Stage 1—Dreaming: Clients fantasize about where they want to live in the future.

How it can help: Builds solidarity; produces positive marital feelings to counter negative ones; relieves feelings of boredom or distress; prompts early planning; builds hope for the future.

How it can hurt: Failure to share dreams leads to problems down the road; unrealistic expectations may lead to disappointment.

What clients need: Encouragement to dream; help in negotiating different visions of the future; exploration of reasons/motives for wanting to move

Stage 2—Negotiating: Partners create a shared vision.

How it can help: Perceiving that dreams may become reality; sharing information and learning; creatively integrating two visions.

How it can hurt: Relocation becomes a source of unresolved conflict; rejected plans lead to resentment and disillusionment; topic is avoided for fear of conflict; autocratic decision making breeds contempt.

What clients need: Assistance with conflict management and negotiation skills.

Stage 3—Planning: Researching and strategizing relocation options within a shared vision.

How it can help: Builds solidarity; partners allocate tasks according to strengths; satisfaction increases as a sign of progress; provides topics for discussion and mutual planning.

How it can hurt: Impatience at slow progress; disagreement over details; frustration at allocation of labor; overload of already busy lives; increased stress; "cold feet" from one or both partners.

What clients need: Regaining "perspective" when relocation stresses spike; help in reallocating tasks, managing expectations, exploring new hesitancies.

Stage 4—Committing: Financial investment is initiated; house for sale; closing on new house; signing papers

> **How it can help**: Feelings of relief; reduction in uncertainty; mark of progress; shared excitement
>
> **How it can hurt**: Feelings of regret; fear of failure; loss of control; new financial hardships
>
> **What clients need**: Financial planning assistance; encouragement; reduction of nonrelocation stressors; relaxation strategies; managing priorities to avoid information overload.

Stage 5—Settling: Completing the move; making a new home.

> **How it can help:** Shared task (e.g., packing and unpacking); mutual satisfaction at the completion of a long term project; resumption of familiar relational and lifestyle patterns; opportunities for enjoyable collaboration (e.g., furnishing a new home; locating local restaurants).
>
> **How it can hurt:** Differences of opinion may reemerge (e.g., over uses of space); reality fails to meet expectations; postmove "let down"; grief over the loss of old friends, neighbors, and ways of life.
>
> **What clients need:** Strategies for preserving the past while welcoming the future; help with grieving; recognition for working well together; recognition of differences in the pace of adjustment to a new home; flexibility and patience with the complicated moving process; reinforcement of their original relocation decision.

Stage 6—Integrating: The partners make new social connections and identify with their new community.

> **How it can help:** Partners depend on each other until new social bonds are formed; new location and friends provide conversational topics; uncertainty is reduced; stress is reduced.
>
> **How it can hurt:** Partners experience different levels of adjustment success; overdependence on partners for social support; costs of new home may exceed expectations; culture shock may persist.
>
> **What clients need:** Ideas for making friends; strategies for increasing independence; financial advice; recognition of the source of culture shock and time to adjust.

SOURCES OF DISTRESS

A central theme of this chapter is that relocation holds the potential to be a symbolic new beginning. Paradoxically, for many married parents, the act of moving to a new home brings closure to a cherished era of family life. Given the importance of this transition, it is not surprising that clients bring a variety of moving-related stressors to counseling sessions. This section discusses the more common sources of distress in detail.

Differing Motives

A common problem involves motives for moving. Connie and Fred thought they were moving for the same reasons, but they discovered otherwise.

Connie and Fred spent years dreaming and planning to build a home on the lot they had acquired earlier in their marriage. To Fred, building a home in an up-and-coming part of town made good financial sense. Their investment would pay off in a few years when the house sold for a high price. Connie looked forward to a change in lifestyle. The new neighborhood was adjacent to a flourishing arts district, close to friends, and near the mountains she loved to hike. The plan was postponed multiple times so the kids could avoid changing schools, but with the children launched, Connie and Fred felt the time was right to build, but an unforeseen downturn in the economy was giving Fred second thoughts. He wasn't sure about taking on the financial burdens associated with building a custom home. Fred hinted that they might instead remodel an older home in a more modest neighborhood. Connie felt disappointed and frustrated. She argued for sticking to the original plan, even if it meant accepting some financial risk. Fred dug in his heels. He wanted to reduce the financial pressure.

Connie and Fred had different motives for moving, but as long as the economy held steady, the differences could be ignored. They needed help recognizing these differences and how they spawned different emotional reactions to changing conditions. (Their conversations were colored by his feelings of financial insecurity and her frustration at another delay in plans.) However, with some assistance, they discovered a creative solution that resolved the impasse: Sell the lot and buy an existing but more affordable home in the same general area.

At midlife, some people feel compelled to change careers, often in a search for a more meaningful and fulfilling life. A career change in itself can upset the marital status quo (see chapter 5). When it involves relocation, the potential for spousal conflict is heightened.

Paula and Eduardo had varying ideas about how they would spend the next period of their lives. Years earlier, upon the news that they were expecting their second child, Eduardo suspended his dream of becoming an artist and dropped out of art school. For 2 decades, he devoted himself to family life and made a good living in real estate, so Paula was astonished to hear that Eduardo, now in his mid-40s, wanted to return to the prestigious art program he had left as a young man. He wanted the couple to move out of state. Paula was concerned for their financial future. Just the thought of leaving family and friends left her in tears. She loved Eduardo and recognized that he had made tremendous professional sacrifice but still thought he was being foolish and selfish.

Couples like Eduardo and Paula find themselves at something of a crossroads. Eduardo's plan would radically change what has become a familiar and comfortable pattern of life. As with Connie and Fred, this couple will need assistance in examining their motives for moving (and staying).

Unrealistic Expectations

Some partners agree on motives but find that their expectations are unrealistic.

Richard and Diane both worked factory jobs in a Midwestern city. Although money was tight in their household, they took pride in their ability to raise two well-adjusted boys. The sons married and moved to nearby suburbs, but the family remained very close, especially after the grandchildren came along. When Richard was laid-off at the age of 54, the payment on their mortgage became burdensome. At the urging of their oldest son, Richard and Diane agreed to sell the house and move in with their son, daughter-in-law, and three young grandchildren. Richard would look for work and help with the kids, while Diane commuted to her job at the manufacturing plant. Despite their high hopes, the arrangement proved impractical. The older couple found the flurry of young children exhausting and the lack of privacy disconcerting. Within just a few months, they decide to move back to the city, in part to avoid damaging their relationship with their son and his family. Unable to afford the payments on a new house, Richard and Diane were forced to rent an apartment. The disappointed couple describes this as one of the darkest periods of their long marriage.

Richard and Diane are an example of a couple with shared motives for moving (to be closer to family, to save money), but the couple and their son had unrealistic expectations. Counseling may have helped them anticipate the problems. Now that the move has failed, this vulnerable couple may need different assistance, such as employment counseling and access to subsidized housing.

Personality Differences: Openness to Change

Personality differences surface during the relocation process, particularly those involving preferences for predictability and novelty. This is the case with Eduardo and Paula, the couple introduced previously. Paula is perfectly content with a small group of friends and a predictable lifestyle. She values financial security and a strong sense of community. In contrast, Eduardo is energized by change. He enjoys novelty and the lure of the unknown. For Eduardo, the idea of moving is pregnant with possibility. For Paula, it brings anxiety and dread. In counseling, they will need to explore ways to integrate these differing orientations. One possibility: Eduardo could move temporarily to complete his art degree, with the couple joining each other on some weekends.

Autocratic Decision Making

The decision to relocate can have profound consequences for marriages and individual partners. In our studies, we sometimes hear from partners who are profoundly bitter after feeling forced to relocate by a dominating spouse. Counselors can encourage couples to fully consider both partners' views and to recognize that autocratic decisions can have long-term negative effects that outweigh short-term gains.

Loss of Friends

Leaving friends can be stressful for couples, especially for those who have limited support from extended family. Before moving, clients should inventory the kinds of support they receive from friends, including advice, companionship, empathy, emotional venting, perspective taking, and even tangible help. Can these be maintained after the move, through phone conversations, e-mail, and visits? If not, are the partners confident in their capacity to develop new sources of support?

Moving to Family: Family Tensions/Expectations

Couples sometimes tell us that moving closer to families of origin brings unanticipated anxiety and stress. Living at a distance from family can be a hardship for some midlife couples, especially when they feel obligated to assist elderly parents. Of course, distance can be a blessing as well, because it preserves privacy boundaries and allows the couple to act with relative autonomy. In some case, couples have unrealistically positive expectations about living closer to family, only to find that the old relational tensions with parents and siblings are alive and well. Clients may need help establishing boundaries and avoiding old patterns of destructive communication. In counseling, they should confront questions such as: Will my family members come to rely on me too much? Will we feel suffocated by the close proximity of our relatives? How will my spouse be affected by my family? What conflicts will resurface and how will I manage them? Step-family dynamics may complicate the process even further, as couples contemplate a varied set of family allegiances, sensitivities, and expectations. See Appendix A for more information on helping blended families.

Increased Closeness

Moving can bring spouses together, sometimes too close together. After years of distracting engagements with children, work friends, volunteer organizations, and friends, some relocated couples find themselves "alone together" in a new home. Many couples have experienced the occasional awkward evening of staring at each other over dinner, not knowing what to say. As they contemplate a move, one or both partners may express ambivalence at the prospect of spending too much time together. Will we run out of things to say? Will we drive each other crazy? And, although these concerns are not uncommon, partners may harbor unexpressed guilt for having them. Moving has a way of magnifying existing relational insecurities. You may be asked to help couples confront them before or after they decide to relocate.

Financial Stresses

Although midstage marriages are often on more solid footing than their younger counterparts, relocation can change a couple's financial status in sometimes alarming ways. Costs often exceed projections. Mortgage payments may rise to less comfortable levels. Basic differences in attitudes toward money often resurface (as was the case with Connie and Fred). You may notice that your married clients experience higher levels of discord because of these almost inevitable financial stresses. Many couples need assistance with reality testing their financial expectations and negotiating a mutually comfortable set of financial commitments.

Negotiating the Relocation Plan: Whose House? Where?

Derek and Sidney spent a good deal of their married lives living overseas, chasing Derek's career in the oil business. Nearly constant relocation made it impossible for Sidney to maintain her own career in the publishing industry; however, Sidney maintained her professional contacts and took on occasional contract projects as an editor. Derek's corporate career came to an early end when he was offered a sizeable early retirement plan. For this midlife couple, the events of launching children, retirement, and relocation coincided to form a perfect storm of midlife indecision. In his mid-50s and tired of the hectic pace of global travel, Derek wanted to settle into a golf community somewhere in the southern United States. Sidney had a different vision. She wanted low-maintenance living in an interesting urban setting—a place where she could kick-start her long-delayed career.

Disagreements about where to live may have surfaced over the course of the marriage because partners nurture different visions for their future. As was the case with Derek and Sidney, the arrival of midlife provides opportunities to fully voice these differences. The differences matter more now because partners finally feel free to act on their dreams. Sidney had put her own career on hold out of support for her husband and their kids, but now she saw an opportunity to advance her own career interests. Suppressed conflicts percolate to the surface when a critical relocation decision looms. As with so many conflicts, compromise may appear to be the best solution, but by this point in life, some clients have grown weary of compromise. Sidney certainly had. In counseling sessions you can encourage clients to try a collaborative approach, one which encourages a deeper evaluation of the interests and assumptions of each partner and sets aside a win/lose mentality. To do so, partners must engage in the kind of problem-solving dialogue discussed in chapter 2.

The ultimate objective is to develop a relocation strategy that meets as many relational needs as possible, without sacrificing the interests of either spouse. For spouses with financial resources, including Sidney and

Derek, a variety of creative options are available. They might purchase two smaller homes in different locations, rather than one larger one, try fractional ownership, or engage in the increasingly popular practice of "home swapping." Other couples must simply do their best to maximize the interests of each individual. Sidney and Derek could do so by purchasing a more affordable smaller home in an urban location and using the money they saved to join a nearby golf club—not exactly what Derek envisioned, but close.

Periods of Separation

At some point during their relocation, certain couples will find that they will be separated. These separations may be caused by a failure to sell, or delay in selling a previous home, or by extenuating circumstances regarding the health or well-being of a different family member. Some separations will be relatively short-lived, but others may be extended to unusually long periods, placing the couple at increased risk of drifting apart, subsequent affairs, or even divorce. Financial stress may be high during times when couples support two households. Other couples have reported that time apart gave them the opportunity to realize how much they value their time together.

Culture Shock

Culture shock is the general anxiety that often accompanies relocation to a dramatically different location. It is marked by emotional and/or physical distress and may interfere with a client's social functioning. It is associated with feelings of helplessness, irritability, loneliness, withdrawal, and obsessions with cleanliness and health, among other things (Klopf, 2001). Clients experiencing culture shock sometimes require short-term counseling. They sometimes need assurance that the situation can improve, help in understanding local norms and customs, supportive connections to other newcomers, mentors from the local community, flexibility, and practice in local social and language practices.

ANALYTICAL TOOLS

Three analytical frameworks can be helpful in interpreting client's relocation experiences.

Applying the Dialectical Framework

We find dialectical theory particularly useful because it acknowledges the ambivalence midlife couples often experience when considering relocation. The decision is rarely easy and is often accompanied by periods of doubt, delay, and indecision. When working from a dialectical approach, counselors encourage clients to identify the "pushes and pulls" that are creating tension in the marriage and suggest ways to manage them.

Predictability versus Novelty

Partners often want both predictability and novelty in their marriage, but they want them at different times and in different proportions. The prospect of relocation tilts the relationship toward the novelty side of the continuum, but as they approach and execute a move, the couple may regret the loss of predictability and try to reestablish it. This will be reflected in the messages you hear in counseling sessions.

BOX 7.3 WHAT YOU MIGHT HEAR FROM CLIENTS: PREDICTABILITY VERSUS NOVELTY

- "What's wrong with the house we live in now? I like things the way they are."
- "I thought we were happy here."
- "I just need a change. The same old thing is boring."
- "I'm sick of looking at these same four walls."
- "We just keep spending money on remodeling the house and new furniture. It's like we really need a change but don't have the courage to move."
- "We need to make new friends" versus "I have all the friends I need."
- "What if we don't like it?" "What if we move, and we're miserable?"

Past Ties–Future Prospects

The sentimentality associated with the past can make it difficult to contemplate a different future.

Valerie and Don moved to their current neighborhood when their son John was in preschool and their daughter Brooke was just beginning kindergarten. Their son Adam came along later that year. The couple became fast friends with many neighborhood families. Photo albums are filled with evidence of how their children all attended school and played sports together. This family has fond memories of neighborhood barbeques, pool and birthday parties, and eventually graduation celebrations. Now, Valerie wants to move, and Don does not understand what is wrong with staying exactly where they are. A few families have begun to leave the neighborhood, whereas others remain, but Valerie claims she just can't take the constant reminder of the way things used to be. She wants a new start—a new project. She wants the opportunity to move to a new community where they might meet new friends. She knows they'll keep in touch with their good friends too, so she doesn't understand why Don is dragging his feet so much.

Like Valerie and Don, many couples need guidance to understand how to move toward the future without throwing away the past. Couples must explore central benefits of the proposed change and discern how elements of the past can be retained while embracing the future.

Family Ties versus Couple Plans

Most couples will identify the home or *homes* where they raised their children as their *family home*. Some partners have trouble envisioning a home without making accommodations for the adult children; for others, that is the whole point of moving. In counseling sessions, midlife parents may cycle between ambivalent feelings of sorrow and excitement, loss and anticipation.

Applying the Resilience Framework

Despite the potential pitfalls, most couples manage midlife relocations with creativity and resilience. Therapists can assist clients in cultivating sources of resilience.

Friends Who Have Moved

Most couples know someone who has relocated after their children left home. These successful movers can serve as sources of advice and encouragement. "Moving mentors" can help couples anticipate relational, social, and financial challenges and suggest strategies for overcoming them.

Financial Advisors

At some point, most relocating couples confront concerns about money. Some couples will need help assessing the effects of relocation on retirement plans; others will need to make adjustments for unforeseen hardships; some will need to become more realistic about the short or long-term costs of selling and purchasing a new home. A competent financial advisor will help them assess, analyze, and adjust financial plans. The capacity to make informed adjustments is a hallmark of resilience.

Communication Tools

Emerging communication technologies make it ever easier to stay connected with geographically distant family and friends. Knowing how to use them effectively makes long-distance moves seem less daunting. Clients who fear isolation can be encouraged to use a range of online communication tools, including online communities, interest-based chat groups, Internet video/audio connections, and picture sharing, in addition to the more obvious e-mail and cell phone options.

Newcomer Support Organizations

Most communities mobilize resources to assist newcomers. This welcoming function may be organized by the Chamber of Commerce, synagogues and churches, civic organizations, school districts, and local governments. Local Web sites hosted by newspaper or government entities often include a section for newcomers. Encourage clients to look for these resources.

Applying the Roles Framework

Role Loss

Downsizing or moving to a newer home may lead to role loss as less home maintenance is required. In addition, many veteran couples describe the childraising years as the most challenging but also the most gratifying period of a long marriage. Midlife relocation symbolizes the beginning of a new relational era, but it is also signals the closure of another. Nothing signals the end of active parenting more decisively than closing the front door of the family home and turning over the keys to a new owner. Your clients may need assistance in recognizing the feelings of signs grief that accompany a midlife move.

WORKING WITH CLIENTS

This section provides a concise summary of the actions you can take in helping your clients through a midlife relocation. Clients may need your assistance with one or more of these 10 moving tasks.

Review Motives

Encourage clients to articulate their reasons for wanting to move. Listen for unexpressed motives (see the list presented earlier). Help partners give voice to their reservations. Help the partners identify points of agreement and disagreement.

Probe Beliefs

Encourage clients to examine their beliefs about moving. What do they believe to be true about their current living situation, and how would a new one be similar and different? What hardships and opportunities do they anticipate? Are these grounded in realistic information? Strongly held assumptions about moving may be the result of previous hardships. Some individuals may be slow to adjust to change. Others have experienced culture shock, depression, or physical illness after a previous relocation, but past experience may not apply well to current circumstances. Unfounded beliefs should be explored. For example, a reluctant mover may be operating on the false assumption that a relocation must be permanent, when in reality, their partner is open to the possibility of moving again.

Inventory Advantages/Disadvantages

Sometimes clients need reminders of time-tested strategies. The act of recording an inventory of the advantages and disadvantages of a potential move, or one location versus another is often enough to illuminate the obvious. Encourage your clients to compile this list and incorporate the results in a session with you.

Check for Realistic Expectations
(Financial, Social, Health)

A reality check can be emotionally threatening, but it is vital. You can support the couple as they review their financial situation, social needs, and health. An accurate evaluation of the financial implications of relocation is necessary, but too often neglected. Many couples will benefit from the help of an impartial financial advisor. A variety of helpful books and Web-based resources are presented in Appendix A. Honest financial discussions can provoke feelings of disappointment, frustration, and even blame, so your support is imperative. The couple's social needs should be assessed. Will they leave friends? Do they make friends easily? Are they willing to be more open to establishing social networks? What are their expectations for social activities? Health should be considered as well. Although moving can be exhilarating, it is no secret that movers endure temporary periods of substantial stress. Alternately, a desire for a healthier lifestyle may inspire a move. This may be to reduce stress or to be closer to outdoor activities.

Are Old Plans Right for New Circumstances?

After checking for realistic expectations, clients will have a clearer idea about merging their dreams with their current situations. Most couples will spend years or decades dreaming about the future they envision for themselves. Some will be fortunate and fulfill these dreams. However, many will encounter unanticipated circumstances and be forced to make adjustments. For some, this means accepting more modest changes in their current circumstances. A major task for counselors at this point is to help clients reconcile their dreams with reality.

Assess Relational Impacts

Throughout this chapter we have described relocation as a relational process. You can help clients examine how the process of moving is adding to, or subtracting from, the quality of their relationships. Is it a source of energy, creativity, and collaboration? Or is the couple bothered by chronic conflict, fatiguing stress, and financial worry. Will moving to a new home isolate one of the partners? Exacerbate current feelings of frustration or dissatisfaction? Will moving provide new and interesting sources of conversation and social connection or simply yield intolerable levels of anxiety? In counseling sessions, you can help the couple identify how their communication processes are aggravating or assuaging the stress associated with relocation. A central task is to help clients visualize how their relationship will change and stay the same if a move is to be made.

Managing Uncertainty: Developing and Monitoring Plans

"Overwhelmed" is a term frequently used by mid life movers. Indeed, a tremendous amount of uncertainty is generated by relocation. The development of an action plan that identifies key tasks, partner responsibilities, completion targets, and sources of assistance is useful in managing uncertainty and associated stress. For example, clients may identify the steps that would be needed to prepare their current house for sale, to include interviewing realtors, identifying needed house repairs, and researching recent sales in the neighborhood. Use counseling sessions to review clients' action plans and make adjustments.

CONCLUDING THOUGHTS

For many couples, the family home is a haven. It is where children are nurtured, memories are made, stories are told, and family bonds are sustained over many years. It is not surprising then that relocation, a literal abandonment of the "empty nest," is a time of ambivalence for some couples. From our own research, we are convinced that, when not handled with care, relocation can be a source of relational distress rather than inspiration. However, more often than not, relocation is an important symbolic move for the midlife couple—one that ultimately launches a new and positive phase of married life. Finding a new home, together, is a concrete way for couples to move their marriage back to centerstage.

QUESTIONS FOR CLIENTS

1 How would you describe your current stage of relocation? (Review Box 7.2 in this chapter.)
2 What are your motives for moving? Are your partner's similar or different?
3 How committed are you to moving? Would you consider staying and remodeling? Why or why not?

4   How will the move affect existing friend and family relationships?

5   How will the move affect you and your partner differently? Have you fully explored these differential effects?

6   Do you work well together as a couple when handling major transitions? Provide an example. How can lessons from the past apply now?

7   Describe the types of support you would like during relocation or remodeling. Have you consulted with enough friends, experts, and advisors to really know what your move entails?

8   Is your financial plan for moving/remodeling your home realistic? Why do you think so?

9   Describe how the relocation/remodel might affect each of your roles in the family? Are these role shifts short- or long-termed?

EXERCISES

Exercise 7.1 Stages of Relocation: Where Are You in the Process?

The goal of this exercise is for you to realize where you are in the process of relocation.

Which of the stages listed below best identifies your experience at this point?

1   How long have you been in this stage? How close you are to moving on to the following stage?

2   What have been the benefits of this stage? The drawbacks?

Try to anticipate your strengths (and potential weaknesses) in the next stage.

Stages of Relocation:

Dreaming: We are dreaming about the possibilities of moving; excited about experiencing something new and moving on from the child-drearing years. Some worries about leaving the house in which we raised our children.

Negotiating: As a couple we've begun to talk about what it would really be like to move. We're figuring out what's realistic in terms of what each of us would ideally want in a move. We've experienced some minor conflict in deciding what's most important when relocating.

Planning: We've begun to research our options and make a plan. We've looked at the housing markets of interest to us and had our house assessed for its current value. We're beginning to manage many details of the project. "Reality" is causing some stress. Actual planning is exciting. We've found a realtor or put the house up for sale on our own.

Committing: We've committed financially. We're spending money on home fix ups or down payment. We may have signed papers on the new house or sold our current house. "We're committed!" We have some feelings of regret and anxiousness over being financially committed. It also feels good to be making progress.

Settling: We're starting to make a new home. We're packing and unpacking. We're finding "surprises" in the new home. Friends are helping with the move, but we're experiencing some "goodbyes" with them. Uncertainty in the new neighborhood is high (Where to shop? Where are the parks? Where do I get my oil changed? How do I find local churches/synagogues?). We're clinging to each other in this new environment, but there has been some conflict as well.

Integrating: We've found some ways to get involved in our new community. We're depending on each other, but we've met some neighbors and made new friends in the neighborhood or at work. We've found some new favorite restaurants and have begun some of the new activities that were part of our motivation for moving.

Exercise 7.2 Identifying Sources of Distress

The goal of this exercise is to understand feelings of anxiety. After identifying source(s) of distress from the following descriptions, talk, as a couple, about how to best help each other manage these perceived obstacles.

1   *Differing Motives*: You and your spouse differ as to why you want to relocate (or remodel).
   ■ Look for ways to collaborate. Try to embrace each person's desires.
2   *Unrealistic Expectations*: You and your spouse have set your expectations in a way that leaves very little chance for fulfillment.
   ■ Rather than giving up your dreams, set intermediate goals that are more achievable.

3 *Personality Differences*: As marriage partners you vary in your openness to change.
- For the person who struggles with change, talk about ways s/he can feel more secure in the move.

4 *Autocratic Decision Making*: Ask yourselves, honestly, to what extent the relocation is a decision that has been made together.
- If the decision has been mostly one sided, discuss how it can be made more democratic.

5 *Loss of Friends*: To what extent will moving result in the loss of friends who provide emotional support?
- Discuss ways to maintain that support during the relocation transition.

6 *Moving Closer to Families of Origin*: What are the potential stressors of moving closer to family?
- Discus how you can keep your marriage a priority when closer to parents, sisters, siblings, etc.

7 *Increased Closeness*: Will the move give you more "couple time" than what you're used to?
- Discuss ways to make this increased togetherness enjoyable for you both. Also, plan ways each of you can maintain your own independent interests.

8 *Financial Stress*: To what extent is moving going to create short-term financial stress?
- Create a budget that provides security during this time of transition.

9 *Separation*: Is being apart for significant times adding stress to your thoughts about this transition?
- Discuss how you can maintain good communication and emotional closeness during the times of separation.

10 *Culture Shock*: To what extent is either of you experiencing culture shock at being in a new neighborhood/city?
- Discuss how to take advantage of new opportunities and maintain some of your more meaningful traditions.

Exercise 7.3 Handling Role Loss

The goal of this exercise is to identify key roles that might be lost or changed during your move.

1   Brainstorm roles that both of you play that are linked to your current residence. For example, if you have a large yard, mowing and trimming is a duty one or both of you must take care of.

2   Next, discuss how important each role is in terms of each partner's personal satisfaction and identity.

3   Now that you've discussed each role's importance, imagine how the role might or might not change with relocation or remodeling (perhaps the new house is a patio home requiring much less yard work).

4   Finally, think through how each role that has been positive, or significant in your life, can be managed in your new home. For example, container gardens in your new patio home may satisfy the urge to garden.

Exercise 7.4 Family and Friendship Impact

The goal of this exercise is to think how key family and friend relationships can be maintained during and after relocation.

1   Begin by making a list of family and friend relationships that provide emotional support for you or your spouse.

2   Next, brainstorm ways that each relationship can be maintained after the move. For example, video chatting may work for staying in touch with your 24 year-old daughter, while bi-annual weekend retreats with friends might maintain key friendships.

Exercise 7.5 Developing an Action Plan

The goal of this exercise is to reduce stress by creating a plan for your current stage of relocation.

1   *Key Tasks*: List key tasks to be accomplished in the short term (within 1 week) or long-term (within the next month).

2   *Partner Responsibilities*: Identify the partner responsible for each task.

3   *Completion Targets*: Select realistic completion target dates for each task.

4 *Sources of Assistance*: Identify available resources for the completion of each task.
- *External Resources*: (e.g., friends, family, finances, community organizations)
- *Internal Resources*: (e.g., the ability to organize and plan, the ability to manage change, optimism)

REFERENCES

Adams, K. (1994). *Moving: A complete checklist and guide for relocation*. San Diego: Silvercast Publications.

Halford, W., & Markman, H. (1997). *Clinical handbook of marriage and couples interventions*. New York: John Wiley & Sons.

Hess, M. & Linderman, P. (2002). *The expert expatriate: Your guide to successful relocation abroad*. Boston: Nicholas Brealey Publishing.

Klopf, D. (2001). *Intercultural encounters: The fundamentals of intercultural communication*. Englewood, CO: Morton Publishing Company.

Levine, L. (1998). *Will this place ever feel like home? Simple advice for settling in after you move*. Chicago: Real Estate Education Company.

Montgomery, B., & Baxter, L. (1998). *Dialectical approaches to studying personal relationships*. Mahwah, NJ: Lawrence Erlbaum Associates, Publishers.

Reliable relocation. *Complete relocation services* [data file]. Retrieved November 17, 2008, from http://www.reliablerelocation.com

Steinberg, L. (2002). Children and parenting. In Bornstein, M. (Ed.), *Handbook of parenting* (Vol. 1). Bethesda, MD: Wiley Publishers.

Wallerstein, J., & Blakeslee, S. (1995). *The good marriage: How and why love lasts*. Boston: Houghton Mifflin Company.

8   Illness and Caregiving

Ray and Carolyn were in their early 50s when a series of misfortunes occurred. Married for 28 years, with three adult daughters and two grandkids, life was "just calming down" when Ray was diagnosed with prostate cancer. Not a year after, Carolyn's widowed father fell and broke his hip. An only daughter, Carolyn became his primary caretaker as he recovered in their home. To complicate matters, during the same year, a granddaughter was diagnosed with a serious congenital kidney problem. Her surgery and subsequent recovery stretched the limited financial and emotional resources of her young parents. Ray and Carolyn felt obligated to help out as best they could. Exhausted, and at times irritable, the couple described this period as an important turning point in their long relationship. Although proud of the strength they found in each other, Carolyn and Ray also became more cognizant of the need to set limits. With the help of a counselor, they realized that the burdens of illness and caregiving had changed the dynamics of their relationship in ways that left them feeling resentful and dissatisfied. The couple pledged to move the health of the marriage to the top of their priority list.

The caregiving challenges faced by Ray and Carolyn are typical of those experienced at midlife, although the close timing of the three crises was certainly unfortunate. Midlife is a time when potentially life-altering diseases are more likely to be diagnosed. Cancers of the colon, breast, and prostate are examples. Chronic health problems like hypertension and diabetes may require intervention and management. In addition, health incidents like stroke and heart attack can disrupt the lives of middle-aged persons. Serious illnesses change roles for both partners, disrupt familiar patterns of interaction, and alter plans for the future. Feelings of uncertainty, fear, and guilt can replace the comfort and confidence that might otherwise prevail in a veteran marriage. In weaker marriages, the experience of illness can expose and magnify existing problems.

When couples tell us the story of their relationships, we certainly hear about the disruptive and taxing effects of illness, but we also hear stories of adaptation and resilience. Indeed, it is important for clients to know that that couples who make middle-aged adjustments in health practices can partially "turn back the clock," decreasing the likelihood that they will be hampered by life threatening illnesses, such as cardiovascular disease (see Box 8.1). Moreover, for many midlife couples the challenges

---

BOX 8.1 HOW DO I USE IT? THE "TURNING BACK THE CLOCK" STUDY

A recent medical study is useful in convincing midlife couples to adopt healthy lifestyle practices as a way to lower risk of mortality and rates of heart disease (King, Manous, & Geesey, 2007). For 6 years the researchers followed a cohort of 15,700 participants aged 45 to 64, measuring lifestyle variables of (1) eating 5 daily servings of fruit and vegetables, (2) body mass index, (3) regular exercise, and (4) smoking. Participants who adopted healthy habits showed statistically significant reductions in disease when assessed 6 years later. The results have implications for those who counsel middle-aged persons, including:

- *Healthy lifestyles are rare*: Only 8.5% of participants engaged in the four healthy practices at the time of study initiation, and an additional 8.4% adopted the habits during the 6 year study period.
- *Adopting new habits pays off*: Only 2.5% of adopters died in the next 4 years (vs. 4.2% for nonadopters). The statistical difference for heart disease was greater (11.7% vs. 16.5%).
- *Some clients need more encouragement*: Some subpopulations were less likely to adopt healthy lifestyles on their own: Males, African Americans, those of lower socioeconomic status, and those with hypertension and diabetes.

of illness yield improved collaboration, mutual admiration, and for both partners, an enlarged repertoire of relational roles. This was eventually the case with Ray and Carolyn, who consider their relationship stronger for having weathered a series of difficult health changes.

As the opening narrative reveals, illness can pressure a midlife marriage along several fronts. The first of these involves an illness of one or both partners. Debilitating illness can have disturbing effects on the victim, who experiences an unfamiliar sense of vulnerability, impotence, and dependence. The spouse adopts the role of caretaker, which often requires a bewildering set of practical skills, new forms of communication, and a deep reservoir of patience. Caregiving can be deeply rewarding, but it is also time-consuming, emotionally draining, and sometimes exasperating. Caretakers often feel "invisible" as the ill spouse becomes the center of attention for family members and service providers.

In addition to managing their own illnesses, couples respond to the health crises of family members, as Carolyn did when her father broke his hip. Midlife couples often feel obligated to care for parents and other elders, and they are counted on by their families to do so. Although they often possess the maturity, resources, and sense of family commitment needed in these situations, parental caregiving responsibilities create stress for even the most well-adjusted midlife couples. This stress can be magnified by cultural and gender norms (Yarry, Stevens, & McCallum, 2007). Often, women are compelled to play primary caregiving roles. As the only daughter in a traditional Hispanic family, it was Carolyn who felt a strong obligation to care for her injured father.

Although offspring may no longer be present in the family home, they can be a source of worry for some midlife clients. When adult children or grandchildren become seriously ill, parents may be called on for assistance. Ray and Carolyn learned that medical insurance failed to cover some costs of their grandchild's surgery. They quickly offered financial assistance from their own savings. When the sick child's parents exhausted their own vacation and sick leave, Ray and Carolyn used their own vacation time to care for her during the day. Of course, most midlife couples provide this support willingly and generously, finding satisfaction in their capacity to provide vital help to their offspring. But when combined with other midlife challenges, these health events can be a source of discord for centerstage spouses, who may disagree over the amount, type, and duration of support that should be provided.

These first paragraphs paint a picture of the harried, overtaxed midlife couple, squeezed by their own health needs and those of older and younger generations. In fact, much has been made in the popular media about the "sandwiched generation"—parents who are caring for adolescents and older parents at the same time. This complex set of caregiving tasks can be psychologically demanding, but it can also be fulfilling when the necessary assistance is available (Williams & Nussbaum, 2001). In reality, sandwiching is rare (Himes, 1994), in part because older persons are living longer, healthier, and more independent lives. Nonetheless, the new wave of longer living elders will need family assistance as they manage the effects of arthritis, type 2 diabetes, glaucoma, hypertension, and cardiovascular disease.

Despite the limited evidence for the traditional sandwich effect, demographic trends are increasing intergenerational caregiving pressures. One of these is the increased dependence of adult children on parental support. Due to a host of cultural, educational, and economic changes, young adults often remain closely tied to their parents well beyond the teen years (see chapter 6). The high rate of birth for single parents is another such trend. Lacking the support of a spouse, young mothers and fathers are more likely to call on their parents when health crises arise. These trends have the effect of lengthening and intensifying the period when midlife parents serve as primary sources of support for their offspring. One consequence is that the "gap" between the end of primary parenting responsibilities and assumption of caregiving responsibilities for elders may shrink. The upshot is that therapists will see more clients who are struggling with this somewhat different, but still demanding, kind of sandwich effect.

This chapter examines how these illness and caregiving challenges influence the relationships of centerstage couples. As in earlier chapters, we first consider sources of marital distress. Next, we apply three analytic frameworks to help professionals interpret the illness-related concerns of midstage couples. The third section presents tasks for clients to complete in therapy or by themselves. The chapter ends with exercises. Resources are found in Appendix A.

SOURCES OF DISTRESS

Midlife illness can cause serious distress for clients, disrupting their marriages, and burdening their spouses, who often serve as primary caretakers. Here we examine some of the more widely reported problems by couples in our studies.

Effects on the Ill Partner

In addition to the obvious physiological effects, including discomfort and limitations on activity, illness causes additional kinds of distress for midlife clients. Counselors and other mental health professionals can help clients articulate these concerns.

Identity Threat

A serious health event, like a heart attack, can threaten a client's sense of self. Phil was a 45-year-old basketball playing "weekend warrior" when he had his first heart attack. He was happy to survive a close call, but Phil soon grew despondent at the loss of his "athletic self," an identity he had been comfortable with since youth. For some clients, midlife illness is a revelation. It marks the end of youth and the beginning of vulnerability. Phil became more cognizant of his hard-charging approach to everything in life—work, sports, and relationships. He realized that the identity that had served him so well might be less optimal at midlife. With the help of his spouse and a therapist, Phil experimented with a new outlook—one which valued moderation and health as much as hard work and achievement.

Unfamiliar Dependence

Illness makes a person dependent. This is unsettling for clients (and their spouses) who are used to controlling their own lives, and the lives of others. Some express feelings of helplessness, frustration, and even humiliation. They may need assistance in developing a graceful approach to illness, one that recognizes that some of life's happenings are beyond individual control. Learning to trust others, to ask for and accept help from the spouse, to be adaptable in the face of changing circumstances— these are some of the lessons learned from illness.

Fear of the Unknown

When a client is diagnosed with cancer or a spouse experiences a stroke, they often report high levels of uncertainty and fear of the unknown.

One obvious set of uncertainties involves the physical effects of disease, but other questions concern the broader relational implications. How will this illness affect my role in the family? My marriage? My ability to work and provide? Still more questions concern recovery. How long will I feel this way? Will the disease recur? Clients may express fear of mortality as they confront the inevitability of death, sometimes for the first time. Counseling can help distressed couples manage uncertainty, enhance feelings of self-efficacy, and develop fear-reduction strategies. For example, a client who faces a job loss due to a debilitating illness may need assistance in imagining a new career and its potential benefits. Other clients are made frustrated or helpless by the medical bureaucracy. You can help them develop the assertiveness and communication skills they need when interacting with doctors and insurance companies.

Loss

Illness related distress is sometimes driven by loss or anticipation of loss. Clients may not realize the significance of these feelings or recognize them as signs of grief. For example, midlife men faced with prostate cancer weigh the loss of sexual function in their deliberation over treatment options. The potential loss of sexual intimacy can weigh heavily on them. Other clients struggle with illness-induced job losses, as well as diminishing social interactions, daily activities, and leisure pursuits. You can help clients grieve these losses, cope with them, and find alternative sources of life satisfaction.

BOX 8.2 HOW CAN I USE IT? WHAT THERAPISTS CAN DO TO HELP CLIENTS STRUGGLING WITH ILLNESS

- Help recognize feelings of uncertainty and fear
- Assist in the process of identity adaptation and expansion
- Facilitate the process of grieving illness-related losses
- Help locate graceful, flexible, and hopeful responses to changed circumstances
- Connect clients with disease-specific resources and support systems
- Develop constructive communication practices for interactions with medical professionals and caretaker spouse

---

Disruption of Key Marital Functions

Marriage serves a variety of important functions, including collaboration, companionship, support, intimacy, and self-continuity (Rosowsky, 2007). Serious illness threatens one or more of these. Consider Melody (age 46) and her husband Jack (age 44), a couple who for 2 decades shared a passion for vigorous outdoor activities like mountain biking, hiking, and kayaking. The pursuit of these sports formed the core of the family vacations they enjoyed with their two children. Their mutual friends were drawn from hiking clubs and other organizations of like-minded outdoor enthusiasts. On one particularly challenging trail ride, Melody's bike slipped off the trail and caromed down a steep, rocky slope. She survived the crash but sustained a serious concussion, broken ribs, and fractured ankle.

During the recovery period, Melody could not drive and was forced to use crutches. A fiercely independent person, Melody was now reliant on her family for such basic needs as transportation, meal preparation, and even bathing. She appreciated Jack's support, but Melody grew impatient with the slow rate of her recovery and worried that the fractures would not heal properly. Melody feared that resuming her previous activities could lead to another serious injury. She felt isolated from friends. As the months passed, Melody became depressed, irritable, and obsessed with her body's recovery.

As Jack reported, Melody's injuries disrupted the normal functioning of their marriage for a period of roughly 6 months. His domestic workload increased considerably because previously shared tasks were now his alone. Their social activities were restricted by Melody's physical injuries and her depressed mood. Their sexual relationship was curtailed. Melody's fixation with her recovery made conversation about other topics difficult. During this period, Melody was largely incapable of providing emotional support to others, including her husband. As she became more depressed, Jack became more concerned.

BOX 8.3 FUNCTIONS OF MARRIAGE DISRUPTED BY ILLNESS

- Collaboration: Task sharing and mutual planning
- Companionship: Joint social activity and friendship
- Support: Emotional support, advice, and practical help
- Intimacy: Psychological and sexual closeness
- Self continuity: Identity confirmation and stability

At an intellectual level, Jack recognized that these conditions were temporary. He felt deep compassion for his wife but also reported a range of less positive emotions (see Box 8.4). Nonetheless, he felt puzzled and sometimes disturbed by the changes he saw in Melody and felt compelled to discuss them with friends and eventually his counselor. Jack came to see that, as Melody's closest supporter, he was an easy target for her feelings of blame and frustration. He knew that Melody feared being out of control and recognized her palpable frustration at being so dependent on others. Indeed, the injury reminded both partners of their mortality and vulnerability. To his counselor, Jack expressed guilt for sometimes becoming impatient with his injured wife.

BOX 8.4 WHAT YOU MIGHT HEAR FROM CLIENTS: EMOTIONAL REACTIONS TO A SPOUSE'S SERIOUS ILLNESS

- Resentment at the burdens of caregiving
- Anger over the ill spouse's health practices which contributed to the illness
- Guilt for not meeting (often unrealistic) caregiving expectations
- Grief over the loss of companionship and plans for the future
- Hopelessness in the face of mounting stresses
- Fear of what the future might hold

As do most couples, Jack and Melody recovered from this relatively brief health crisis, but it did prompt them to rethink their relationship. Melody is less willing to engage in risky recreational pursuits, so they are looking for safer activities to share. With her counselor, Melody is reevaluating her need for control. She and Jack recognize how that tendency sometimes creates distance, even mistrust, in their relationship. Jack has come to better appreciate the many domestic tasks that his wife managed without his help. They are redistributing some of the domestic labor in their household. Indeed, an "upside" for many clients is that a health crisis stimulates reassessment and healthy adaptation.

Health of the Caregiver

Most spouses find fulfillment in being a caregiver for an ill spouse. They often take pride in the support provided to a loved one. However, caregiving takes a toll on the caregiver, particularly when the spouse's illness is long and debilitating. Research makes clear that without appropriate support, caregivers may experience fatigue, stress, despair, emotional burnout, and depression (Schmall & Stiehl, 2003). Recent research even suggests that sustained caregiving can undermine the immune systems of caretakers, making them more vulnerable to illness (Damjonavic, 2007). Caretakers experience disruptions in normal sleep, work, social interactions, and leisure schedules. The clear message is that even the most gifted and emotionally hardy caretakers require respite and support.

Mental health professionals can help midlife clients recognize some of the less obvious ways that the illness of a spouse disrupts, or potentially disrupts, their lives (see Box 8.5). In some cases, clients decline to seek assistance to avoid self-perceptions of failure. Others are unwilling to "abandon" caregiving responsibilities to third parties. It is important to help clients see that self-care is a key to being an effective caregiver. This involves teaching clients to develop strategies for acquiring help from family members. For example, siblings who are unable or unwilling to provide "hands-on" help with parental caregiving can be asked to support the costs of purchasing that assistance, so the tasks do not all become the responsibility of the sibling who is providing care.

BOX 8.5 HELPING CLIENTS RECOGNIZE POTENTIALLY DISRUPTIVE EFFECTS OF ILLNESS AND CAREGIVING

- Expanded responsibility for domestic tasks (housekeeping, finances, correspondence)
- Reduced time for social interactions with friends and family
- Interference with the quantity and quality of work
- Increased time spent on medical appointments, transportation, and insurance matters
- Health effects: Fatigue, vulnerability to illness, and emotional exhaustion
- Degraded communication: Limited topics, irritability, and increased conflict
- Loss of physical intimacy
- Conflicting demands from employer, family, and relatives
- Increased financial stress

Caregiving spouses may be unaware of the formal and informal resources available to them. Professionals can assist clients in locating community agencies and services. Strategies for negotiating assistance from family members can be suggested and practiced in therapy. Clients may also need assistance in developing constructive strategies for coping with stress (see *Working with Clients*, below).

Loss of Financial Resources

Some clients will be stressed by the tangible side effects of illness, including loss of income. A client who practices a trade, that involves physical labor—a carpenter or bricklayer—may be forced by a heart condition to accept a job at a lower rate of pay.

In addition to creating a loss of work identity, this kind of change can increase pressure on the spouse to generate more income. A stroke could interrupt or end the career of an accountant or teacher, disrupting a couple's income stream and forcing adjustments in lifestyle. For many couples, including those with decent incomes, illness can transform a relatively comfortable life to a financially precarious one (Newman & Chen, 2007). Even clients who are insured may struggle to pay large medical bills for themselves, their children, or their parents. Of course, financial strains can pressure couples who previously handled their finances well. These clients need assistance with understanding how financial pressures are contributing to marital discord. They may benefit from community services, which help families in crises. Assistance with managing health-related expenses and negotiating with the medical bureaucracy may be useful as well. In some cases, the income-reducing medical problem of one spouse prompts a career change in the other. Victoria and Tim adapted to illness in that way.

BOX 8.6 VICTORIA AND TIM: A CASE STUDY IN ADAPTATION TO ILLNESS

"I think being able to change and accept change is fundamental to a good marriage," said Tim, who describes himself as a methodical lover of structure. As a young man, Tim's good friend Victoria encouraged him to be more flexible, urging Tim to move out of his family's home and cheering his desire to become an amateur pilot. Victoria found his new adventuresome streak very appealing, and despite some obvious differences in personality, they eventually wed. The couple faced a serious financial hurdle after 2 decades of "uneventful marriage." Tim was exposed to an industrial chemical that damaged his lungs and forced him to leave a lucrative engineering job. After an initial period of confusion, the couple collaborated on a new financial plan, featuring a return to the workforce by Victoria and a less vigorous part-time consulting role for Tim. Just 5 years later, it was Victoria who was diagnosed with cancer and the pattern was reversed. Tim returned to a "regular job," partly for the insurance benefits. Models of resilience, Victoria and Tim overcame and met the financial effects of illness with flexibility, collaboration, and creativity.

Cultural Expectations

Clients' values and expectations concerning illness and caregiving are shaped by culture and gender. Culturally competent service providers are sensitive to these differences and tailor their helping effort to the clients' cultural realties. Indeed, coping strategies are most useful when they are responsive to cultural values. Some caregiving approaches accepted in the cultural mainstream (e.g., moving a parent to an assisted living facility) will be repugnant to certain minority clients. In the United States, cultural difference have been observed in the caregiving practices of European Americans and the minority populations of Hispanic, African, Asian, and Native Americans. Table 8.1 identifies differences in values and expectations that might vary based on culture. Of course, cultural variation is also observed between these minority groups and within any given subpopulation. Additional culture-specific information is found in the *Resources* section in Appendix A.

One pervasive cultural difference is the value placed on familism, which involves loyalty to, and reciprocity within, the extended family. Familism tends to be weaker among European American clients and particularly strong in clients of Hispanic, Asian, or Native American origin. One consequence is that spouses in minority families may be less inclined to seek help from formal social services when caring for an ill partner. Instead, spouses and family members may feel a strong obligation to provide such help. African American clients may be influenced by the important supportive roles played by members of the extended family, including grandparents and "fictive kin" (family friends who assume

Table 8.1

POTENTIAL CULTURAL DIFFERENCES RELATED TO ILLNESS AND CAREGIVING

- Willingness to use formal social support services
- Expectation that female family members will be caretakers
- Respect for the authority of medical professionals
- Preference for traditional forms of healing
- Expectation that parents will be cared for by children
- Role of extended family in caregiving and responsibility to care for extended family.
- Contributions of fictive kin
- Preference of "emotion-focused" caregiving strategies
- Belief in illness as "God's will"
- Role of prayer and religious community in caregiving

family support roles). Among some populations, for example traditional Hispanics, daughters and other female relatives are strongly identified with caregiving roles. Because of exploitative practices of the past, some minority clients will be suspicious of government services and medical authorities. They may prefer traditional forms of medicine and culturally familiar sources of advice and support.

Culturally competent therapists can help clients develop coping strategies that are realistic within their cultural milieu (Yarry et al., 2007). You can help clients understand how conflicts between personal needs and cultural expectations are causing feelings of guilt or inadequacy. A client who is feeling isolated may appreciate your suggestions for culturally appropriate sources of social support, such as a community center serving his or her ethnic community (for examples, see *Resources in* Appendix A). When cultural values discourage overt expression of conflict between a caregiver and care recipient, you can suggest other forms of communication (e.g., intervention by an elder or religious leader). For traditional female caretakers, psychological coping strategies, which help caretakers create positive emotions (such as storytelling or imagining an improved future), may be more feasible than requesting help from family members. Finally, it is important to recognize that traditional response to illness and caregiving may vary by degree of assimilation, leading to significant tensions among generations of the same cultural group.

BOX 8.7 HOW DO I USE IT?

Culturally competent practices for service providers (Yarry et al., 2007)

- Be comfortable asking about cultural values
- Explore cultural and family meanings of caregiving; assess generational differences
- Suspend dominant culture expectations (e.g., regarding gender equality in caregiving)
- Explore the role of religious beliefs in client coping
- Help the client identify tensions among personal needs and cultural expectations
- Connect the client with culturally appropriate resources and services
- Help clients develop tactics for managing family expectations and conflicts
- Suggest culturally appropriate coping strategies (e.g., elder intervention, emotion focused)

ANALYTICAL TOOLS

Illness leads to a variety of conflicted feelings and opposing relational forces, some of which are revealed in the discourse used by midlife clients. By listening for these relational dialectics, counselors develop insights about how the effects of illness are shaping marital interactions. In this section, we review some of the more commonly expressed dialectical tensions. We also examine how resilience and role concepts can be useful in helping clients understand the relational impact of a health crisis.

Applying the Dialectical Framework

When describing the more challenging episodes in their long relationship, veteran couples sometimes reference periods of illness (Waldron & Kelley, 2008). The dialectical tensions described below express the ambivalent feelings couples reported in interviews with our research team. In therapy, the discourse used by couples or individual partners provide clues about these underlying struggles. Labeling these dialectical tensions provides clients with a way to "make sense" of emotions and recurring patterns of interaction. Ultimately, the counselor can help clients manage oppositional tendencies that may be pulling them apart during a crucial time in the marriage.

Compassion versus Blame

For care providers, expressions of concern conflict with a sense that the ill partner is partly to blame for his or her illness. The care recipient may express feelings of regret even as he or she expresses resentment at "blame the victim" implications.

Hope versus Despair

The partners alternate between hoping for future improvement and despairing that what has been lost will not be regained. Hope is expressed in assurances and plans for the future. Discourse about unexpectedly slow recovery and lost capacities is associated with despair.

Autonomy versus Interdependence

The ill partner acknowledges a new dependence on others, including the spouse. Couples often embrace this interdependence with terms like "teamwork." Yet, both partners are likely to chafe at new restrictions on their autonomy and a diminished capacity to control their own lives. Marital discourse may reflect the caretaker's need for respite. In contrast, the care recipient may resent what feels like excessive intrusion or, conversely, he or she may express excessive dependency on the spouse.

Duty versus Affection

Spouses are sometimes troubled by a sense that caregiving is being performed out of obligation rather than love. In practice, obligation and love are typically copresent motivations for caregiving. Partners may regret the loss of intimacy that accompanies the transition to caretaker–care recipient relationship. The ill partner may both appreciate and resent being treated as a "patient." Both partners may express longings for more "normal" patterns of interaction.

Openness versus Protectiveness

Illness stresses and fatigues both parties, increasing the odds of irritability, rudeness, and tactless criticism. Frustrated caregivers may just want to be open about their feelings, to "lay it all out on the table," to "just say what I feel." At the same time, they feel pressured to censor negative speech out of concern for the patients' vulnerability. The ill partner may engage in similar kinds of self-editing out of respect for the caretaker's extraordinary commitment. Others will not exhibit this protective instinct. For them, the misfortune of illness is a license for continuous complaints and bad behavior. Clients who are unsuccessful in managing the openness versus protectiveness dialectic will report increasingly uncomfortable interactions and a growing list of unaddressed grievances. You can help them identify and redress the imbalance.

BOX 8.8 WHAT YOU MIGHT HEAR FROM CLIENTS: THE OPENNESS VERSUS PROTECTIVENESS DIALECTIC

- "She acts like she is walking on eggshells. I may be sick but that doesn't mean I want to be protected from everything that is going on in our lives."
- "He complains all of the time, and I am getting fed up. I am doing the best I can. But I don't want to make things worse by calling him on it."
- "All she talks about is how her body is feeling."
- "It seems like she is blaming *me* for the fact that she is sick. I resent that and it hurts."
- "I feel like we are afraid to share our fears about the future and that is creating some distance between us."

Acceptance versus Resistance

A willingness to accept the limitations of the illness may conflict with a commitment to "beat" the disease. However, partners may differ over the extent and timing of medical treatments and the degree to which they should share responsibility for illness management efforts (e.g., changing diets, remembering medicines, engaging in physical therapy).

BOX 8.9 HOW DO I USE IT? STRATEGIES FOR MANAGING THE DIALECTICAL TENSIONS OF ILLNESS

- Identify the source of tension: Help clients recognize feelings of duty and affection
- Choose the constructive side: Explore reasons for hope rather than despair
- Strike a balance: What limitations should be resisted? Which should be accepted?
- Reframe the tension: Caregiving as a choice rather than a restriction
- Seek external resolution: Find a support group for direct expression of hostile feelings

Clients need assistance in recognizing how their enactment of a dialectical tension might be creating such relational difficulties as reduced feelings of intimacy or increased conflict. One approach is to help one or both partners find ways to emphasize the relational "pull" that is most helpful at the current moment. For example, couples faced with a terminal illness may learn to value the time they have together, rather than despairing over the time they will lose. In addition, external mechanisms may be helpful in relieving some dialectical tensions. By joining an appropriate support group, the ill partner is able to vent negative feelings and meet hope-providing role models (see Garstka, McCallion, & Toseland, 2001). Doing so makes it easier for the ill partner to be more polite and hopeful (less direct and despairing) in interactions with the caregiving spouse.

Another strategy is to reframe or redefine the situation in a manner that integrates the opposing relational pulls. The traditional husband who told us that caregiving for his ill wife was a "privilege," was making this kind of move. He originally resisted caregiving chores like cooking, shopping, and cleaning. He had little experience with these tasks and spent considerable time and energy on allocating them to family members or finding paid help. With time, he realized how much effort his wife had invested in these tasks over the years and how his own life had been made easier by her uncomplaining approach to this domestic labor. The insight helped him not only accept these new roles, but also to reframe them as opportunities to pay his respects and express his appreciation. When these tasks were defined as expressions of love, they were easier to accept and resistance no longer made sense.

Applying the Resilience Framework

Marriages and similar relationships can be sources of resilience during health crises (Carpenter & Wingyun, 2007). Therapists can help clients identify and develop the relational resources that will help them and their marriage prevail. See Box 8.10 for examples.

BOX 8.10 DEVELOPING THE HEALTH PROMOTING CAPACITIES OF MARITAL PARTNERS

- *Advocacy:* Help the ill partner articulate questions and concerns to health professionals
- *Information seeking:* Locating health related information in virtual and real formats
- *Advice:* Sharing personal experience and obtaining advice from personal contacts
- *Compliance:* Reminding, monitoring, and encouraging compliance with medical instructions
- *Modeling:* Demonstrating healthy behaviors, including eating, exercise, and stress reduction
- *Emotional support:* Listening; empathy, expressions of concern; assurance about the future
- *Tangible support:* Driving, lifting, cooking, and help with daily activities
- *Financial support:* Defraying costs of insurance, prevention, treatment, drugs, and housing

---

The story of Bonnie and Clay illustrates how the resources of a midlife marriage can be mobilized in response to illness.

Mobilizing Relational Resources: A Case Study

Clay was depressed, but not surprised when medical test revealed that his prostate was in fact cancerous. He had been having symptoms for years, but it was only because of Bonnie's insistence that he had been "religious" about his annual checkups. Fortunately, the cancer was detected early. Clay and Bonnie reviewed the available treatment options, using information she had obtained from websites and a local support group. Her cousin, a practicing urologist was helpful and so were two friends who had weighed the options and chosen surgery over radiation-based treatment. Clay lamented the potential side effects of surgery, including the sexual ones. But Bonnie reminded him that a prostate wasn't necessary for sexual pleasure and assured him that their sex life would continue. At the doctor's office, Bonnie helped her husband remember the many questions he wanted to ask, and at the hospital, she remained in Clay's room, making friends with the nurses and keeping an eye on things as he recovered from the surgery. As Clay recuperated at home, Bonnie drove him to follow-up appointments and monitored his compliance with doctor's instructions. During this period, the couple spent quiet moments savoring their 26 years together and planning for the future.

Bonnie performed most of the health-promoting functions described above. But some clients can be overwhelmed by illness and their partner's reactions to it. Counselors can help by assuring them that concrete actions can be taken to help an ill spouse and making specific suggestions. Although some of the contributions made by a spouse like Bonnie are obvious, others are not. For example, clients might not appreciate the importance of advocacy during a health crisis, when the ill spouse may be feeling overwhelmed or even intimidated. In addition, Bonnie's social network yielded important information and expertise. Her constant presence at Clay's bedside optimized his chances for receiving high quality care by medical staff that are sometimes overloaded with work and information. Her assurances helped him be hopeful about the future.

Applying the Roles Framework

When couples talk about the impact of illness in their marriage, role-related stresses are almost always implicated, even if they are not explicitly labeled. You may hear evidence of the following:

Role Overload

A health crisis spurs the well partner to significantly expand the number of roles he or she performs. The resulting role overload leads to increased stress, fatigue, and sometimes resentment. In many families, women perform more domestic roles than men, including caregiving, kin-keeping, and housekeeping roles. This domestic labor is contributed above and beyond the contributions they make in their (external) work roles, a phenomenon sociologist Arlie Hochschild (1993) famously labeled the "second shift." The illness of a family member can amplify this inequality.

Indeed, many American women, including a woman we will call Christa, are "superproviders," driven to the edge of exhaustion nearly every day.

Christa returned to school recently to complete the bachelor's degree she postponed years ago, when she returned to work full-time to help her family's precarious financial situation. On the day we spoke with her, a typical day, Christa rises early to make breakfast for her family and pack their lunches. As is her habit, she sends a quick and chatty e-mail to her 24-year-old daughter, who is in Germany serving in the military. Christa drops her 17-year-old son at high school (his car is in the shop), then heads to the college campus for morning classes. During a hurried lunch, she phones her father who is recovering from a recent heart attack and calls a pharmacy to check on his prescription. Then, Christa dashes for the computer center where she works a part-time job. At 3:30 P.M. , she leaves to collect her son. After a quick stop at the pharmacy, they head home where Christa makes dinner and, with a barrage of quick phone calls, organizes a holiday picnic for the extended family. Her husband Rick arrives home around dinnertime, and Christa spends most of the meal listening as Rick shares his mixed feelings about terminating one of his employees. Then it is off to the high school Booster Club meeting, where Christa reports for the fund raising committee, then back to the campus library for a study session with fellow students from algebra class.

Should Rick become ill, or one of his parents need care, Christa's already exhausting role commitments will expand further, perhaps to a point of crisis. Superprovider clients like her need help in prioritizing roles, delegating some responsibilities to family members, and "permission" to simply do less.

Role Rigidity

Illness requires flexibility and role adjustment. Unwillingness to give up a role, or at least share it, can be problematic for clients and their families. Examples of role rigidity include caretakers (often women) who refuse to share their caregiving burdens due to feelings of obligation, loyalty, or guilt; "heads of the household" (often men) who insist on remaining in control despite the limitations imposed by illness; and the tendency of some midlife clients to reprise the role of "child" in caregiving interactions with parents, where mature and independent judgment may be needed.

Role Loss

Clients will sometimes describe an unsettled, sad, or anxious feeling when confronted with the loss of a role. In some cases, role loss is a side effect of illness—one that receives less attention than the more obvious physical or financial losses that illness can bring. One example is the loss of sexual identity that can accompany surgery for breast or prostate cancer. As discussed earlier, some illnesses result in loss of a work role. Intensive caregiving sometimes makes it difficult to maintain friendship networks and leisure activities, resulting in the loss of social roles. In each case, an important aspect of a client's identity is threatened by illness.

BOX 8.11 WHAT YOU MIGHT HEAR FROM CLIENTS: ROLE-RELATED CONCERNS

- Exhaustion, hopelessness, or resentment (emotional burnout) due to role overload
- Frustration at the need to compress more roles into less time
- Guilt over failure to meet role expectations of the self or others
- Resistance to the role changes required by illness or caregiving
- Sadness over the loss of valued aspects of identity

WORKING WITH CLIENTS

In this chapter, we have documented some of the many effects of illness and caregiving on midlife marriages. Although we have focused mostly on challenges, we know that most couples learn to cope and many look back on an illness as a stimulus for productive change. Client situations will vary depending on the nature and severity of the illness and the kind of caregiving required. Despite this variety in circumstances, midlife clients often need professional help in completing one of more of these eight coping tasks. See *Appendix* and *Exercises for Clients* for additional ways to help clients with caregiving challenges.

Articulate Meanings and Emotions

A first task is for clients to consider the meanings and emotions associated with illness. Listen for the dialectical tensions described previously. Identify what the illness means to the partners and how it changes or reinforces their relational identity. Try questions such as: *How does the illness affect how your husband sees himself? Does it change the way you view the future of your marriage? How is your communication different now than it was in the past?*

Check for emotional reactions. What emotions do the partners express and which ones are they struggling to articulate? What emotions are they choosing to edit or censor? Consider "negative" reactions such as fear, loss, uncertainty, blame, silence, or sadness. Also look for signs of resilience in the form of hope, determination, expressions of support, planning for the future, and expressions of solidarity.

As suggested earlier, reactions to illness and caregiving are influenced by culture. Ask about how family members and relatives think about the illness. What do they think about its causes, treatments, and the roles played by patients, caregivers, and traditional and untraditional sources of medical care? What experiences has the client had with illness and how is that reflected in the assumptions she or he brings to the role of caregiver or care recipient?

Recognize Personal and Relational Stressors

Clients may not fully recognize the ways illness is causing broader distress in themselves and their marriage. You can help clients recognize changes in interaction patterns, the allocation of time, opportunities for social contact, roles, and relations with extended family members and friends. Distress may be heightened by the coping behaviors of the ill person. Excessive use of alcohol, hostility towards family members, chronic complaining, the use of guilt, and blaming are secondary sources of stress for caretakers. In addition, counseling helps couples understand how illness results in a loss of intimacy and restricted communication patterns. He or she can also help clients devise creative responses to these relational restrictions. For example, to expand the range of conversation beyond medical concerns, a couple might schedule more visits from friends, watch thought provoking films, or read and discuss the same book.

Inventory Sources of Resilience

Counseling can help couples find strength in such sources as their (1) history of overcoming past challenges, (2) capacity to be flexible, (3) supportive friends and family, (4) their tendency to balance each other's weaknesses and strengths, and (5) personal qualities such as determination, creativity, ability to learn, patience, and kindness.

Negotiate Realistic Expectations

Some clients need assistance in identifying the expectations that are driving their behavior. Does an ill client have realistic expectations of the pace of his or her recovery and the degree of help that can be provided by the spouse? Is a caregiving spouse overestimating his or her ability to complete caregiving tasks on top of other responsibilities? What roles and tasks are being given priority? Which are being neglected? What do the care provider and the care recipient believe is normal behavior for their respective roles?

When working with couples who are offering assistance to their parents or adult children, counselors should pursue answers to additional questions. How are the partners influenced by the caregiving assumptions of their extended families? Have these been discussed or just enacted? Are caregiving obligations the source of distress or conflict in the marriage? Are traditional gender norms placing the female spouse in the role of primary or exclusive caretaker? How does that affect her mental outlook, capacity to perform other roles, and willingness to ask for and accept help? Is pressure to reciprocate important in the family and how does it obligate a couple to provide care for relatives and parents? To what extent is caregiving shared by siblings and other family members? How is a couple's commitment to caregiving affecting their commitment to each other, positively and negatively?

You can encourage clients to discuss and agree to limits on caregiving. How much time, money, and effort can they provide to parents and other family members? What signs will indicate that their limits have been exceeded? What kind of help will they need from other family members and how will they negotiate it? When will they seek help from professionals? What community resources will they use to relieve the demands on their personal resources?

Connect With Sources of Support

Clients who are facing illness may need encouragement and direction as they seek emotional support, tangible assistance, and advice. Informal and formal support groups are available to people battling common midlife illnesses (see *Appendix A*). The counselor can help reluctant clients understand how participation in a support group can facilitate such tasks as managing uncertainty, venting emotion, understanding the medical infrastructure, and avoiding isolation. These groups relieve some of the pressures that caretaker spouses feel as the primary or sole source of support.

Clients may have difficulty asking for or accepting support. Some need evidence that such support would be helpful. In addition, some clients believe that asking for help is a troubling sign of failure or weakness. With them, the counselor can explore the possibility that the quality of caregiving may actually improve if the spouse seeks and accepts some aid. Other clients lack the communication skills needed to negotiate with siblings or other relatives. Role playing may prove helpful here, particularly if these interactions are likely to be emotional, as sometimes happens when the caretaker is bitter about the lack of assistance offered thus far or fearful of confrontation.

Practice Unfamiliar Behaviors and Roles

Role reversal is common when illness strikes. Relinquishing familiar roles can be identity threatening. Yet, counseling can help clients accept the necessity of giving up familiar roles and adopting new ones. A stay-at-home spouse may be required to enter the workforce earlier than planned or a working partner may adopt an expanded domestic role. In each case, counselors and other supporters can provide encouragement during what may be an anxiety provoking transition. Therapists can help clients express the loss of control and grief that sometimes accompanies role loss. With regard to the examples just mentioned, the domestic and work roles will no doubt be performed differently by the new occupants. One goal of counseling may be to help clients communicate acceptance by minimizing criticism of the spouse's approach and limiting unsolicited "advice."

Illness and caregiving require spouses to engage in any number of unfamiliar practices. Through counseling, the client can become aware of these and perhaps find opportunities to rehearse them. Some examples:

- Saying "no" to requests for help
- Asking questions of medical professionals
- Defending a caregiving spouse from pressure applied by in-laws and other relatives
- Introducing and developing nonmedical topics of conversation
- Listening patiently to the medical concerns of an ill spouse
- Providing emotional support
- Requesting and accepting help from family members and friends
- Exercising patience during recovery from illness or injury
- Admitting to fears and resentments
- Accepting uncertainty about the future

Practice Self-Care

Service providers should be vigilant in looking for the signs of caretaker stress. They should encourage self-care and make specific suggestions for managing caregiving burdens. The physical and mental health of the caretaker is enhanced by such factors as adequate sleep, exercise, opportunities to express emotions, and time to oneself. Caretakers who sustain other meaningful roles at work, church, or community may be more resilient, particularly if these roles can performed without guilt. Respite services, formal or informal, provide this opportunity by freeing the caretaker's time and assuring that the needs of the ill partner are tended to. For some clients, self-care involves tending to spiritual matters. They are strengthened by prayer, attendance at religious services, and consultation with spiritual leaders.

Tend to the Marriage

As we have made clear, surviving a health crisis can actually strengthen a midlife marriage. But, a serious health problem is one of the midlife events that can threaten the vitality of marriage. Distracted and stressed by the demands of caregiving, partners stop tending to their relationship. Earlier, we documented the potential health benefits of a functioning marriage, so it is obvious that relational neglect undermines this important source of resilience. When clients are too distracted to notice, counselors can direct attention to the health of the marriage. Partners can be encouraged to preserve the relational traditions that sustained them before illness struck. Depending on the illness, these could include weekend dates, long talks over dinner, planning vacations, or time shared with good friends. Friends and family can be enlisted so caregiving spouses can find time for themselves.

Midlife couples need help in anticipating stressors and preserving valued relational qualities, even as they adjust their marriage to new realities. Using the metaphor which guides us throughout this book, counselors can help these couples move their marriage from the periphery back to centerstage.

CONCLUDING THOUGHTS

In this chapter, we have paid relatively little attention to the dynamics of individual diseases, focusing instead on the more generic relational effects of illness and caregiving. This emphasis is consistent with our larger purpose of helping counselors interpret and respond to the commonly reported challenges of midlife marriage. Of course, we do recognize that couples coping with a diagnosis of breast cancer have a different experience than those facing prostate cancer, or those managing chronic illnesses, like diabetes. For that reason, we provide references to disease-specific information in *Appendix A*. Obviously, medical specialists and disease-focused organizations are the most informed sources of health information for couples facing a particular illness. Nonetheless, we believe that the information presented here applies to most of the health problems that challenge midlife couples.

Some of the practices recommend in this relatively lengthy chapter are intentionally brief, because detailed recommendations are developed elsewhere. For example, our suggestions that counselors help spouses become comfortable with new communication behaviors are developed in chapters 2 and 6, respectively. Another example: We mentioned in this chapter that caretakers sometimes find themselves blaming the ill spouse for his or her illness, particularly if the disease could have been prevented by a healthier lifestyle. In such cases, forgiveness, a topic developed in chapter 3, may need to be addressed in therapy.

Negative health events sometimes expose fault lines in a weak marriage. Partners who get by during times of good health and relative stability may lack the communicative and psychological resources needed to manage a medical crisis. For these couples, learning to cope with illness may be the first of an ongoing series of relational adjustments made under the guidance of a counselor. In some cases, health problems are a stimulus for overdue adjustments. Finally, we have emphasized throughout this chapter the importance of communication, community resources, and the acquisition of social support. This partly reflects our own disciplinary biases and our cultural experiences. However, to revisit an earlier discussion, it is important to recognize that these kinds of external help seeking are discouraged or simply considered unnecessary within some family or subcultural contexts. In such cases, those service providers who have contact with caretakers might focus on emotion-focused rather than social or service-based coping (see Yarry et al., 2007). The objective is to help clients feel better about, and cope more effectively with, the situations they face. Emotional relief might come from fulfilling the expectations of one's family, accepting "God's will," emphasizing the positive aspects of the present and future, and avoiding negative rumination. These too can be important sources of resilience as clients grapple with the challenges of midlife.

QUESTIONS FOR CLIENTS

1   What are the challenging and rewarding aspects of caring for your partner?
2   How has the illness affected your relationship? Does it change the topics of conversation or the way you talk?
3   How has illness affected your individual identity? Have you discussed this with others?
4   In what ways do you feel you are collaborating with your partner in response to the illness? Describe ways in which you feel the two of you have adapted.

5 Does the caregiving partner have time for self care? Does he or she have time to spend with friends? Has he or she considered joining an illness-specific support group?

6 What would make your daily life less hectic? Help with laundry and household chores? Errand running? Having meals prepared? Have you considered investing in domestic help to ease this burden?

7 Who is included in your support system? Professionals? Church networks? Clergy? Family? Friends? Domestic help? How is caring for elderly parents and/or your adult children compounding your own health challenges?

8 What are your fears associated with being ill or caring for your ill partner? Have you discussed them?

9 Describe your interactions with the health care system. What is working and what is frustrating you? What communication strategies do you need to learn? What help could you find among your experienced friends?

EXERCISES

Exercise 8.1 Movie Night

The goal of this exercise is to think about illness and its effects on marital relationships by watching a film that shows positive and/or negative examples of couples' responses to illness.

Watch a film (see suggestions below) with an illness theme. Take notes on what you think are the most important illness-related concepts. Discuss with your partner.

- How do partners communicate their feelings (fear, frustration, sadness, anger, gratitude, joy) regarding illness and caregiving? Discuss the variety and sources of these feelings.
- Do the partners adjust their roles to accommodate the illness? How?
- How do they communicate with doctors and medical professionals? Could they do it better?

- Where do the couples find emotional support? Are friends and family helpful? Would yours be helpful? How?
- How do the couples find joy and intimacy during times of illness?
- How do the caregivers in the film find relief?

Recommended films

- *Philadelphia Story*—Homosexual couple battles prejudice and health deterioration of HIV.
- *The Notebook*—Depicts a couple facing the challenge of Alzheimer's Disease.
- *The Family Stone*—Loving, vibrant family and couple face breast cancer.

Exercise 8.2 Build on Past Successes

The goal of this exercise is to use your past experiences to help you respond to current illness.

Reflect on times in your marriage when one partner provided short-term care for the other. This may have been after a surgery, during pregnancy (bed resting, postpartum), or a time when one partner had the flu.

- What feelings are evoked by this experience?
- How did it feel to be the dependent partner? The caregiver?
- Did this experience strengthen the bond between you or stress your marriage? Explain.
- What did you learn?

Exercise 8.3 Learning from Those Around You

The goal of this exercise is to learn from friends and family who have dealt with long-term illness.

1   Describe an instance (or instances) when you have witnessed another couple engage the challenge of serious illness and caregiving.
2   What strengths did they display?
3   What behaviors seemed most supportive or helpful? Least supportive or helpful?
4   Which traits and behaviors do you hope to emulate or avoid?

Exercise 8.4 Identifying Sources of Distress

The goal of this exercise is to discuss sources of distress that may accompany long-term illness.

> Talk as a couple about the following issues. Focus on understanding your partner's experience.
> To what extent does the ill partner struggle with the following issues?
>
> - Identity threat (I am frustrated at not being the person I once was.)
> - Increased dependence (I find it difficult to accept help.)
> - Fear of the unknown (I am anxious about issues such as finances and when I'll be able to return to work.)
> - Loss (I am afraid the illness will impact our sexual relationship, leisure activities, or social connections).
>
> To what extent is the caregiver struggling with the following issues?
>
> - Expanded responsibility (I feel overwhelmed with having to pick up new responsibilities).
> - Loss of social support (I have had less time with friends and family).
> - Fatigue (I'm tired emotionally and physically).
> - Changes in intimacy (I miss being able to confide in my spouse or be physically intimate).

REFERENCES

Carpenter, B. D., & Wingyun, M. (2007). Caregiving couples: Have service providers learned how to help? *Generations, 31,* 47–53.

Damjanovic, A. K. (2007). Accelerated telomere erosion is associated with declining immune function of caregivers of Alzheimer's disease patients. *Journal of Immunology, 179,* 4249–4254.

Garstka, T. A., McCallion, P., & Toseland, R. W. (2001). Using support groups to improve caregiver health. In M. L. Hummert & J. F. Nussbaum (Eds.), *Aging, communication, and health* (pp. 75–100). Mahwah, NJ: Lawrence Erlbaum Associates.

Hochschild, A. (1993). *The second shift.* New York: Penguin books.

Himes, C. L. (1994). Parental caregiving by adult women: A demographic perspective. *Research on Aging, 16,* 191–211.

King, D. E., Mainous A. G., & Geesey, M. E. (2007). Turning back the clock: Adopting a healthy lifestyle in middle age. *American Journal of Medicine, 120,* 598–603.

Newman, K., & Chen, V. T. (2007). *The missing class: Portraits of the near poor in America.* Boston, MA: Beacon Press.

Rosowsky, E. (2007). Loss of the 'supplementary spouse' in marriages in later life. *Generations, 31,* 38–40.

Schmall, V. L., & Stiehl, R. E. (2003). *Coping with caregiving* (Pacific Northwest Cooperative Extension Rep. No 315). Retrieved November 18, 2008, from http://extension.oregonstate.edu/catalog/pdf/pnw/pnw315.pdf

Waldron, V. R., & Kelley, D. L. (2008). *Communicating forgiveness*. Thousand Oaks, CA: Sage.

Williams, A., & Nussbaum, J. F. (2001). *Intergenerational communication across the lifespan*. Mahwah, NJ: Lawrence Erlbaum Associates.

Yarry, S. J., Stevens, E. K., & McCallum, T. J. (2007). Cultural influences on spousal caregiving. *Generations, 31,* 24–30.

9   Reimagining the Empty Nest: Helping Clients Think Differently

In chapter 1, we criticized the empty nest as a metaphor for midlife marriage. We found the concept to be unnecessarily gloomy, with its focus on emptiness and too simplistic in emphasizing parenting to the exclusion of other dimensions of married life. Of course, metaphors are intended to simplify life's complexities. When applied to complex relationships, they draw attention to selected features and obscure others (Appleton & Bohm, 2001). Metaphors also encourage different and more creative thinking about familiar relationships. Our purpose in this brief closing chapter is to develop more fully several alternative metaphors for midlife marriage. By introducing them in counseling sessions, you can help married clients reimagine their relational future. Well-chosen metaphors create possibilities where clients previously perceived only limitations. They encourage varied ways of thinking where clients previously perceived only narrow choices. Some metaphors foster hope by focusing attention on opportunities rather than losses. A second purpose is to end the book on a hopeful, practical note by revisiting the best practices of resilient couples, previously introduced in chapter 1.

ALTERNATE METAPHORS

First, we consider the metaphors introduced earlier in this book: Recoupling, retooling, and the centerstage.

Recoupling

The metaphor of *recoupling* implies that midlife is a time of "coming back together." This notion resonates with couples who once enjoyed a stronger and closer relationship. The trials of parenting and career commitments may have left them feeling disconnected and distant. The process of recoupling assumes a certain basic "fit"; partners may take comfort from the idea that they are in some fundamental ways the same two people that met and fell in love many years before. At the same time, the metaphor implies a need to become closer.

The tightening up of loosened relational ties may require some preparatory work, perhaps in the context of therapy. One task is to update relational identity. Some spouses supplement their "parenting partners" image by emphasizing the other shared commitments that will keep them close in coming years. As suggested in chapter 4, these could involve new and meaningful engagements in education, community service, faith communities, career development, or recreational pursuits. A second task is to improve the communication practices that increase and sustain intimacy, some of which may become rusty due to inattention and poor maintenance (see chapter 2). To reduce emotional distance, the partners may need help in forgiving past transgressions; disclosing emotions, dreams, and uncertainties; and making conflict management a safer practice.

Recoupling implies rechoosing one's mate and recommitting to the union. This conscious decision to stay married, despite a significant change in circumstance can be relationally empowering for some couples. Those who previously felt compelled to stay together for the sake of the children, may feel an enhanced sense of commitment after choosing the marriage for other reasons. Some couples acknowledge this decision with the renewal of wedding vows or a second honeymoon.

The notion of recoupling also implies rebuilding or refurbishing in the same way that a worn and loose mechanical fitting is made secure by the replacement of old parts with newer and more supple ones. In this way, the metaphor raises the hopeful prospect of a "new and improved" marriage. What parts will be replaced in the refurbishing process? Those that have become rigid with age should be the first to go. These might include inflexible gender roles, mindlessly destructive patterns of communication, obsolete assumptions about beauty and youth, and calcified plans that no longer respond to the needs of both partners. The implications for counseling are obvious. Locate the worn-out, dysfunctional assumptions and practices which are causing distance and friction. Replace them with updated ideas and communication skills.

Retooling

This metaphor reminds a midlife couple that relational skills can become dated as the lifecourse progresses. It draws its meaning from the work place, where most employees have accepted the necessity of continuing education and openness to new ways of thinking. In this sense, retooling implies a kind of "relational learning" that is proactive, anticipatory, and empowering. Counseling is conceptualized as an effort to prepare the marriage to thrive, or at least survive, the changing times. For some couples, counseling is a way to fine-tune a "pretty good marriage," instead of a last-ditch effort to avoid a crisis.

Of course, distressed couples feel an urgent need to make adjustments at midlife. Now that the kids are gone, familiar ways of communicating are no longer working and the partners have grown weary of the marriage. The retooling metaphor, although arguably simplistic, can be particularly appealing to couples who see that their communication skills are failing them. Reluctant clients (men in particular) who are leery of counseling, sometimes find retooling to be a sensible, constructive, and safe goal of therapy. The need to update one's skills, so familiar in other aspects of modern life, might motivate a skeptical wife or husband to fully engage in the process.

We see retooling as a particularly helpful metaphor for the adjustments couples must make in response to major life events. We discussed the adjustments required of both partners when a spouse loses a job or returns to school (chapter 5). Living with uncertainty and learning new domestic roles are two examples. Changing family obligations (chapter 6) requires the couple to adopt new tools, such as contracting with boomerang children. Midlife relocation (chapter 7) and caregiving challenges (chapter 8) require couples to think and act differently as they negotiate financial issues, locate sources of advice and support, and address unfamiliar sources of relational conflict.

Centerstage Marriage

The centerstage metaphor has been most prominent in our approach to understanding midlife marriage. The metaphor implies at least two new kinds of relational thinking. The first recognizes the developmental and temporal transitions that occur at midlife. The active parenting years are ending. The couple is no longer young, but certainly not old. Careers are in mid-arc. Retirement is now visible on the horizon, but most couples have decades of work and saving ahead of them. Their bodies are visibly aging, and by midlife, couples have time to adopt healthier habits. In short, these couples are experiencing the middle of the marital life span. They have lived together long enough to accumulate a significant inventory of mistakes and accomplishments. Most have plenty of time to plot a new relational trajectory.

Of course, the centerstage metaphor borrows imagery from the theater, a frequent source of inspiration for social scientists, including the sociologist Erving Goffman (2008/1967), who viewed human interaction as a kind of performance staged by cooperative actors responding to cues and following social scripts. We find the theater metaphor useful too, but for different reasons. Most basic is the opportunity it creates to imagine midlife as a time when a marriage once again becomes the center of attention. After years of putting the marriage backstage, in the wings, or, perhaps, in the orchestra pit, it is time for a couple to make their marriage the headline event.

Centerstage is where the action happens. For years, the marriage was dominated by the children while the spouses waited in the green room for their names to be called. In seeking counseling at midlife, couples make a decision to retake the stage, to seek the attention they deserve, to refine their roles and hone their performance, to make the "show" go as smoothly as possible. Of course, the centerstage also implies bright lights and increased exposure. Spouses may feel some pressure, a bit of stage fright as the supporting actors leave them to carry the show. From this point of view, the counselor is like an acting coach. He or she offers encouragement, urges the actors to take more risks, provides ideas for expanding roles and altering the script, locates flaws in synchrony, and suggests alternate modes of expression. Placing marriage on the centerstage gives it priority at a time when priorities are changing; it helps a couple make the adjustment needed for success in the long run.

Although they certainly differ, these three metaphors share an emphasis on the capacity for change. Recoupling emphasizes the relational changes that allow a couple to renew feelings of intimacy and collaboration. Retooling suggests a willingness to learn new relational attitudes and skills in response to changing conditions. Taking the center stage involves a change in priorities. To negotiate these inevitable changes, partners must draw on a deep reservoir of good will. But a more important facilitator of change will be their capacity to communicate well. In the preceding chapters, we have identified a host of crucial communication practices. A short list would include expressing social support, negotiating shared tasks, communicating assurance, managing conflict, listening well, sharing emotions, discussing expectations, and engaging in dialogue.

Indeed, we see evidence of the recoupling, retooling, and centerstage metaphors in the relational narratives we have collected over the years. But it has become obvious to us that those couples who have sustained successful unions over many years of life share certain best practices. We introduced these in chapter 1 and revisit them here, as a way of ending this book on a hopeful and positive note. Our intention is to leave the reader with a clear sense of how each of these practices is instrumental in helping couples optimize the centerstage of marriage.

BEST PRACTICES REVISITED

Renew Relationship Commitment

As we mentioned in chapter 1, some successful couples told us "recommitment stories," tales of trying times or wavering allegiances, followed by pledges of renewed commitment to the marriage. Recommitment takes many forms, including marriage renewal ceremonies, second honeymoons, or finding a new home to share (chapter 7) for the next stage of life. Less public signs of commitment come in the form of regular assurances (chapter 2) and renewed pledges to abide by relational agreements (chapter 3). For some resilient couples, the act of seeking counseling in itself signals a new commitment. Rechoosing the marriage is an act of affirmation and, importantly, it suggests a hopeful view of the relationship's future.

Prioritize the Relationship

As we have documented throughout this book, midlife brings daunting challenges for some centerstage couples. Caring for elderly parents can be an all-consuming task (chapter 8) as can custodial grandparenting (chapter 6) or finding a new job (chapter 5). Unless a couple actively resists, these life events can overwhelm a marriage with stressful demands. Emotionally exhausted, many couples understandably neglect their marriage during these times. Nevertheless, those who survive them tell us that the health of their marriage remained a top priority. As we suggested in chapter 2, they sustain their relationships by sharing tasks, creating positive experiences, communicating assurances, and using other relationship maintenance behaviors. When the marriage shows signs of stress, they take remedial actions, such as spending the weekend alone together or renegotiating limits on the support they can provide to family members (chapter 6). Simply said, successful centerstage couples make the health of their own marriage a high priority.

Negotiate Changing Expectations

As we have seen, personal and relational expectations often shift at midlife. In this book, we have documented changes in career aspirations, financial goals, careers, gender roles, and friendship networks, among many others. In chapter 7, we suggested that the decision of whether or not to relocate sometimes surfaced differences in expectations. Differences about how to spend free time (chapter 4), how to parent adult children (chapter 6), and the nature of the sexual relationship may arise. Resilient partners attend to these differences in expectation, sometimes in therapy. They exhibit a degree of flexibility and a willingness to discard assumptions that no longer apply. Reassessment and negotiation are common themes in their relational narratives.

Find a Common Voice

In our studies, successful couples often describe solidarity in the face of crisis or opposition. They find a common voice in their interactions with boomerang children (chapter 6) and doctors (chapter 8). Of course, they experience conflicts around these and other issues, but they resolve their differences privately, not publicly. As we mentioned in chapter 1, these couples avoid the temptation to negotiate "side deals" with family members and they support each other in conversations with family and friends. In short, they stick together.

Maintain an External System of Support

Resilient couples build supportive relationships outside the marriage. Many of them told us about sharing the responsibility of maintaining relationships with friends and family members. They recognize that a strong support system is crucial in times of crises, including illness (chapter 8). Their social support network is a consideration as they make decisions about relocation (chapter 7), returning to school (chapter 5), and leisure activity (chapter 4). When couples describe midlife transitions that went smoothly, the social support provided by family members is nearly always a crucial element of the story.

Develop the Habit of Dialogue

As we described in chapter 2, dialogue is the kind of communication that promotes understanding during times of disagreement (chapter 2). Successful couples seem more concerned with understanding than winning, and their communication practices reflect this orientation. They tend to work as a team to define their conflicting goals and common interests. They are honest about disagreements and committed to making fully informed decisions. They limit conversational disruptions, defensiveness, verbal attacks, and other bad habits. They have learned to be patient listeners (chapter 2). Even in times of conflict, successful couples seem to be on the same team, collaborating to find a workable solution.

Sustain Intimacy

The preoccupations of parenting can gradually diminish marital intimacy. Rebuilding it can be a daunting task, but many couples tell us that they became better at sustaining intimacy during the centerstage of their marriage. Sometimes their success is hinged on the difficult process of forgiving hurtful behaviors of the past (chapter 3). For some couples, counseling was needed to facilitate self-disclosure, increased empathy, and a willingness to rediscover their sexual relationship. As we suggested in chapters 1 and 2, successful centerstage couples seem to cultivate emotional and physical closeness. They recognize signs of emotional distancing and talk about them. They respect a partner's need for an "emotional break," but they also expect emotional honesty. Feelings are acknowledged and explored.

In closing, we simply note that each of these practices promotes flexibility and adjustment at a time of life when it is definitely needed. These seven practices are just some of the lessons we have learned from observing hundreds of centerstage couples. They are the resources that couples draw upon as they enact the metaphors of recoupling, retooling, and taking the centerstage. You can help couples develop these practices in counseling sessions and workshops. We can only hope that the chapters of this book, with their resources and exercises, have provided some of the tools you will need to serve the rapidly growing population of centerstage couples.

REFERENCES

Appleton, C., & Bohm, E. Partners in passage: The experience of marriage in midlife. *Journal of Phenomenological Psychology*, 32, 41–70.

Goffman, E. (2008/1967). *Interaction ritual: Essays on face to face behavior*. New Brunswick, NJ: Aldine Transaction Publishers.

CHAPTER 2: RESOURCES

1 *The Seven Principles for Making Marriage Work: A Practical Guide from the Country's Foremost Relationship Expert.* Gottman, J. (2000). New York: Three Rivers Press. (ISBN-10: 0609805797)
   - Written by professor of psychology at the University of Washington
   - Includes questionnaires and exercises

2 *Ten Lessons to Transform Your Marriage: America's Love Lab Experts Share Their Strategies for Strengthening Your Relationship.* Gottman, J. (2007). New York: Three Rivers Press. (ISBN-10: 1400050197)
   - Strategies for improved communication
   - Conflict management
   - Case studies

3 *Are you Really Listening?: Keys to Successful Communication.* Donoghue, P.J., and Siegel, M.E. (2005). Notre Dame, IN: Sorin Books. (ISBN-10: 1893732886)
   - Helps identify poor listening
   - Strategies to improve listening

4 *We Can Work It Out: How to Solve Conflicts, Save Your Marriage, and Strengthen Your Love for Each Other.* Notarius, C., & Markman, H. (1994). New York: Perigee Trade. (ISBN: 0399521372)
   - Four styles of conflict interaction
   - Setting up a couples meeting
   - Insight about the impact of arousal

5 *Interpersonal Conflict.* Wilmot, W., & Hocker, J. (2007). New York: McGraw-Hill. (ISBN-10: 0073135542)
   - Comprehensive guide for managing conflict
   - Conflict styles and tactics
   - Guide for negotiating mutual satisfaction

6 *Building a Stronger Marriage/Focus on the Family/30th Anniversary Broadcast Set*/4 *CD broadcast set includes:*
- Grounded in culturally conservative principles
- Topics include:
  - "Happily Married Opposites"
  - "Experiencing a Fulfilled Marriage"
  - "How To Save Your Marriage"
  - "Building Hedges Around Your Marriage"
7 *Relational Communication Self-Assessment.* www.austincc.edu/colangelo/1311/relationalcommtest.htm
- Short quiz
- Emphasis on communication
- Discussion questions

CHAPTER 3: RESOURCES

1 *Communicating Forgiveness.* Waldron, V. R., & Kelley, D. L. (2008). Los Angeles: Sage Publications. (ISBN: 9781412939713)
- Conceptualizes forgiveness as communication
- Real-life narratives from personal interviews
- Specific guidelines for forgiveness
2 *The Sunflower: On the Possibilities and Limits of Forgiveness.* Wiesenthal, S. (1997). New York: Schocken Books. (ISBN: 0805210601)
- Holocaust survivor raises questions of forgiveness
3 *No Future Without Forgiveness.* Tutu, D. (1999). New York: DoubleDay. (ISBN: 0385496907)
- Lessons from South Africa's Truth and Reconciliation Commission
- Focus on possibilities for reconciliation
4 *Worldwide Forgiveness Alliance.*   www.forgivenessday.org
- Forgiving substance abusers
5 *Stanford Continuing Studies Program/Stanford Center for Integrative Medicine and Stanford Health Improvement Program.* www.learningtoforgive.com
- Stanford University forgiveness scholar Dr. Fred Luskin
- Health benefits of forgiveness
6 *Beliefnet.com.*   www.beliefnet.com
- Religious traditions and forgiveness
- Inspiration to forgive

7 *Marriage Builders.* www.marriagebuilders.com
- Surviving infidelity
- Healing and reconciliation

8 *Alcoholics Anonymous.* www.alcoholics-anonymous.org
- Forgiveness with alcohol/substance abuse
- Support groups

9 *The Forgiveness Web.* www.forgivenessweb.com/default.htm
- Reading forums and message boards
- Support groups
- Workshops

10 *Journey Toward Forgiveness.* http://journeytowardforgiveness. com/setting-out/
- Documentary videos
- Stories and instruction

11 *ForgivenessNet.* http://website.lineone.net/~andrewhdknock/ index.html
- Christian, Jewish, Hindu, Buddhist, and Islamic scripture regarding forgiveness
- Forgiveness stories and poetry

12 *The Forgiveness Project.* www.theforgivenessproject.com
- Forgiveness in the news
- Video links
- Inspirational forgiveness stories

13 **Restorative Justice Online.** www.restorativejustice.org/resources/ world
- Restorative justice discussion
- Restorative justice stories from around the world
- Restorative justice resources.

CHAPTER 4: RESOURCES

1 *The 7 Best Things Happy Couples Do.* Friel, J., & Friel, L. (2002). Daytona: HCI Inc. (ISBN 13: 978–1-55874–953-5)
- Based on scientific study of couples
- Promoting happiness through activity

2 *Chicken Soup for the Soul: Empty Nesters: 101 Stories about Surviving and Thriving When the Kids Leave Home (Chicken Soup for the Soul).* Canfield, J., Hansen, V.M., Rehme, C.M., & Evans, P. (2008). New York: Simon & Schuster (ISBN-10: 1935096222)
- 101 stories of surviving and thriving

3   *10 Things that Happy Couples Do.*   www.thecutekid.com/
parenting/ happy-couples-secrets.php
- Suggestions to strengthen marriage
- Low- and no-cost activities

4   *Meetup.com.*   www.meetup.com
- Meet other local adults (nationwide)
- Travel groups and support groups
- Book clubs

5   *Sensual Activities for Couples.*   www.beautyden.com/
sensual-couples.shtml
- Suggestions to liven up romance/intimacy
- Creative ways to pamper your partner

6   *The Soko magazine.*   www.thesoko.com/thesoko/
article989. html
- Fun summer activities for couples
- Creative couple time and communication

7   *Bella Online: The Voice of Women.*   www.bellaonline.com/articles/
art57920.asp
- Physical activities
- Entertainment events
- Relaxation getaways for couples

8   *Sur La Table.*   www.surlatable.com
- Cooking classes
- Network for cooking clubs

9   *Hiking/Backpacking Clubs.* Find one in your area by going to
www.hikingandbackpacking.com
- Various levels (aggressive or relaxed)
- Adventure and photography

10 *Fred Astaire: Franchised Dance Studios.*   http://www.fredastaire.
com/
- Various types of dance for couples of all ages
- Search local city offices for classes

11 *Visit museums.*   www.museumspot.com
- Educational, historical, cultural sites
- Locate museums in any geographical area

12 *Bowling Leagues/Clubs.*   www.amf.com/corporate/index.htm
- Leagues and clubs for couples

13 *Couples Spas.*   Search locally at www.discoverspas.com/
romanticspas.shtml
- Intimacy, relaxation, sensuality

CHAPTER 5: RESOURCES

Responding to Job Loss

1   **The "Ways of Coping" Questionnaire.**   www.mindgarden.com/products/wayss.htm
■ Questionnaire administration time takes approximately 10 minutes
■ Stimulus for discussion in clinical, training, and workshop settings

2   *Occupational Outlook Quarterly.* Department of Labor Statistics
www.bls.gov/opub/ooq/ooqhome.htm
www.bls.gov/opub/ooq/2007/winter/grabbag.htm
■ Locate high-growth careers
■ Current statistics
■ Aid for entrepreneurs

3   *Federal Trade Commission.*   www.ftc.gov/bcp/edu/pubs/consumer/credit/cre26.shtm
■ Guidance for choosing a credit counselor
■ Debt management plans

4   *CareerBuilders.com.*   www.careerbuilder.com
■ Resume builder/skills assessment
■ Online databases/job search resources

5   *HeadHuntersDirectory.com.*   www.headhuntersdirectory.com
■ Worldwide index of employment agencies

6   *The Riley Guide.*   www.rileyguide.com/support.html
■ Comprehensive site for job searchers
■ Where to file for unemployment

7   *Linkedin.com.*   www.linkedin.com
■ Connect with employers, peers, and job seekers

Returning to School

8   *Traditional Degrees for Nontraditional Students: How to Earn a Top Diploma From America's Great Colleges At Any Age.* Fungaroli Sargent, C. (2000). New York: Farrar, Straus & Giroux (ISBN: 0374299897)
■ Stories from 100 adults aged 25 to 85 who returned to school
■ Classroom tips
■ Management of family relationships

9 *The Adult Student's Guide to Survival and Success (6th Ed.).*
Siebert, A., & Karr, M. (2008). Portland, Oregon: Practical Psychology Press. (ISBN: 0944227381)
www.adultstudent.com
- Online companion
- Specific tips for students and educators

10 *U.S. Department of Education.*
- www.ed.gov/students/prep/college/thinkcollege/return/edlite-college.html
- www.ed.gov/students/prep/college/thinkcollege/highschool/edlite-index.html
- Step-by-step instructions for returning students
- College search information/virtual college tour
- Financial aid and entrance exam information
- Business, trade, and technical school information

11 *Formal Sources of Support on College Campuses for Re-entry/Nontraditional Students (Exemplars).*
A Returning student office at Cleveland State Community College
www.clscc.cc.tn.us/departments/student_services/adult_student_services/index.asp
B Re-entry student club at Arizona State University
www.asu.edu/studentaffairs/lss/ARE.html
C Re-entry workshops at California State University, Long Beach
www.outreach.csulb.edu/Undergraduate_Admission/Adult_Re-entry
D Mentor support at UNC Charlotte
www.oases.uncc.edu/amps/home.htm

12 *National Center for Educational Statistics.* http://nces.ed.gov/collegenavigator
- College navigator
- Career and occupational outlook handbook

13 *College Board.* www.collegeboard.com/student/csearch/index.html
- Major and career profiles
- Summary of college requirements

14 *National Public Radio (podcast).* www.npr.org/templates/story/story.php?storyId=6387526
- Estimates financial benefits of college degree
- Podcast explains $23,000 per year salary advantage

15 *Bernard Osher Foundation.* www.osherfoundation.org/index.php? reentry
- Scholarships for nontraditional students

CHAPTER 6: RESOURCES

1 *Working With Custodial Grandparents.* Hayslip, B., & Patrick, J.H. (2002). New York: Springer Publishing Company. (ISBN: 0826116841)
- How to handle stress
- Support group helps
- Everyday strategies
2 *To Grandmother's House We Go and Stay: Perspectives on Custodial Grandparents.* Cox, C. (1999). New York: Springer Publishing Company. (ISBN 0826112862)
- Financial strain
- Lack of preparation
- Emotional and psychological stress
3 *CustodialGrandparents.com.* http://custodialgrandparents.com/forum/
- Support blogs for custodial grandparents
- Development and maintenance support networks
4 *Grandparents Raising Grandchildren: Implications for Professionals and Agencies.* www.uwex.edu/ces/gprg/article.html
- Helpful tips for TANF (Temporary Assistance for Needy Families)
- Benefits
- Legal issues
5 *Grandparents Raising Grandchildren: Assessing Resources in your Community.* www.fcs.uga.edu/pubs/PDF/CHFD-E-59–6.pdf
- TANF
- Financial assistance
- Food stamps
- Health insurance
- Tax credit
6 *Grand Parent Again.* www.gradparentagain.com
- State by state child/grandparent access laws
- Local support groups

7 ***U.S. Department of Health and Human Services Administration for Children and Families.***   www.acf.hhs.gov
- (TANF) temporary assistance for needy families
- Title IV-A and XVI of the Social Security Act

8 ***Boomerang Nation: How to Survive Living with Your Parents ... The Second Time Around.*** Furman, E. (2005). New York: Fireside. (ISBN-10: 0743269918)
- Humorous anecdotal stories
- Guide to help ease family/boundary frustrations

9 ***Kiplinger.com***   www.kiplinger.com/columns/drt/archive/2007/dt070516.html
- Advice for handling boomerang children

10 ***When Our Grown Kids Disappoint Us: Letting Go of Their Problems, Loving Them Anyway, and Getting on with Our Lives.*** Adams, J. (2003). New York: Free Press. (ISBN-10: 074323281X)
- Practical guidance about negotiating relationships with adult children
- Advice for accepting realities

CHAPTER 7: RESOURCES

1 ***Will This Place Ever Feel Like Home?: Simple Advice for Settling in After Your Move.*** Levine, L. (2002). New York: McGraw Hill. (ISBN: 0658020986)
- Anticipating the effects of moving (on self, spouse, adult kids, pets)
- Strategies to balance work and move
- Support to recreate the comfort of home
- Ways to establish new friends and community

2 ***Moving: A Complete Checklist and Guide for Relocation.*** Adams, K. G. (1994). San Diego, CA: Silvercat Publications. (ISBN-10: 0962494569)
- Planning the move
- Weekly countdown and checklists
- Budgeting guidelines and packing advice

3 ***The Expert Expatriate: Your Guide To Successful Relocation Abroad.*** Hess, M. B., & Linderman, P. (2002). Yarmouth, Maine: Intercultural Press. (ISBN-10: 1857883209)
- How to budget for a move
- Dos and don'ts of relocation

4 *When Life Changes or You Wish It Would: How to Survive and Thrive in Uncertain Times.* Adrienne, C. (2003). New York: Harper Paperbacks (ISBN-10: 0060934565)
 ■ Managing uncertainty
 ■ Adapting to new environments

5 *Cities Ranked and Rated: More than 400 Metropolitan Areas Evaluated in the U.S. and Canada.* Sperling, B., & Sander, P. (2007). New Jersey: Wiley. (ISBN-10: 0470068647)
 ■ "Best and worst" charts
 ■ Cost of living statistics
 ■ Quality of life indicators

6 *RelocationEssentials.com* www.relocationessentials.com
 ■ Customized relocation planner for specific needs
 ■ Community search: Information about cost of living, crime reports, etc.

7 *U-Turn Ahead.* http://uturnahead.com/2008/06/best-blogs-and-websites-for-midlifers
 ■ Blogs on midlife decisions, including relocation
 ■ Discussions of relocation opportunities and pitfalls

8 *Relocation Quiz.* www.letlifein.com/2007/12/17/to-relocate-or-not-to-relocate-take-this-quiz
 ■ Assess relocation readiness

9 *HomeExchange.com* www.homeexchange.com
 ■ Information on home swapping (vacation or long term)
 ■ Step-by-step procedures, testimonies, and references
 ■ Membership required

10 *About.com: Architectural Tips for Building Your New Home.* http://architecture.about.com/od/buildyourhouse/a/buildyourhome.htm
 ■ Advice on understanding contracts
 ■ Tips on building costs
 ■ How to check building codes

CHAPTER 8: RESOURCES

General Medical Reference

1 *WebMD.* www.webmd.com
 ■ Medical guide for screening in midlife
2 *Health Insite (Australian Government).* www.healthinsite.gov.au
 ■ Nutrition and fitness in midlife

3   *Gayot.com.*
   ■ Healthy restaurants and cooking ideas
   ■ Physical and mental health
4   *Cancer Information Service* (1–800-4-cancer)
   ■ 24-hour question and answer service
5   *How to Communicate With Your Doctor: A Study in Assertiveness.*
   www.hodu.com/assertiveness-medical.shtml
   ■ How to use "PowerPhrases" to encourage dialogue
   ■ Tips on getting questions answered
   ■ How to broach uncomfortable subjects

Disease Specific

Heart Disease/Heart Attack

6   *American Heart Association.*   www.americanheart.org
   ■ Health and lifestyle information
   ■ Heart attack warning signs
   ■ Heart and stroke encyclopedia

Breast Cancer

7   *Susan G. Komen.*   http://cms.komen.org/komen/index.htm
   ■ ABCs of breast cancer
   ■ News and events
   ■ Message boards/support groups
8   *National Breast Cancer Foundation.*   www.nationalbreastcancer.org
   ■ Tips for early detection
   ■ Advice for newly diagnosed
   ■ Survivor stories

Prostate Cancer

9   *Prostate Cancer Foundation.*   www.prostatecancerfoundation.org
   ■ Support group
   ■ Risk factors and symptoms
   ■ Treatment options

Diabetes

10   *American Diabetes Association.*   www.diabetes.org
   ■ Recent treatments

- Recipes
- Daily tips

11 ***National Diabetes Education Program.***   http://ndep.nih.gov/campaigns/SmallSteps/SmallSteps_index.htm
- Awareness campaigns
- Thorough description of diabetes and pre-diabetes
- Symptoms

Hypertension

12 ***American Society of Hypertension Inc.***   www.ash-us.org
- Statistics
- Strategies of prevention
- Guidelines

Stroke

13 ***American Stroke Association.***   www.strokeassociation.org
- Preventative education and symptoms
- Life after stroke

14 ***National Stroke Association.***   www.stroke.org
- Gender- and culture-specific information
- Survivor stories and recovery information
- Effects on caregivers/families

Understanding Cultural and Gender Differences in Response to Illness

African American

15 ***African-American Women's Health and Social Issues.*** Fisher Collins, C. (2006). Westport, CN: Praeger Publishers.
- Encouragement for women
- Literary perspective on coping
- Indications and treatment of disease

16 ***Medline Plus (African American Health).***   www.nlm.nih.gov/medlineplus/africanamericanhealth.html
- Differences in health culture, health care access, environmental, and genetics
- Nutrition

Asian American

17   *Asian American Family Services.*   www.aafstexas.org
- Healthy lifestyle classes
- Counseling and mental health needs
- Services for adult, youth, family, abusers, etc.

Hispanic American

18   *Medline Plus (Hispanic Health Information).*   www.nlm.nih.gov/
medlineplus/hispanicamericanhealth.html
- Clinical trials and screening
- Health statistics

Native American

19   *University of California, San Diego, Moores Cancer Center.*   http://
cancer.ucsd.edu/Outreach/PublicEducation/CAMs/
nativeamerican.asp
- Alternative therapies
- Side effects and pain control
- Benefits/risks of treatment

Gender specific

20   *U.S. Department of Health and Human Services.*   www.4woman.gov
- Campaigns and events
- Screening/diagnostic tools

21   *Men's Health Network.*   www.menshealthnetwork.org
- Men's health library
- Violence and addiction prevention

Caring for the Caretaker

22   *National Alliance for Caregiving.*   www.caregiving.org
- Communication during illness
- Transportation assistance
- Financial resources/insurance/legal information
- Support groups for caregiver
- Reviews of books, videos, and brochures

23 *Family Caregiving 101.*   www.familycaregiving101.org
   ■ List of family resources
   ■ Question and answer blog
   ■ Support groups
24 *Focus on the Caregiver.*   www.aarp.org/families/grandparents/ focus_on_the_caregiver/a2004–01-20- supportgroups.html
   ■ Finding a support group or starting meetings
25 *Help for Sandwiched Couples.*   http://mediastorm.org/ 0009.htm
   ■ Support groups, blogs, and personal narratives

Index